'Or quoi, si je prens les choses autrement qu'elles ne sont? Il peut estre; et pourtant j'accuse mon impatience, et tiens premierement qu'elle est également vitieuse en celuy qui a droict comme en celuy qui a tort: car c'est tousjours un'aigreur tyrannique de ne pouvoir souffrir une forme diverse à la sienne.' ('And what if I get things wrong? That could well be the case; and yet I blame my own impatience and reckon above all that impatience is as much a fault in the person who is right as in the person who is wrong: for it is always a tyrannical sourness to be unable to endure a way of thinking different from one's own.')

– Montaigne, *Essais*, Book 3, ch. 8, 'De l'Art de Conferer'

ANTWERP
AND THE GOLDEN AGE
Culture, Conflict & Commerce

RICHARD WILLMOTT

UNICORN

Published in 2025 by Unicorn,
an imprint of Unicorn Publishing Group
Charleston Studio
Meadow Business Centre
Lewes BN8 5RW
www.unicornpublishing.org

ISBN 978-1-916846-67-8

10 9 8 7 6 5 4 3 2 1

Typeset by Matthew Wilson
Printed in Malta by Gutenberg Press

Front cover: The Crane on the Antwerp Quay by the Frozen Scheldt by
Sebastiaan Vrancx, 1622 (Rijksmuseum, Amsterdam)

Endpapers: Antverpia, a bird's eye view of Antwerp and the citadel by Joris
Hoefnagel, before 1597 (University Library of Antwerp: Special Collections)

Contents

Illustrations

Acknowledgements

My manifold debts to the scholarship of others are revealed in my bibliography (although any errors are all my own), but three diligent editors are worthy of particular mention. I could never have written the book in its present form without the herculean labours of Jan Hendrick Hessels, who edited the numerous letters addressed to Ortelius and his nephew Ortelianus held by the Dutch stranger church of Austin Friars, *Epistulae Ortelianae*, and the yet more time-consuming efforts of Max Rooses and Jan Denucé, Directors of the Plantin-Moretus Museum, who engaged in the enormous task of transcribing all of Plantin's letters in nine books over a number of years.

I am also most grateful to all those who have sent me material from libraries that I was unable to visit. Foremost among these should be the librarian at Eupen, who sent me the article about Gillis Hooftman by Willi Berens, 'Ein Großer Eupener' from *Geschichtles Eupen I*, a hard copy of which I have never been able to find. Had I realised at the time that this would provoke the curiosity that led to my writing this book, I would have taken more care to record their name, an omission for which I apologise. I am grateful as well to Anne van Buren of De Acht Zaligheden and Elspeth Orwin of Auckland Public Libraries. One library that I could visit in person was the Chained Library at Hereford Cathedral, and I must thank Jennifer Dumbelton for her helpfulness in showing me volumes of the Complutensian Polyglot Bible and of Plantin's *Biblia Regia* and Gordon Taylor for taking photographs.

I also offer thanks to Cecile van der Harten, who kindly organised a visit to the Rijksmuseum store at Lelystad, and I owe particular debts of gratitude to Gijs van der Ham, the curator of *80 Jaar Oorlog* at the Rijksmuseum, who found the time to show me around what proved a most thought-provoking exhibition (and which could be said to underlie the writing of this book).

Thanks also to Rudie van Leeuwen, who thoughtfully sent me an English translation of his article, '*Moses and the Israelites* by Maerten de Vos: The *Portrait Historié* of the Panhuys Family from 1574'. And although I had already completed the preliminary drafts of this book when I visited it, I was able to learn more when I went round the excellent *Ode aan Antwerpen* exhibition curated by Micha Leeflang at the Catherijneconvent in Utrecht, which placed de Vos's great painting of Moses, Aaron and the Tablets of the Law at its heart.

I am also grateful to Liz Russell, who read an early draft, to Catherine Evans for reading a later one, and to Claudia Thompson for casting an eye over my Dutch translations (my errors are not her fault). I owe a particular debt to Ian Strathcarron for his willingness to take on what he described as a 'suitably eccentric' project for Unicorn, and to the excellent team at Unicorn of Ryan Gearing, who oversaw the project, Katie Greenwood, who sourced the images, and Michael Eckhardt, who patiently sorted out the manuscript. Finally, I must thank my wife, Isobel, for her tolerance while I was writing and for accompanying me to various foreign galleries and museums in pursuit of my prey.

Names and identifications

The English reader is likely to come across a good many unfamiliar names in this book, and, to add to the potential confusion, many of these names take various forms. I have tried to be consistent in my naming of them, but this has sometimes proved a challenge.

Place names

These are relatively easy to deal with. Where there is a form of the name generally used in English, I use it; for example, Antwerp and neither Antwerpen nor Anvers; Brussels and neither Brussel nor Bruxelles; and Genoa, not Genova. Elsewhere, the form used by the native population is preferred; for example, the German Aachen and neither the Dutch Aken nor the French Aix-la-Chapelle. Holland was originally the dominant state of the United Provinces that became the Netherlands, and so I have avoided using it to name what has now become the Netherlands. Unhelpfully, the Netherlands was originally the name used to signify all the territories once ruled by the Dukes of Burgundy and then the Habsburgs, and so I normally refer to the Low Countries when I mean the territories that are now the Netherlands, Belgium and Luxembourg. I do, however, sometimes use Dutch as a general term for those coming from either the Dutch- or Flemish-speaking parts of the Low Countries, as well as for their language and its various dialects.

Names of people

These pose a much greater problem because not only are there different forms commonly used (for example, Jacob Coels lived in London and is quite often referred to by the Anglicised names James Cool or Cole), but there are also Latinized names used by humanists (who frequently wrote to each other in

Latin) such as Ortelianus, the nickname for Coels because he was a favourite nephew of Abraham Ortelius (Ortels in Dutch). Where somebody is well known by a particular name (for example, Abraham Ortelius, who produced the first atlas), I use that; elsewhere, I use the form that has become most familiar in my own reading. The Antwerp merchant Gillis Hooftman was sometimes referred to as Aegidius van Eyckelberg (Aegidius is the Latin form of Giles), but since there are references to other members of his family who do not normally carry the cumbersome family name of van Eyckelberg, I have stuck to the name that they all used: Hooftman. Emanuel van Meteren always spells his first name with one 'm', and since Christophe Plantin came from France, I use the French form of his name rather than the Dutch or English. William of Orange (also known as William the Silent) refers to the leader of the Dutch rebellion and not to his great-grandson who married Mary, the daughter of James II, to become William III of England and who is also often referred to as William of Orange. In choosing the spelling Lucas d'Heere and not De Heere or D'Heere, I follow the spelling used in the contemporary manuscript copy of his *Tableau Poetique*. I refer to the Habsburgs and not the Hapsburgs.

By now, the astute reader will have realised that there is no absolute principle governing my decisions, although I have tried to be consistent throughout the book in the naming of each individual. (You may refer to the *Dramatis Personae* following this section if you are puzzled by an unfamiliar name.)

Different Christian confessions

There is another possible confusion over names which concerns the terminology used to differentiate between the different Christian groups during the Reformation. When Luther first published his famous ninety-five theses in 1517, he was not intending to establish a new 'Lutheran' church, but to put forward propositions for discussion that might lead to reform within the existing church. Similarly, individual Christians did not wake up one day and suddenly decide to be a 'Lutheran' or a 'Calvinist', but gradually changed their opinions about such disputed matters as exactly what was happening when the priest blessed the bread and wine at Mass, and the relative importance of faith and works in the search for salvation. Consequently, scholars do not always agree on the terminology to describe these changing positions. In this book, I shall use the term 'Catholic' to describe those who accepted the Pope's authority, 'Lutheran' to describe those who accepted the teaching and authority of Luther, and either 'Reformed' or 'Calvinist' to describe those who followed the teaching of the Swiss reformers such as Calvin and Zwingli. The general term for the Reformed in France was 'Huguenots'. I shall try to avoid the term 'Anglican', referring simply to the English church since, convenient though the term is, the Church of England today is so different from what it was in the sixteenth century that the term is inevitably misleading. Despite its historical inaccuracy, I occasionally use 'Protestant' as an umbrella term for all those rejecting the Pope's authority.

It should also be pointed out that 'humanism' will not refer to the modern atheist or agnostic assertion of the worth of humanity independent of God, but to the Renaissance study of human history and thought through the liberal arts and especially the revival of classical learning; it is in no way opposed to Christian belief. The usage just about survives in the title of the Oxford course called *literae humaniores*, which is the study of the languages, history and philosophy of Greece and Rome. A hint of the humanist desire to improve Latin as a language of science and thought can be seen in the occasional apology for poor style by some of the correspondents in the *Epistulae Ortelianae*.

Dramatis Personae

The following list is intended to aid the reader if they come across an unfamiliar name and need a little information to place them in the story. Generally speaking, I have not listed those who appear only once, whose identity will be explained at the time.

Alba, Duke of: The general sent by Philip II to the Low Countries to suppress Protestantism and resistance to royal authority, who would later become Governor of the Low Countries.

Anjou, Duke of: The youngest son of Henri II of France; unsuccessful suitor of Elizabeth I of England; invited to replace Philip II as hereditary ruler of the United Provinces of the Low Countries, he proved treacherous and died soon after being forced to flee the country.

Assonleville, Christoffel d': Lawyer and influential member of the council that governed the Habsburg Low Countries under Margaret of Parma.

Aylmer, John: Tutor to Lady Jane Grey; exiled under Mary, and Bishop of London under Elizabeth.

Barrefelt, Hendrik Jansen van (Hiel): Leader of a breakaway group from the Family of Love and a mystic theologian.

Bomberghen, Cornelis van: A Calvinist merchant who was a business partner of Plantin.

Botticelli, Sandro: A Florentine painter of the early Renaissance.

Brederode, Hendrick van: A leader of the confederacy of Low Countries nobles who presented a petition to Margaret of Parma demanding an end to the persecution of Protestants (the *Geuzen*).

Burghley: See Cecil.

Camden, William: English antiquarian and author of *Britannia*.

Çayas (Zayas), Gabriel de: A scholarly secretary of Philip II.

Cecil, William, Baron Burghley: Queen Elizabeth I's principal adviser for much of her reign.

Cisneros, Cardinal Francisco Jiménez de: Statesman, religious reformer and scholar; founder of the first university of Alcalá de Henares in Spain and initiator of the Complutensian Polyglot Bible.

Clinton, Edward, Earl of Lincoln and Lord High Admiral: English patron of Lucas d'Heere.

Coudenberg, Pieter: Botanist.

Coxcie, Michiel: A Flemish painter who served both Charles V and Philip II (*c.* 1499–1592).

Cranmer, Thomas: First Protestant archbishop of Canterbury under Henry VIII and Edward VI; martyred by Mary I.

Dousa, Janus (Jan van der Does): Governor of Leiden during the Spanish siege and first president of its university.

Dudley, Robert, Earl of Leicester: Favourite of Elizabeth I and leader of the expeditionary force to support the Dutch.

Erasmus, Desiderius: A scholar from Rotterdam (1466–1536) who insisted on the importance of establishing reliable biblical texts; he was critical of the Catholic Church, but thought reform should come from within and opposed Luther.

Espés, Don Guerau de: Spanish ambassador to Elizabeth I.

Eyck, Jan and Hubert van: Brothers who painted *The Adoration of the Mystic Lamb* in St Bavo's Cathedral, Ghent.

Farnese, Alessandro, Duke of Parma and Piacenza: Son of Margaret of Parma, general of Philip II's forces in the Low Countries and Governor (1578–92).

Granvelle, Antoine Perrenot de: Cardinal and statesman; adviser to Margaret of Parma and subsequently to Philip II; a man of great learning and patron of Plantin and Lipsius (who as a young man was his secretary).

Guicciardini, Lodovico: Italian merchant who settled in Antwerp and who wrote a detailed description of the Low Countries and their culture illustrated with city maps.

Haemstede, Adriaan van: Pastor of the Dutch stranger church at Austin Friars accused of Anabaptist sympathies and expelled from England.

Heere, Lucas d': Painter and poet from Ghent.

Heyns, Peeter: Owner of an influential girls' school in Antwerp, as well as a poet and playwright.

Hoefnagel, Joris: Miniaturist, illuminator and poet from Antwerp.

Hooftman, Anna: Daughter of Gillis and wife of Orazio Palavicino; she subsequently married Sir Oliver Cromwell (uncle of the Lord Protector of the same name).

Hooftman, Bartholomaeus: An elder brother of Gillis, and a merchant and alderman of Trier.

Hooftman, Gillis: Wealthy Antwerp merchant, financier and ship-owner.

Hooftman, Hendrik: An elder brother of Gillis; merchant who fled Alba's persecution.

Hooftman, Margaretha: Daughter of Bartholomaeus Hooftman and wife of Peeter Panhuys.

Lefèvre, Guy, de la Boderie: French scholar of oriental languages and poet; with his brother Nicolas he was one of the correctors of the *Biblia Regia*.

Leicester: See Dudley.

Lipsius, Justus (Joost Lips): Eminent classical scholar and philosopher.

Mander, Karel van: Pupil of d'Heere who wrote *Het Schilder-boeck*, which contains a collection of brief biographies of painters.

Margaret of Parma: Illegitimate daughter of Charles V; became Duchess of Parma by her second marriage. Governor of the Low Countries (1559–67) until the arrival of Alba; mother of Alessandro Farnese, a subsequent Governor.

Marlowe, Christopher: Elizabethan playwright and poet.

Marnix van St Aldegonde: Statesman and writer; William of Orange's right-hand man and Governor of Antwerp when it was besieged by Farnese.

Marot, Clément: French Protestant poet, some of whose psalm translations form part of the *Genevan Psalter*.

Melanchthon, Philip: Lutheran theologian.

Meteren, Emanuel van: Dutch merchant based in London who became consul for the Dutch community in London and wrote the first history of the Dutch revolt.

Moerentorf, Jan (Moretus): Married Plantin's eldest daughter and inherited the Antwerp printing press. His descendants continued to run the press until 1867 when it was sold to the city of Antwerp and became a museum; the presses, typefaces and much paperwork had been scrupulously preserved by the family.

Montano, Benito Arias: Chaplain to Philip II, he was the biblical scholar and philologist sent to Antwerp to supervise the printing of the *Biblia Regia*.

Moretus: See Moerentorf.

Niclaes, Henrik: Founder of the Family of Love.

Nispen, Margaretha van: Third wife of Gillis Hooftman; her eldest child, Anna, married Palavicino.

Noot, Jan van der: A Protestant, he was one of the first poets to write in Dutch.

Noue, François de la: Huguenot leader and war hero.

Ortelius, Abraham: Antwerp cartographer, author and scholar.

Parma: See Farnese.

Perez, Luis: Spanish merchant based in Antwerp; close friend of Plantin.

Palavicino, Orazio (Sir Horatio Palavicino): Noble Genoese merchant and financier; became an English denizen and served as an ambassador for Elizabeth I; married Anna Hooftman.

Panhuys, Peeter: Merchant and partner of Gillis Hooftman, whose niece he married.

Plantin, Christophe: A Frenchman, he was the pre-eminent printer of Antwerp.

Postel, Guillaume: A learned French scholar of ancient oriental languages and a religious universalist.

Racket, Johanna: Niece of Gillis Hooftman and wife of Johan Radermacher.

Radermacher, Johan: Apprentice of Gillis Hooftman and subsequently his agent in London and right-hand man.

Raphelengien, François (Raphelengius): Husband of Plantin's eldest daughter and skilled orientalist; took over Plantin's Leiden printing house and became Professor of Hebrew there; later converted to Calvinism.

Requesens, Luis de: Governor of the Low Countries after Alba (1573–6).

Rivière, Jeanne: Wife of Christophe Plantin.

Rogers, Daniel: Son of John Rogers, the first Protestant martyr under Mary I, and of Adriana van Weyden, who was a first cousin of Abraham Ortelius and Emanuel van Meteren. He wrote Latin poetry and acted as an agent for Elizabeth I in her negotiations with Protestant German princes.

Ruytinck, Simon: A minister at the Dutch stranger church at Austin Friars in London; wrote a brief biography of van Meteren.

Spinola, Ambrogio: Genoese soldier and successful Spanish general.

Viglius de Zuichem: An influential Netherlandish statesman under the Habsburgs.

Vivien, Johan (Vivianus): Friend of Ortelius and Radermacher; writer and collector of antiquities and especially coins.

Vos, Maerten de: Antwerp painter.

Walsingham, Francis: English ambassador to France at the time of St Bartholomew's Day massacre and subsequently principal secretary to Elizabeth I; Elizabeth's most important adviser apart from Cecil.

Zayas: See Çayas.

PART 1

AT THE HEART OF A CIVILISATION

CHAPTER 1

Prelude

The first portrait

As the taxi made its way through the rectangular gridiron of an industrial estate, we turned another right angle and there in front of us was a huge barrier. The driver turned and asked if we were sure that we had the correct address. I confirmed that we were sure, observing that I had a print-out of the email appointing the time and place.

'May I see it, please?' she enquired in the impeccable English that one comes to expect from the entire Dutch nation. Satisfied, she drove slowly up to the barrier, which began to slide open as we approached. We drove through, turning in a gradual circle through the enormous forecourt. A couple of people were waiting to welcome us at the top of some external steps, and so we climbed them, identified ourselves and were welcomed in. There, as we waited to meet the director, we read about the history of the building we now stood in. It had been constructed to protect the new euro coins and notes that were distributed once the new currency became legal tender in December 2001, hence the elaborate security arrangements and the huge loading yard for the lorries needed to distribute an entire nation's cash. Now the building was instead keeping safe the numerous works of art for which there was no room on the walls of Amsterdam's Rijksmuseum, and it was one of these that we had come to see.

Back in England, I had ascertained that the Rijksmuseum possessed a family portrait by the sixteenth-century Antwerp artist Maerten de Vos, and rather than travelling to Amsterdam on the off-chance of seeing it, I had emailed the museum to ask if it would be on display. I received a prompt answer informing me that it would not. I replied to express my regret that I would not be able to see the wedding portrait of my eleven times great-grandfather and great-grandmother. This quickly brought a reply with an invitation to view the portrait at the Rijksmuseum's store in Lelystad, which I gratefully accepted, much impressed by the speed and courtesy of the museum's staff. And so it was that we stood there as one of those great sliding racks with a number of pictures hanging on it was slowly drawn out and the portrait celebrating the marriage of Gillis Hooftman and Margaretha van Nispen in 1570 gradually emerged into sight (ill. 1). While we were there, we were told that both these forebears appeared in another much larger group portrait by the same artist which was to form part of an exhibition at the Rijksmuseum that winter, entitled *80 Jaar Oorlog* ('The Eighty Years' War'[1]). It is this second portrait which is the starting point of this book.

The second portrait

In the museum of the Catherijneconvent in Utrecht hangs the large oil painting that I went to see in the *80 Jaar Oorlog* exhibition at the Rijksmuseum. Its strong colours seem to confirm the suggestion that the painter worked for a while in Tintoretto's studio. It is entitled *Moses Showing the Tablets of the Law to the Israelites*, and at first glance it appears to be a straightforward imagining of the scene when Moses brings down the Tablets of the Law (the Ten Commandments) for a second time before he asks the Israelites to make offerings for the construction of the ark in which to carry and protect them. However, a closer examination immediately reveals an anomaly, for whereas Moses and Aaron in the centre are wearing what might be imagined to be clothes of the Old Testament period, we notice that between them and all around them are other people in more modern (i.e. sixteenth-century) clothes, many of them wearing ruffs typical of the 1570s. Looking more carefully, we now see that the full title describes the picture as showing Moses and the Israelites 'with portraits of members of the Panhuys family, their relatives and friends' (ill. 2).

What we have in front of us is a *portrait historié* – a painting in which contemporaries of the artist are depicted taking part in a historical scene. This needs to be distinguished from the earlier custom in which it was not uncommon for the donor of an altarpiece, for example, to be painted in devout prayer at the side of a painting and often to a smaller scale. These earlier figures are not participating in what is shown, but are observing it, just as the worshippers in the church are being invited to do. In a *portrait historié*, however, the modern characters are shown participating in the scene that is being painted. An earlier example would be Sandro Botticelli's *Adoration of the Magi* painted one hundred years earlier in 1475/6, an altarpiece commissioned by Gaspare di Zenobi for his family's funerary chapel in Santa Maria Novella in Florence. Not only is Gaspare shown amongst those adoring the Christ child, but according to Giorgio Vasari in his *Lives of the Painters*, the three Magi themselves can all be identified with members of the powerful Medici family.[2] This painting is different in one respect, though: in Botticelli's painting, it is only the artist himself who looks directly at the viewer, as if challenging us to join the worshipping great ones, but in de Vos's painting, all the contemporary figures look out from the painting. Right in the middle between Moses and Aaron stands the figure of Johan Radermacher, who looks directly at us over the right shoulder of Aaron. It is as if they are all urging the viewer to take heed of the Ten Commandments.

A picture with a modern layman at the centre was clearly never intended as an altarpiece in a church; this is a private painting, a fact made clear when on examination we see that some of the figures have their names and ages discreetly painted on their clothes. All of these turn out to be members of the family of Peeter Panhuys and it was, in fact, a descendant of the Panhuys family, Jonkheer Peeter van Panhuys, who gave the picture to the Mauritshuis Museum in 1836. For this reason, it is often referred to as the *Panhuys Paneel* and, in the interests of brevity, that is how I shall now refer to it.

Other sources

At this point, I began to investigate the origins of the connection between Gillis Hooftman and Peeter Panhuys, the business partner who had married his niece, and Maerten de Vos, the painter of both pictures. I soon found that the answer was literally staring me in the face from the centre of the *Panhuys Paneel*. The literature all pointed to Johan Radermacher, the tall man between Moses and Aaron who looks directly (and rather sternly) at the viewer. He was an erstwhile apprentice of Hooftman and subsequently his London agent. At an earlier period, Hooftman had wished to have a series of biblical paintings in his dining room (that new extravagance in the homes of the wealthy which also provided a private place near the back of the house where friends could discuss controversial matters in privacy). He asked Radermacher to suggest a good artist. While working in Antwerp as a young man, Radermacher had come to know Abraham Ortelius and they had become good friends. Consequently, it was only natural that Radermacher should turn to Ortelius for advice, and it was the latter, with his links across the intellectual world of Western Europe, who suggested that Maerten de Vos would be just the man to paint pictures for Radermacher's boss.

We can be sure of this because much later, after the death of Ortelius, his nephew Jacob Coels (often referred to as Ortelianus) asked Radermacher for memories of his uncle, and the latter told him the story in one of a number of letters that Coels kept, adding them to the large number of letters that Ortelius himself had carefully saved. This wonderful cache of letters, the *Epistulae Ortelianae*, was in due course passed on to the Dutch stranger church at Austin Friars in London for safe keeping. Most of these letters are in Latin, but a number are in 'modern' languages (i.e. sixteenth-century Dutch, French, Italian, German and Portuguese). Mercifully for readers today, their admirable nineteenth-century editor Jan Hendrick Hessels added to the heroic task of editing these letters the provision of full summaries of each one in English.[3] This painstaking transcription of a remarkable collection of letters provides a portrait of European civilisation at the time, as well as throwing light on the literal portrait that is the starting point of this study. There are more letters than these, however, that throw light on the likenesses in the portrait.

One of the figures in the *Panhuys Paneel* is the printer Christophe Plantin, and his letters are a further major source of information. Whereas the *Epistulae Ortelianae* consists mainly of letters written to Ortelius and his nephew, the letters in the enormous collection that Max Rooses, another diligent nineteenth-century editor, began to publish in the 1880s, the *Correspondance de Christophe Plantin*, are mainly copies of letters written by Plantin rather than to him. Other written material that I shall be drawing on includes the *memorieboeken* (family records) of Peeter Panhuys and Emanuel van Meteren (the first historian of the Dutch revolt), the *alba amicorum* (friendship books) of Radermacher, Ortelius and van Meteren, and some of the poetry of Lucas d'Heere and Joris Hoefnagel (who were both poets as well as painters).

Exploring the context

So, who are all these people that de Vos painted in the *Paneel*, and what do we learn from their lives? Some answers to the first of these questions are suggested below ('Who is who'). They range from the certain to the highly speculative, although there is fairly general agreement about many of their identities. My aim in the first part of this book is to explore what can be found out about the civilisation and conflicts of the time prior to the painting of the *Paneel* by looking at the lives and writings not just of the group shown in the *Paneel* but also of their wider circle. Next, in a shorter second part, I shall look at what happened after that moment. What can be said straight away is that these contributors to Antwerp's rich civilisation would be scattered by political and religious conflicts that led to an extended period of warfare and ultimately to the establishment of the northern provinces of the Habsburg Low Countries as the separate country that became the Netherlands.

The Habsburgs had inherited the Low Countries from the Dukes of Burgundy, and the territory that they ruled approximately covered what is now the Netherlands, Belgium and Luxembourg. Despite the seventeen constituent states being collectively described as the Low Countries, and despite the fact that they all shared the same hereditary overlord, they were some way from being what would normally be described as a country. Each state, and sometimes each city, had its own laws and privileges granted to them over time, and some of the northern states had only been annexed much more recently, the last being Gelderland, which had only finally been conquered by Charles V in 1543 after a long and vicious struggle with the Duke of Gelre. In addition, they were divided by language – not just French and Dutch, but also Frisian and Oosters (or East Dutch), and further east even Low German. They were also soon to be divided by bitter divisions between Calvinists and Catholics. These factors combined to ensure that it was only in exceptional circumstances that they joined to resist Spanish authority; in general, though, their own local interests over-rode any wider concerns.[4]

In 1559, the twenty-five-year-old Lucas d'Heere (the fifth man from the right standing at the back) had painted Philip II of Spain, the Habsburg overlord of the Low Countries, as King Solomon being offered gifts and homage by the Queen of Sheba, an allegorical figure representing the Low Countries. When he depicted this harmonious relationship of overlord and grateful subjects, he could hardly have imagined the moment twenty-six years later, in 1585, when Johan Radermacher (the central figure) would be part of a delegation negotiating the surrender of Antwerp to one of Philip's generals in exchange for an agreement that all Protestants would be allowed four years in which to settle their affairs and leave. This agreement was to prove more or less the point of no return in establishing a line between what became the Calvinist north (the future Netherlands) that would renounce Philip's lordship, and the Catholic south (the future Belgium) that would remain loyal to him, although there were still many weary years of war ahead. The aim of this book is to look at what was lost by this conflict.[5]

Who is who on the *Panhuys Paneel*?

The list below is intended both as an introduction and for reference as you read on. You may also wish to refer to the *Dramatis Personae* (p. 11) when you come across an unfamiliar name. The ascription of identities ranges from the certain (the names and ages of members of the Panhuys family are painted on their clothes) to the probable, the possible and, finally, but by no means of least interest, the distinctly speculative – let the reader beware![6] Therefore, this section needs to be prefaced with a warning. This book is about the civilisation that the people painted in the *Paneel* epitomise, as illuminated by their letters and other writings. It is *not* about the precise identification of every figure in the picture, nor is it exclusively about the people represented in it. If, therefore, some of the identifications I suggest below are wrong, this does not mean that, like some politicians, I am adhering to 'my' truth as opposed to provable facts. Three of the most doubtful identifications below are of Emanuel van Meteren, Benito Arias Montano, and Justus Lipsius. All three of them, however, were closely associated with other people who are generally agreed to be shown in the *Paneel* and, more importantly, are integral members of the civilised circle that is the real subject of this book. (My fourth completely unprovable identification is of Johanna Racket, but what I say about her is not dependent upon the identification.) Fuller explanations will emerge as the book continues, but where identification is particularly uncertain, I have put question marks below.

A provisional identification of figures on the Panhuys Paneel (ill. 2)
Standing at the back from the left
1. Joris Hoefnagel
2. Israelite
3. Black woman carrying a red amphora
4. Gillis Hooftman
5. Another black woman carrying a large jug
6. Emanuel van Meteren (or Jean de Castro or Maerten della Faille)
7. Johanna Racket (with back turned; niece of Gillis Hooftman and wife of Johan Radermacher) with young daughter
8. Jeanne Rivière (wearing a cap; she is the wife of Christophe Plantin)
9. Israelite (?) woman pointing
10. Unknown man in contemporary (?) dress, or an Israelite
11 & 12. Two Jewish women behind Moses
13. Moses (seated)
14. Unknown man gesticulating (just to right of Moses' head; possibly Justus Lipsius as a young man)

Standing at the back from the right
1. Self-portrait of Maerten de Vos
2. Peeter Panhuys
3. Rembert Dodoens
4. Israelite man
5. Lucas d'Heere

6. Bartholomaeus Hooftman
7. Israelite woman (behind, carrying a jug)
8. Unknown man. (I would dearly like to suggest that this simply dressed figure's evident interest in the text that he gestures towards means that he is intended to represent Benito Arias Montano, or at least his insistence on the primacy of textual scholarship, but deliberately painted to look unlike him since he was worried about the Inquisition at the time and would not wish to be associated with the others, but I have to concede this is *highly improbable*.)
9. Christophe Plantin
10. Israelite
11. Peeter Heyns
12. Aaron
13. Johan Radermacher (just to right of Moses' staff)

When these characters first enter the story, they will be identified by the numbers above preceded by an 'L' or 'R' (left or right, respectively): e.g. Gillis Hooftman (L4).

Left foreground with children

Margaretha van Nispen (the third wife of Gillis Hooftman) and her children Anna, Cornelis and Gillis Hooftman (junior). (There is some doubt about the identity of the two boys, but these are the names of Margaretha's first three children according to *Batavia Illustrata* or *Oud Batavien* (p. 1028),[7] which was published in 1685 and at the time was very approximately the Dutch equivalent of *Burke's Peerage*.)

Right foreground

Margaretha Hooftman (sitting in a yellow dress), a niece of Gillis Hooftman by his brother, Bartholomaeus,[8] and the wife of Peeter Panhuys, surrounded by a number of her children, including Peeter (standing behind her with his father's hand on his shoulder), Anna (kneeling in front of her mother and holding a jug), Margaretha (behind her sister), Bartholomaeus (between his mother's knees) and Gilles (on her lap). The *putto* (naked child) leaning against her is not a cupid, but perhaps a cherub to represent the soul of a daughter who had died in early childhood (strange though it seems to us, such cherubs were invariably portrayed as male).[9] Sitting to the immediate left of Margaretha is her mother, Barbara Daelberg (with her head resting on her hand, wearing a headdress). This last portrait is posthumous.

CHAPTER 2

A merchant family and its network:

Gillis Hooftman and Peeter Panhuys

...iam nova Roma resurgat
Scaldis ubi refluo flumine voluit aquas.
...'Now a new Rome arises
Where the tidal waters of the Scheldt ebb and flow.'

Orbis in exiguo maximus orbe viget.
'The great globe thrives within the small one.'
– Daniel Rogers[10]

The quayside scene in Sebastiaan Vrancx's picture of the crane and harbour gate on the Scheldt at Antwerp (1616–18; **ill. 3**) is one of frantic activity. Barrels and chests are everywhere as a horse drags a heavily loaded cart, and baskets and goods are carried in every direction; one dockworker is bent low under a heavy bale of cloth wrapped in bright red material, and another carries a huge chest. Two men shake hands, and others stand around discussing business. A sailor holds the hand of a woman as she cautiously walks down a gangplank to a moored ship. Dogs go about their doggy business, while one mother breast-feeds her baby, and others hold their children firmly by the hand. More ships can be seen on the river beyond. and in the middle distance is the fort known as Het Steen. Further along the bank, a windmill can be seen, and the right bank of the river curves away into the distance. Looming large on the left is a great double crane and to the right is the harbour gate leading into the city through the strong walls.

It was here in the heart of all this activity that the influential merchants Gillis Hooftman (1521–81) and Peeter Panhuys (1529–85) had lived forty years earlier in their great house, the Pollenaken, and made such a major contribution to the wealth of Antwerp. And where did Hooftman and Panhuys negotiate the business deals, loans and financial arrangements that lay behind the frantic trading activity shown in Vrancx's picture? After 1531, merchants like Hooftman no longer had to strike deals in the street or a warehouse because Antwerp had led the way in building an exchange, their Bourse, where merchants and bankers could meet all comers to exchange commodities, find the best bargains, arrange financial credits overseas, or borrow money to set up new businesses at home (ill. 4). If imitation is the sincerest form of flattery, then Sir Thomas Gresham, the English financier whose ingenious transactions on the Antwerp money market helped fund Elizabeth I through various financial difficulties, paid just such a tribute when, in 1565, more than thirty years after Antwerp, he opened a similar Bourse in London. After a visit by Elizabeth I, it became known as the Royal Exchange. The importance of the Antwerp Bourse was emphasised when Joris Hoefnagel (L1) chose to include the same Daniel Rogers poems quoted at the start of this chapter in his bird's-eye view of Antwerp which was printed by Plantin some time before 1597 (ill. 5).

When a merchant like Gillis Hooftman accumulates wealth, he looks for things to spend it on, and so he asked his agent, Johan Radermacher, to find a painter for the pictures that he wanted to decorate his dining room. His instructions were those of a typical businessman: he wanted someone who would work faster than the best-known Antwerp painter of the day, Frans Floris, but also someone whose work was not too expensive.[11] This is not only a reminder that you do not become as rich as Hooftman did without being careful with your money, but also that civilisation does not come cheap, and in Antwerp it depended very much on successful international trade.

The wealth that art seeks out can also, of course, derive from land or conquest, but it is worth noting that all the gold and silver looted from the Americas by the Spanish at this time was poured into their wars with France and in keeping the Ottoman Empire at bay in the Mediterranean, even before vast sums were spent trying to control the Netherlands (and which may well have contributed as much to inflation as to civilisation).[12]

Trade, as opposed to looting, depends on mutual contacts, and with the exchange of goods there often comes the exchange of ideas. For a society as a whole to become civilised, the peaceful cross-fertilisation of ideas is as crucial as the leisure provided by trade-generated wealth. And Antwerp, with its many resident foreign merchants, was supremely successful in creating the tolerant environment in which goods and ideas could be exchanged with profit to boost both the cultural and trading wealth of the city.

Antwerp's mercantile wealth depended partly on its happy position just a little way up the Scheldt estuary, with sea routes to the Channel and North Sea, west to Spain and across the Atlantic to the Americas, and finally even north to the White Sea. There were also good overland routes through Germany to the south and east, and connections through France in the west and on to Italy. In short, Antwerp was ideally placed to become the great trading centre of northern Europe, and so it did. There was a *frequentia omnium gentium*, a gathering of people from across the globe, as that Anglo-Netherlandish emissary of Elizabeth I, Daniel Rogers, was to put it in his poem about how merchants flocked to the Antwerp Bourse to trade (see note 1). Of course, Antwerp's location would have been insufficient without the drive and energy of its merchants, and the favourable site and burgeoning trade drew in ambitious merchants from far and near, not only from the Netherlandish provinces, but also from Germany, France and England, as well as from other great trading cities and ports such as Genoa and Venice. As the printer Christophe Plantin puts it in his 'Ode to the Council and People of Antwerp':

C'est grand honneur, Messieurs, do voir tant d'estrangers
Des quatre Parts du Monde (avec mille dangers)
Apporter ce qu'ils ont d'esprit & de puissance
Pour render vostre ville un Cornet d'abundance,
De sçavoir & de biens.
('It is much to the credit of the city that so many foreigners from the four
corners of the world, facing a thousand dangers, bring their ingenuity and
energy to make the city a cornucopia of plenty, knowledge and goods.')[13]

To encourage these foreign entrepreneurs and the money that they brought, Antwerp gave favourable trading concessions, even sometimes at the expense of their own merchants. Almost 1,000 foreign merchants were based in Antwerp and the city helped them to establish their own *naties* (nations) or bases where they could find accommodation and warehousing for their goods. These 'nations' were separate corporations within the city with their own buildings, administration and jurisdiction.[14] The city was also open to new ideas and willing to turn a blind eye to the unorthodox religious beliefs of some of its visitors.

However, not everyone who came to Antwerp to seek their fortune came from that far away. Hooftman and Panhuys came from an area roughly between Eupen, Walhorn and Aachen. These days, Eupen is at the centre of a small German-speaking enclave in east Belgium whereas Aachen is less than ten miles across the border in Germany. This region was in the Duchy of Limburg, but today this information is not especially helpful since there are now both Dutch and Belgian provinces called respectively Limburg and Limbourg, neither of which actually coincides with the earlier territory. The earlier Duchy of Limburg passed into the territory of the Duchy of Brabant, with the Duke of Brabant being one of Philip II of Spain's many inherited titles. (Eupen and Walhorn only became part of modern Belgium after the First World War, when the region was taken from Germany and given to Belgium.) Nowadays, Walhorn is a small village less than five miles from Eupen, itself a modest, although attractive, town. Modern borders, and indeed the concept of Belgium and Germany as separate countries with national boundaries, are quite alien to the period under discussion. Although Philip II's father, the emperor Charles V, was the common ruler of all these territories, and merged the titles that he had inherited with the intention of making a single unified state through his 'Pragmatic Sanction' of 1549, the Eighty Years' War split them apart again (later, the incursions of Louis XIV would slice away some of the western territories into France). Nor did linguistic boundaries coincide with national ones in the way that English people have come to expect because of their isolation across the Channel: even today, some people in this region speak Limburgish amongst themselves, a variant of Dutch/German, which like Dutch and Platt-Deutsch (Low German) gradually evolved from German. It was a form of Dutch itself, however, that was to become the dominant dialect and official language in northern Belgium and the Netherlands.

Hooftman moved from Eupen to Antwerp as a young man, whilst Panhuys, his younger partner and nephew by marriage, came from Walhorn. The wealth they created enabled them to commission pictures by increasingly well-known Antwerp painters such as de Vos, although, as we have seen, they were careful about the price they were willing to pay. The pictures that they commissioned also had a serious purpose behind them: they were not just decorative but were normally related to their wider intellectual interests and especially their religious concerns.

In the *Paneel*, for example, we not only see Moses at a key moment in Jewish and Christian history – when he brings down the Ten Commandments from Mount Sinai – but also one of the greatest printers of the age, Christophe Plantin, surrounded by some of his authors: the botanist Rembert Dodoens; the schoolmaster, translator and playwright Peeter Heyns; and the artist and poet

Lucas d'Heere, as well as learned merchants such as Johan Radermacher and Gillis's brother, Bartholomaeus Hooftman, another merchant.

Like a number of other merchants, Radermacher was a humanist with an interest in classical literature and history, as well as what could be learned from them. Humanist interests of this period went far beyond mere backward-looking antiquarianism: it has been suggested, for example, that Prince Maurice, who was to transform the rebel Dutch troops into a disciplined army that could cope with the Spanish, studied the account of Roman military tactics and training by Justus Lipsius, one of Plantin's authors, for principles and inspiration, if not for tactics.

So, what were the sources of the wealth that drew together so many exceptionally talented people, making sixteenth-century Antwerp a centre of civilisation as well as of trade, its new city hall as fine as any 'gorgeous palace' of Shakespeare's imagining? At the core of Antwerp's prosperity was the trade in wool and woollen cloth from England. Even today, you would be hard put to travel through the hillier regions of the English or Welsh countryside without seeing flocks of sheep. In sixteenth-century England, when most people's principal preoccupations were still shelter, food and clothing, just about the only commodity that could be easily transported and sold for profit was wool or the cloth woven from it (timber and stone were much more difficult to transport and were usually used locally). As such, wool lay at the heart of the English economy and the woolsack represented the commercial wealth of England and Wales. (It is not for nothing that the Lord Chancellor still sits on the Woolsack when presiding over the House of Lords.)

Much of England's wool was exported through Antwerp, where it arrived either unwoven or as cloth. The latter was sent either ready for immediate sale or for 'finishing' in the workshops of the Low Countries.[15] Dyeing cloth meant that another key import was alum (usually a term for hydrated double-sulphate salt of aluminium, which could only be mined in a few places), which was the only known mordant for fixing dye and therefore essential for the local industry. In 1491, Maximilian of Austria had granted Antwerp the staple (i.e. exclusive trading rights) for alum, and being at the centre of this trade had strengthened Antwerp's growing commercial dominance.[16] By the sixteenth century, the basic trade in cloth and alum was beginning to be augmented, partly, of course, by what English merchants bought with the money made by selling wool. The range of what was being sold started to expand rapidly as the result of the explorations and colonisation of the Portuguese down the west coast of Africa and beyond to the East Indies, as well as by Spanish and Portuguese conquests in South America.[17] Not only Portuguese spices, but also South German copper and silver were valuable commodities traded through Antwerp.[18] There was also trade from southern Europe and the Mediterranean, where Venetian and Genoese galleys had been fighting both literally and commercially for many years while trading with North Africa and the Ottoman Empire. Goods from this region might travel overland or directly by sea; for example, writing at the end of the sixteenth century, John Stow mentions Italian 'galley men' in his *A Survey of London* who landed their merchandise in Thames Street at a place called Galley Quay.[19]

Many imports, however, reached England via Antwerp, the most successful and prosperous port in northern Europe, and it was here that Hooftman and Panhuys came in the mid-sixteenth century with a view to making their fortunes. We can see the latter on the right-hand side of the *Panhuys Paneel*, named after him, of course, as its commissioner. He stands there (R2), looking out at us, dressed in brown, with lace at his cuffs and wearing a ruff, and with a reddish-brown cloak over his left shoulder. His left hand rests reassuringly on the left shoulder of his rather apprehensive-looking eldest son, also named Peeter, and he holds his son's right hand with his own right hand. (He can be identified with absolute confidence by the fact that his name is painted on the fold of his cloak running upwards towards his shoulder.)

On the left-hand side of the *Paneel* stands Gillis Hooftman (L4), wearing a red cloak and with a bushy, gingerish beard. At first sight, his careworn face which stares out at us looks almost detached from the body to which it belongs, but on closer examination we see that this is because its owner has the stooped neck of an older man who has spent many hours in his office poring over his maps and accounts. Nevertheless, he still has an imposing physical presence. Apart from his natural concerns as a ship-owner and merchant in a time of widespread war and upheaval, we know that Hooftman had good cause to look careworn, as he had suffered some heavy financial losses in the years prior to the painting. One of his ships had sunk off the coast of Zeeland in 1571 and another, valued at 30,000 florins, was wrecked on shifting sands near Saaftinghe[20] in 1574, while in the same year he had also had to contribute 1,500 florins to the forced loan from the city of Antwerp to the Spanish Governor-General, Requesens, after unpaid Spanish troops had mutinied immediately after they had won a crushing victory at Mookerheyde and marched on Antwerp.[21] The earlier painting by de Vos of Hooftman and his third wife, Margaretha van Nispen, mentioned above (**ill. 1**) makes it possible to identify him confidently, as do two portrait medallions (**ills. 6 & 7**; see also p. 52[22]). The inextricable entanglement of politics and religious conflict with commerce in the Reformation period is well illustrated by the lives of international merchants and bankers such as Hooftman and Panhuys. As such, it is not surprising that Hooftman looks preoccupied.

Hooftman (1521–81), possibly the youngest of eight siblings, had probably come to Antwerp a year or two before 1540 (he was already registered as a citizen of Antwerp by 15 July 1541).[23] According to the nineteenth-century Belgian *Biographie Nationale de Belgique*, he started his career as a *colporteur et boutiquier* (pedlar and small shopkeeper), but soon became a rich international merchant and owner of a large merchant fleet.[24] This rags-to-riches story requires two major qualifications. The first is that he probably joined one of his older brothers, Hendrik, in Antwerp. We can assume that the latter was already thriving commercially since in 1562 he bought the Pollenaken for 10,000 guilders.[25] This was a substantial house in Steenstraat in a prime position on the banks of the Scheldt where Hooftman lived with Hendrik. Steenstraat was a quayside street that led to Het Steen, the fortress and jail on the banks of the Scheldt. It was evidently a large house since later, after Hendrik had left Antwerp to avoid the religious persecution enforced by the Duke of Alba, Peeter Panhuys and his family lived there with Hooftman and his family. Being right on the quayside, it almost certainly served as a warehouse as well as a home.[26] It appears, then, that Hooftman's first ventures may have been in partnership with an already successful elder brother.

The second qualification to the story is that it was not unusual at the time to share risk not simply through shared ownership of cargo, but also by sharing ships. In these circumstances, it might be hard to quantify accurately the number of ships owned by a single merchant, or to be sure that Hooftman really owned one hundred of them (as some accounts claim), small though they were by today's standards. Nevertheless, by the end of his life, Hooftman was evidently very rich and could afford to take on the risks of shipwreck and privateers by himself, thus avoiding the inconvenience of needing to negotiate the coordination of voyage times and destinations with other merchants.

Hooftman's initial success seems to have been based on the timber trade in the Baltic, although he later came to trade much more widely in anything from woollen cloth to Bibles. Merchant ships were vulnerable, however, not only to bad weather and errors of navigation, but also to the dangers of war and piracy. The Livonian War (1558–83) made the Baltic dangerous,[27] while conflict between Spain and France (which was also engaged in a civil war) also posed threats.

Given these events, it is easy to understand Hooftman's compulsive reference to his maps which was described by his agent, Radermacher, in a letter of 1603 telling Ortelianus how the latter's recently deceased uncle,

Abraham Ortelius, first came to produce his ground-breaking atlas. At this time, maps were often attached to a linen backing and then fixed on wooden frames so that they could be hung on walls, or otherwise they were rolled up; in other words, they were not easily portable or available for instant reference. Radermacher describes how, at times of conflict, Hooftman would anxiously spread out his maps:

> He also bought all the geographical maps that could be had so that he could calculate from the distances the freight of merchandise and the dangers they were exposed to. They also enabled him to make judgements about the news that was brought him daily about the European wars, especially in France. And as he lived at a time of many such events, he would compare all the maps he could get hold of. As he didn't tolerate any delay, he would unfold them to examine them during the course of his meals or whenever there was debate about crossing certain territories, or in the middle of conversation with friends, or even when a thought occurred to him when he was by himself.[28]

The ongoing struggle for domination of the Baltic explains why, at about the time of the painting of the *Panhuys Paneel*, Hooftman started to plan an alternative route for importing goods from Russia via the White Sea. This may have been suggested to him by an early and fairly accurate map of the seas around northern Russia (*Septentrionalium Regionum Descrip.*, ill. 9) that was published by Abraham Ortelius in his *Theatrum Orbis Terrarum* ('Theatre of the Lands of the Globe', first edition, Antwerp, 1570). The *Theatrum* was the first world atlas and was arguably prompted by Hooftman's having earlier commissioned Ortelius to put together a book of maps, and possibly also by his paying for some of Ortelius's earlier visits to Italy in search of these artefacts. Radermacher certainly thought so; in another letter to Ortelianus, he returns to the inconvenience Hooftman experienced when consulting maps that were too large to spread out easily on a crowded table:

> Myself, I suggested a means of removing in some way this inconvenience. If one reduced everything in the maps to a smaller format, one could then reassemble them, once they had been drawn, in a book which could be handled in no matter what place. Hence the task was entrusted to me, and through me to Ortelius, of obtaining from Italy – which was then particularly rich in beautiful things – and from France as many maps as could be found printed on one sheet of paper. In this way originated a

volume of about thirty maps which is still in the possession of Hooftman's heirs. The use of this collection proved to be very commodious both for my master, on the tables of his office or in his bedroom, and for myself, squeezed as I was in my diminutive office. It gave our friend Abraham [Ortelius] the opportunity of taking a decision with useful consequences for those who had a general interest in the topic. He reduced the largest geographical maps of the best-known authors, which rarely had had the same format or dimensions as each other, on to single sheets of paper, in a single volume. In the year 1570 he published a collection of 52 maps – if I am not mistaken – each of which bore the name of its author, accompanied by commentaries. Before this, as far as I know, he had not himself edited more than three maps, that of Egypt, that of Asia (begun earlier by Giacomo Gastaldi) and that of the World.

According to a later letter from Radermacher, this privately commissioned book of thirty-eight maps which predated the *Theatrum* was still in the possession of the Hooftman family in 1604, albeit much worn.[29]

Hooftman's support of Ortelius in his map-making enterprise seems to have been typical of his utilitarian view of learning. Nevertheless, Radermacher writes of his erstwhile master that although not a man of letters himself, he was supportive of academic study, especially when applied to such matters as navigation.[30]

It was in 1577, two years after the *Paneel* was painted, that Hooftman set up a company with the van de Walle brothers to trade with Russia (see p. 147), but the painting reveals the close relationship that already existed between Hooftman and Panhuys. The most basic source of information about Panhuys is to be found in his *memorieboekje* (memory notebook),[31] in which he started recording autobiographical information in 1566, perhaps prompted by the death of his mother that year or by the birth of his eldest son, Peeter. He first notes the death of his father, Servaes Panhuys, thirty years earlier at Limburg, where he had been an alderman (Peeter was seven at the time). At the age of thirteen, he went to Antwerp where he lived with a lawyer, presumably as an apprentice in the law. He then records how, in 1549, he went to London, where he lived with Gillis Hooftman until he returned to Antwerp in 1558. (Hooftman is listed as the richest of the foreign merchants living in London, but will certainly have frequently returned to his large house in Antwerp.) Panhuys also records his marriage in 1561, three years after his return to Antwerp, to Hooftman's niece, Margaretha Hooftman (right foreground, wearing a yellow dress and seated surrounded by her children). Margaretha was the daughter of Bartholomaeus Hooftman (R6) and Johanna du Bois. He adds that the wedding feast was held the next day in Gillis Hooftman's house, the Pollenaken, at the latter's expense.

Panhuys was clearly the junior of the partners; for one thing, he was eight years younger and would have only been twelve when Hooftman became sufficiently established in Antwerp as to become a citizen in 1541. The reasons for Hooftman's decision to take Panhuys on as a partner are not known, but it is not difficult to find likely explanations. The latter will have learnt the intricacies of the business while he was in London with Hooftman, who must have been satisfied with his ability and commitment, not to mention his useful experience of trading abroad. Hooftman may also have felt the need for a new partner after his elder brother, Hendrik, refused to compromise on his Reformist principles when the Duke of Alba was sent to enforce religious conformity (he and his brother had been identified earlier as prominent Calvinists by a Spanish agent). Hendrik had deemed it advisable to withdraw to Limburg, where a number of his siblings were still living.[32] In such uncertain times, Hooftman needed someone to share in running the business. Trust was an important issue for an international merchant with distant offices in foreign countries, and a partner from near where he was brought up, who had learnt on the job under his supervision and whose family he had presumably known as a boy, would have appealed more than someone whose background he did not know. In London, Panhuys will also have met Radermacher, Hooftman's former apprentice who was now his trusted agent and friend. Confidence will have been further strengthened when Panhuys married Hooftman's niece, Margaretha.

The portrait of Panhuys painted by Frans Pourbus in 1562 (**ill. 10**) suggests that he may well have brought money into the partnership as well. Painted a year after his marriage to Margaretha, it shows a young man dressed soberly in black, but looking elegant and wearing three heavy gold chains; there is a coat of arms in the top-right corner. Both the image and the fact that it was commissioned from the fashionable painter Frans Pourbus suggest a man of assured status, who had almost certainly been well-off before he became Hooftman's partner, and who certainly shared Hooftman's pleasure in art.

Both of them appear to have already become Protestant at this point. One of Margaret of Parma's spies reported:

> Gillis Hooftman and Peeter Panhuys, merchants in Antwerp, have belonged to the Calvinist sect for many years. During the wars in France, they provided the Huguenots with money through the hands of Pierre

Assesatz, a wealthy merchant in Toulouse and a member of the sect, to wage war against the king. After that they financially supported and still support the ministers during the riots over there. They are in contact and correspond with [van] Brederode, Van den Bergh and the rest [other leaders of Protestant resistance in the Low Countries]. They have been to the Prince of Orange many times and they are among those who urge the population not to let any soldiers in.[33]

Whether it is really true that Hooftman had 'belonged to the Calvinist sect for many years', rather than being Lutheran, seems doubtful, but it is understandable that a Catholic spy might fail to distinguish between different forms of Protestantism.[34] What is clear is that there would have been religious sympathy between Hooftman and Panhuys. The Pourbus portrait of Panhuys presumably shows him as he wished to be seen: a wealthy merchant, but also a serious-minded and devout one.

Hooftman's own preoccupations as a merchant can be seen not only in his desire for a partner in whom he could have absolute confidence, but in his patronage of books devoted to the applied learning needed by ship-owners and their captains, and also the enormous range of knowledge and skills needed by a successful merchant, such as the ability to convert weights and measures and cope with different currencies, along with an understanding of different languages and legal systems, quite apart from nautical and geographical knowledge.[35] As well as encouraging Ortelius to search out the best maps for his atlas, Hooftman supported Michiel Coignet, a mathematician and cartographer from Antwerp, in publishing his *Nieuwe Onderwijsinghe op de principaelste Puncten der Zeevaert* ('New Instructions on the Principal Points of Navigation'). In an appendix to this book, Coignet argued that with an accurate timekeeper it should be possible to determine longitude (although the invention of an accurate chronometer still lay well in the future). He also shared Hooftman's interest in navigational instruments, and describes in the appendix his invention of a nautical hemisphere which in theory could be used to calculate longitude.[36] The fact that Coignet does not appear in the *Paneel* may reflect religious difference (he appears to have been a Catholic), but is more probably attributable to the fact that he was not at the time that well known by Panhuys or Hooftman (his book on navigation had not been completed at the time the *Paneel* was painted and would not be published until 1580).[37]

Patronage of a different sort can be seen in Hooftman's commissioning of two portrait medallions of himself (**ills. 6 & 7**). The first is by Steven van Herwijk[38] in pewter and is dated 1559 with this inscription: EGIDIUS

HOFTMAN AETATIS SUAE XXXVIII 1559. The second is in lead and inscribed GILLIS HOOFTMAN AET LIX AN M D LXXX; it was commissioned towards the end of his life from Jacob Jonghelinck.[39] Midway between these two portrait medals comes the wedding portrait of 1570, of Hooftman and his third wife, Margaretha van Nispen, by Maerten de Vos (ill. 1). (It is one of the ironies of the Reformation is that the austere piety that saw church paintings whitewashed and forbade statues of saints opened the way instead for portraits of prosperous merchants.)

The choice of van Herwijk and Jonghelinck for the medallions suggests that Hooftman was not influenced by religious prejudice, since the first was a Protestant and the second firmly Catholic, working amongst others for Cardinal Granvelle, the first minister of Margaret of Parma, who did his best to suppress Protestantism. Van Herwijk, the engraver of the earlier medallion, had found it expedient to avoid persecution for his Protestantism by spending time both in Poland, where he engraved medals for Sigismund II and members of the royal family, and in England, where he engraved a medal of Elizabeth I. In an article on these medallions, Luc Smolderen questions the attribution to van Herwijk on the grounds of quality, and draws attention instead to the similarity of pose and style with a medallion showing Calvin by an unknown artist. But if this is correct, we can still be fairly sure that the engraver of this first medallion was Protestant. Jonghelinck, on the other hand, was definitely Catholic: he not only worked for Cardinal Granvelle, but also made the large, triumphalist statue of the Duke of Alba that was placed in Antwerp as an emphatic reminder of his victory over the Dutch rebels at the Battle of Jemmingen, when William of Orange's brother, Louis of Nassau, was forced to withdraw from the Low Countries (see p. 80). It was cast from the bronze cannons captured at the battle, but was taken down on the instructions of Luis de Requesens, Alba's successor, who recognised that its provocative nature was counter-productive. It was subsequently melted down in about 1576. Smolderen also doubts this second attribution, partly on the grounds of style, but also on the grounds that a committed Catholic such as Jonghelinck would not have accepted a commission from the Protestant Hooftman. Nevertheless, given that the latter seems always to have conformed outwardly by attending Catholic Mass and observing fast days, this does not seem a particularly compelling argument.[40]

These medallion portraits can be seen as typical commissions of a successful sixteenth-century merchant, but Hooftman's interests transcend the vanity of the successful, self-made businessman. On the reverse of the second medallion, a ship is shown sailing below a cluster of clouds from which rain down rocks and lines, representing either torrential rain or possibly thunderbolts (**ill. 8**). On either side of the clouds are the initials G and H, and below is an anagram on the name Gylis Hooftman, HA LOF SY MIN GOT ('Ah, praise be to my God'). The picture is very much in the style of contemporary emblem books and presumably it is meant to express Hooftman's gratitude to God for his prosperity despite the dangers of war and bad weather.[41]

More light-hearted than this image or any of the paintings that Hooftman commissioned from de Vos was a *trompe l'oeil* painting that Karel van Mander tells us he commissioned from the architect and painter Hans Vredeman de Vries, who was a master of perspective. According to van Mander, the picture showing an open door leading to a courtyard beyond was so convincing that amongst others it fooled the Prince of Orange.[42]

Margaretha van Nispen, Hooftman's third wife (seated on the left side of the *Paneel*), also patronised the arts. She chose to send her daughters to De Lauwerboom (The Laurel Tree), a girls' school founded by Peeter Heyns (R11) in Antwerp and then later re-founded in Haarlem. We know this because when Heyns published three plays that he had written for educational purposes, one of the dedicatees was Margaretha and he refers to teaching her daughters. This suggests that Heyns regarded Hooftman's widow as a patron. So, evidently, did the composer Jean de Castro (possibly L6), who dedicated two of his volumes of two-part chansons in 1592 to Margaretha's children: one to Cornelis and the other to Marguerite and Beatrice.[43] The latter, written for two high voices, was presumably intended to be sung by the dedicatees themselves. The dedication suggests real affection: 'l'amitié grande que [vous] me daignez porter, laquelle j'experimente largement de jour an jour'.[44] It would be foolish to build too much on the necessarily complimentary sentiments of a dedication to a patron, but the assertion that he experiences the friendship not simply in general terms, but unstintingly from day to day, suggests genuine affection.

The wealth for such patronage came from widespread trade and not just with Russia – Hooftman and Panhuys also did business in Morocco, Spain, Portugal, France, England, Scotland, Ireland and Gdansk.[45] We know that Hooftman's involvement in the wool and cloth trade with England was particularly important, and he was to become the richest foreign merchant to have a base in London at that time (a certificate of assessment of foreigners for tax purposes rates him and his partners at £300, £100 more than the next-richest foreign company in London). It was therefore understandable that during some of the negotiations to resolve disagreements over differential cloth taxes and export licences between the Habsburg Low Countries and England, it was he who led a group of merchants who were upset by discriminatory cloth taxes. They approached the ruling Council of State in Brussels to put a case for their receiving the equivalent privileges in London to those that the English Merchants Adventurers, his commercial rivals, received in Antwerp. They also appealed directly to the Privy Council in London, but they received short shrift: Elizabeth's councillor, Cecil, dismissed the complainants as 'worthy not only to be banished out of England but also out of their own countries for their doings'. Even more irritating for Hooftman must have been the fact that following a grant from the Queen, the majority of licences for exporting English cloths had to be purchased from the Merchant Adventurers, who would have had every reason to make life difficult for him. The lords of Antwerp strongly objected to his making a fuss, however, since the city's prosperity had been built upon a policy of giving foreign merchants much freer access to the city's markets than other cities did to theirs at that period, and they believed that continuing prosperity depended on preserving the goodwill of those using Antwerp as a transit port to export their goods as far afield as Italy and the Levant.[46] The lords would have been uncomfortably aware of the dependence of the home cloth trade on wool imports from England, and the last thing that they would have wanted was to start a trade war and drive away business. As such, they assured the English that Hooftman and his fellow merchants were simply 'particular men, which seek but their particular commodity'.[47]

In the end, the Colloquy between the Netherlands and England (the high-level trade negotiations between three representatives on each side) was adjourned in June 1566 without agreement, but with the English commissioners passing on a warning that the trade agreement and the Spanish/English political alliance were inter-related.[48] The difficulties between England and the Habsburg Low Countries may have been primarily commercial to start with, but as Elizabeth's representatives at the Colloquy made clear, they were inseparable from political issues, and this in turn meant religious issues as well. It was in the same year that negotiations were put on hold that the Spanish agent Jerónimo de Curiel sent his report denouncing several Antwerp merchants, including both Gillis and Hendrik Hooftman, whom he accuses of supporting Huguenots and other Protestants and of being in contact with the *Geuzen*, the rebels opposed to Philip II.[49] Curiel adds that Hooftman possessed goods in Spain, but as a precaution had let these be entered under the name of a third party. He was counted among the richest and most important merchants of the city, but regardless of this Curiel felt he should be kept under surveillance. Curiel also accused Hooftman's son-in-law, Antonio Anselmo from Limburg, of an interest in Calvinism. (Anselmo was later to be the guardian of Anna, Hooftman's first daughter by Margaretha van Nispen, shown kneeling beside her in a green dress on the left of the *Paneel* in the foreground.)

Religious complications intensified sharply in 1566. It was at the end of June, just after the Colloquy was adjourned, that Protestant preachers began to pull huge crowds to the fields just outside Antwerp to listen to sermons. The attempts of the lords of the city to prevent this were ineffective. On Monday 8 July, in response to rumours that the Regent was sending troops to Antwerp to regain control, the trained bands of the city forced the lords to hand them the keys to the city gates and made preparations to resist any assault. In fact, the Regent lacked the troops for an attack and instead sent the Prince of Orange, William the Silent, as the Burggraf of the Duke of Brabant (i.e. the official representative of the King of Spain, one of whose titles was Duke of Brabant), to restore order to the city. Orange was still outwardly Catholic at this time, but respected by both sides, and there was relative calm until he left. Then, on 20 August, an outbreak of iconoclasm started at the collegiate Church of Our Lady (the current cathedral) before going on to affect several other churches. To make matters worse, the iconoclasm was followed by some looting, which induced a widespread fear of a social uprising (and not merely a religious one). This could be seen as a social reaction to the unemployment caused by the earlier action of the Council in Brussels against English wool imports that had caused great hardship in Antwerp, and also as a consequence of a series of poor harvests, but nevertheless there is no doubt of the religious ferment that lay behind it as well.

Hooftman's own reactions, I suspect, were divided between concern for his commercial activities and properties, and sympathy for the Protestant position. When the Prince of Orange returned at the end of August to restore order, a compromise agreement conceded that three churches in the city should be made available to the Calvinists and three to the Lutherans. It is at this point that Sir Thomas Gresham, a key agent of Elizabeth I in commercial and financial matters, reports to Cecil that he was invited to a dinner by the Prince of Orange at which Hooftman was also present, because the Prince was anxious to protect the prosperity of the city by encouraging the English merchants to stay. Gresham was non-committal, but gave clear advice in his report to Cecil afterwards that English exporters should now look elsewhere for an alternative port:

> [You] shall do very well in time to consider some other realm and place for
> our commodities, whereby Her Majesty's realm may remain in peace, which

in this brabling time is one of the chiefest things Your Honor [i.e. Cecil himself] had to look unto, considering in what terms this country do now stand, in which is ready one to cut another's throat for matters of religion.

Gresham also reports to Cecil that Hooftman had asked him at this same meeting: 'How do you think Mr. Gresham, for as much as the Queen's Majesty and her realm is of this religion [i.e. Protestant], do you think that she will give aid to our noble men, as she did in France for the religion's sake?' In his diplomatically non-committal reply, Gresham asked him whether the lords of the city had ever asked the Queen for such help and added that he was 'no counsellor nor never dealt with such great matters'.[50]

Despite his advice to Cecil about moving trade elsewhere, Gresham himself still had financial interests in Antwerp, not least since he wished to raise money for Elizabeth I, and one of her creditors was Hooftman himself. Under the terms of a contract agreed on 4 August 1566, the English crown owed the latter the considerable sum of 42,337 florins.[51] In the aftermath of the iconoclastic disturbances later that month, and with the imminent arrival of the Duke of Alba, Richard Clough, Gresham's agent in Antwerp, reports his difficulty in raising money to pay off the previous loans, mentioning that Hooftman was one of those demanding payment from him and that he was reduced to offering creditors no more than 'fair words'. Gresham resourcefully found money outside the Low Countries to cope with the immediate problem, but by December 1566, Hooftman had only been persuaded 'with much ado' to postpone repayment for a mere two months until February 1567. Then, as the political situation became more dangerous, the problem for Queen Elizabeth eased. Hooftman was the largest Antwerp creditor of the English crown, but probably became aware of the insurance value of having so much capital lodged abroad in a Protestant country.[52]

According to the Lutheran chronicler Godevaerd van Haecht, Hooftman was neither Catholic nor Calvinist, but a prominent member of the Lutheran faction in Antwerp.[53] Van Haecht adds that Hooftman withstood pressure from the Calvinist faction and did not defect. On the contrary, he took an oath of allegiance to the Spanish king, attended Mass and confession, and observed the fast days, unlike his brother Hendrik, who fled in 1566 to avoid such compromises.[54] It is a possibility that Hooftman, like so many at the time, was less than fully certain about his religious beliefs, but would have known in any case that Luther's teaching distinguished between religious and secular authority (both Luther and Melanchthon made it quite clear that the secular authorities must be obeyed or otherwise chaos would follow, as indeed it had during the German Peasants' War in 1524–5). What is clear is that despite his outwardly Catholic observances, Hooftman had been a Protestant for quite some time, but was no revolutionary.

Although Luther's social conservatism and insistence that political authorities should be obeyed will have appealed to Hooftman, one would have expected Calvin's teaching on lending money at interest to be much more congenial to an operator in Antwerp's growing money market than Luther's outright condemnation of such activities, which he describes as invented by the devil. Nor indeed is Luther much more sympathetic to making a profit in trading:

> A man should not say, 'I will sell my wares as dear as I can or please,' but 'I will sell my wares as is right and proper.' For thy selling should not be a work that is within thy own power or will, without [beyond] all law and limit, as though thou wert a God, bound to no one. But because thy selling is a work that thou performest to thy neighbour, it should be restrained within such law and conscience that thou may practise it without harm or injury to him.[55]

Calvin, however, is much more relaxed about making a profit; according to him, 'Whence do the merchant's profits come, except from his own diligence and industry?'[56] In other words, the problem is not wealth, but its misuse. He also recognises the need for a banking system; interest-free loans should be made to the needy, but it is entirely reasonable to share in the profits that someone else has made with the money that has been borrowed from you.[57]

It was presumably in observing Luther's decree that the authority of the state should be obeyed that Hooftman and Panhuys chose, like William the Silent himself, to continue to have their children baptised in the state-endorsed Catholic churches until the Protestant churches were established with state approval. We know, for example, that Johan Panhuys, with whom his mother was probably pregnant at the time that the *Paneel* was painted, was born on Christmas Eve 1575 and baptised on the second day of Christmas at the Catholic church of St Walburgis in Antwerp (the first Panhuys child to be baptised by a Protestant minister would be Barbara in 1579). Similarly, it was only after William the Silent had received formal permission from the States General that Catherina Belgica became the first of his children to be baptised in a Reformed manner.[58] This formal observation of the state's legal requirements sounds much more like Lutheranism than the uncompromising attitude of the Reformed. It would be a mistake, in any case, to think that those who had been brought up as Catholic would suddenly abandon its customs without a preliminary period of doubt and a good deal of soul-searching. Belief in the importance of baptism for salvation would be deeply engrained and emotionally difficult to ignore in a period of high infant mortality, especially if you feared that your baby might otherwise be barred from heaven.

Although Hooftman probably shared the views of William the Silent and Panhuys about conforming to Catholic authority, it is nevertheless clear that on at least one occasion the rebel party trusted him with confidential information and used his resources as an international merchant for political purposes. Emanuel van Meteren reports in his history of the Dutch rebellion that when Flushing (Vlissingen) was being besieged by Alba's troops in 1572, Hooftman was asked to provide the besieged port with weapons and ammunition, which he managed through the agency of a Captain Worst, when he secretly arranged for a ship to be sent with essential military supplies, despite the fact that he was based in Spanish-controlled Antwerp.[59] It was not without cause that the Spanish agent, Jerónimo de Curiel, was keeping an eye on Hooftman. Hooftman may have been more Lutheran than Calvinist, but he was definitely not a supporter of the Spanish regime.

It would have been loyalty to the city in which he had made his fortune, rather than approval of Spanish rule, that led to his positive response to the city's request for financial help to pay off the Spanish soldiers in Antwerp, who had been demanding their back pay with menaces in April 1574. The new vice-regent, Requesens, had asked for a loan of 400,000 pounds Artois[60] to ensure that 'all peril of looting and other inconveniences that might come' would be prevented – a request that sounds remarkably like a demand for protection money.[61] Hooftman was appointed to be a member of a committee instructed to find ways of maximising the city's income and cutting expenditure, but he was also one of those citizens who made a personal contribution to raise the necessary money, a deed that can only be seen as being done for the public good to ensure peace. Spain was notoriously bad at repaying its debts, and nobody would have expected this so-called loan to be regarded in any other light than as a one-off tax.

The political and religious positioning of Peeter Panhuys was to become more apparent in a later crisis – the siege of Antwerp in 1584–5 (see Chapter 10). Panhuys, like Hooftman, was registered as a citizen of Antwerp soon after his arrival, and later served the city as both alderman and treasurer. Almost the only things that he records in his *memorieboek* apart from family births and deaths are some property transactions and his election to various positions in the Antwerp government, regardless of whether the authorities were Catholic or Protestant.

The apparent willingness of Hooftman and Panhuys to compromise over religious matters has led some to speculate that they might have been members of the Family of Love. The Familists (as they were known) were not so much a Christian sect as a group of like-minded Christians – both Catholic and Protestant – who thought the inner spiritual life so important that differences in outward ceremonies were supremely unimportant. For this reason, they instructed their members to obey the civil authorities in matters of religion.[62] The *Paneel* is itself a fascinating, if ambiguous, piece of evidence. It shows a gathering of people who, despite their varying religious affiliations might, in theory at least, all be Familists. This idea will be tested as we look at the lives of others portrayed by de Vos in the *Paneel*, but first I shall look at the life and beliefs of the painter himself.

CHAPTER 3

Maerten de Vos:

The painter of the Panhuys Paneel *and other* portraits historiés

Although J.W. Zondervan suggested that the figure on the extreme right of the *Panhuys Paneel* (ill. 2) was the philosopher Justus Lipsius, it seems very clear, as Rudie van Leeuwen and Armin Zweite argue, that it is a self-portrait of the artist himself, Maerten de Vos, as is confirmed by a comparison with his self-portrait in his painting of the Flood in the Schlosskapelle (castle chapel) at Celle, in which he points in admonition at the panicking wicked as the Ark sails away (ill. 11).[63]

* * *

The painter of the *Panhuys Paneel* was Maerten de Vos (R1). He was born in Antwerp in 1532, and first trained there under his father. The wealth brought by trade had made the city the centre of a flourishing art market, so much so that the Schilderspand (Painters' Building), with no fewer than one hundred shops, was opened for the sale of artworks in 1540.[64] In his *Het Schilder-boeck* ('Book on Painting'), Karel van Mander writes that 'the famous and great city of Antwerp, made rich by its trade, saw the most eminent artists gather within its walls because art desires wealth'.[65] Guicciardini, meanwhile, noted that 'in this region alone are more painters of every kind than in many other provinces put together'.[66] Elsewhere, van Mander writes that Antwerp had become 'the nurse of the arts, just as Florence used to be in Italy, and has brought to birth masters of the most wide ranging arts'.[67]

Leaving Antwerp as a young man, de Vos visited Italy between about 1552 and 1558, where he worked in Tintoretto's studio in Venice, according to the latter's not always reliable biographer, Carlo Ridolfi.[68] He subsequently visited Rome and probably Florence as well. It may well be that it was while working under Tintoretto that he learned his mastery of colour.[69] While in Italy, he may have also spent some time in the company of Pieter Bruegel. The facts become more certain once he had returned to Antwerp in 1558, when he became a master in the Guild of St Luke (the guild for painters). The paintings for Hooftman's dining room discussed below provided, according to Radermacher, his first big breakthrough, leading to commissions from other merchants. (An older painter, Frans Floris, was already well established with a large workshop and had had a near monopoly of history painting in Antwerp until about this time.) Radermacher may be making an exaggerated claim, however, in implying that he helped to give him his first big break, since it was around this time that the artist was commissioned to work in the chapel of the Lutheran Duke William of Brunswick-Lüneburg at Celle. At this point, it seems probable that de Vos was also Lutheran, but after the return of Antwerp to Catholic control in 1585, he went on to become the principal painter of Catholic church art in the city, replacing work destroyed by iconoclasm, which strongly suggests that he later reverted to Catholicism (or at least conformed outwardly).

The *Panhuys Paneel* is not the first *portrait historié* by Maerten de Vos. In 1566, Gillis Hooftman had asked his London agent and former apprentice, Radermacher, for help in finding a good painter who would work faster than the most fashionable artist of the day, Frans Floris, and who might also be cheaper. Amongst the friends that Radermacher had made in Antwerp before he was sent to London was Emanuel van Meteren (L6?), who had been raised with his orphaned cousin, Abraham Ortelius, the geographer and humanist who compiled the first atlas. Consequently, Radermacher and Ortelius became friends, and it was to be on the latter's advice that Radermacher suggested de Vos to Hooftman. Ortelius may well have first met de Vos and Pieter Bruegel when travelling in Italy in the early 1550s,[70] and it was he who recommended de Vos as the artist to provide five paintings for Hooftman's dining room. Radermacher gives a detailed account of how it all happened in two letters to Ortelius's nephew, Ortelianus (see p. 6), who wanted to know more about the career and intellectual interests of his recently deceased uncle.[71]

Although Hooftman conformed outwardly to Roman Catholicism (see p. 42), he was almost certainly Protestant. Moreover, Radermacher definitely was Protestant, being an elder of the Dutch Reformed Church for much of his life, first at the Dutch stranger church at Austin Friars in London and subsequently elsewhere (see Chapter 4). In one of the letters written to Ortelius's nephew, Radermacher explained that he had chosen five episodes from the life of St Paul as told in the Acts of the Apostles to be depicted in the five paintings, and that some forty of the faces of the characters were those of Hooftman's family, servants and friends.

Either two or three of these five paintings survive, and from them certain key themes emerge that were of importance to Protestants, especially at a time of persecution. For instance, St Paul was himself persecuted by his fellow Jews for preaching faith in Jesus as the Son of God.[72] In addition, Paul was the authority for the key Protestant belief in justification by faith (rather than works), and for the Protestant conviction that statues and images of the saints should not be venerated. At least two of these themes are apparent in the picture of *St Paul at Ephesus* (ill. 12). In this, the craftsmen who make and sell little silver shrines for the goddess Artemis (called Diana by the Romans) are being incited to riot; this is because if Paul is successful in teaching them that man-made gods aren't gods at all, and that the true God should be worshipped in spirit only, the image-makers will be out of a job. On the right-hand side of the picture, Paul's disciples are hustling him away from the mob that is being urged on by the silversmith Demetrius. At the very left of the picture, one or possibly two of the town council are gesturing extravagantly, but ineffectively, in protest at the disturbance. The city clerk, who finally persuades the crowd to disperse, is very careful to avoid upsetting the crowd, and goes along with the belief that the great image of Diana that is worshipped at the temple fell miraculously from heaven (see Acts 19:23–41). Although his stance seems sensibly cautious for a man trying to stop a riot, he could be seen by ardent Reformers as typifying those who fail to take a stand on a matter of belief.

This scene of violent activity is combined with an episode reported a little earlier in Acts, when seven would-be exorcisers had decided to exploit the power of Jesus by invoking his name. The evil spirit that they were trying to exorcise had replied that he knew who Jesus was but didn't know who they were, after which the possessed man attacked them violently, stripping them and beating them out of the house. In their subsequent remorse and fear, many who had practised magic arts decided to burn their books. In the background on the right is a huge bonfire on a framework, presumably of the type used by the authorities for public book-burnings and designed to maximise the draught and ensure a good blaze. Singed sheets from the fire can be seen floating in the air, and some have landed near the front of the picture.

The picture dates from 1568; the signature and date can be seen on the torn sheet to the right of centre at the very bottom of the painting: M D V F. / 1568 (that is, 'Maerten de Vos fecit [made this] in 1568'). In other words, this was painted after the *Beeldenstorm*, the great iconoclasm of 1566 when Protestant reformers in Antwerp attacked churches, destroying statues and paintings of saints, to express disapproval of those who venerated images and asked saints for their prayers, instead of praying directly to God (or who in some cases simply prayed to the saints instead of to God).[73] Mass books were also a target for destruction, since the Catholic belief in transubstantiation (i.e. the belief that the consecrated bread and wine of the Mass became the actual body and blood of Christ) was considered by some Reformers to be an unwarrantable superstition. As images of the saints in the form of statues and paintings were the principal target of the iconoclasts in 1566, St Paul's argument with the silversmiths who made images of Artemis was obviously open to being used as an authority to support Protestant iconoclasm.

Nevertheless, clearly neither Protestant nor Catholic could claim St Paul's story entirely for themselves. The burning of the magicians' books, for example, could equally be interpreted as a justification for the Catholic censorship and public burning of books deemed to be heretical. So, were these paintings used to trigger theological discussions? Although we cannot be sure, they almost certainly were. It is hard to see why else Hooftman should have chosen to decorate his dining room with religious paintings. The idea of having a separate *eetcamer* (dining room) was a relatively recent one, and was only an option for those wealthy enough to own a large house. It is not surprising, therefore, that it became a place to impress one's guests not just with fine food and expensive crockery and glass, but also with splendid pictures on the walls. These pictures, however, are not merely intended to impress; according to Radermacher, they follow a carefully planned theological scheme, drawing on the story of St Paul in the Acts of the Apostles. In other words, they are clearly intended to provoke discussion amongst Hooftman's guests. It is worth remembering at this point that by no means everybody had finished making up their minds about religious matters; these pictures, by simply reminding those who saw them of the New Testament stories, were open to a variety of nuanced interpretations.

There is a literary precedent for this in Erasmus's *Colloquies*, the dialogues which were originally intended as learning exercises to teach students how to converse in Latin. At first, they were published without Erasmus's permission, but he then started to add to them and supervise their publication himself. They gradually came to serve a double-purpose, whereby he took the opportunity to introduce moral as well as linguistic teachings into them. As he claimed in the dedication to the 1524 edition, 'This book makes better Latinists and better persons.'[74] One of these colloquies was the *Convivium Religiosum* ('Godly Feast'), in which a character called Eusebius (from the Greek word meaning 'pious') welcomes some friends for a meal. As they look around his garden and then his house, they see frescoes that provoke moral and theological discussions. Whilst they eat, they hear a passage from Proverbs on which they comment verse by verse. Later, one guest produces his pocket copy of the Pauline Epistles, which leads to further scriptural discussion. At one point, they discuss the danger of a purely outward religion which is satisfied with ceremonies alone, a reminder that although Erasmus disagreed with Luther and thought it wrong to break away from the Catholic Church, he was not uncritical of its faults and thought it needed reform, albeit from within. But the meal is a 'feast' as well as 'godly': Eusebius urges his guests to enjoy their food and one of them replies, 'When the whole man is refreshed [i.e. spirit as well as body], this is abundant refreshment indeed.'[75]

This idea of the godly feast, or love feast, seems to have developed for a while and then fallen into disuse. Some time later, evidence of the desire for theological discussion around the dining table can be found amongst the records of the Dutch church at Austin Friars in London. Simon Ruytinck, a later minister of Austin Friars who was a friend of van Meteren, sets out quite detailed plans for a special meal once every few months, when selected members of the congregation would meet for godly fellowship and discussion. This was quite a bit later and does not seem to have lasted very long, but shows that the concept had not been forgotten.[76]

An earlier parallel can again be found in England, where Thomas Cromwell engaged in just such discussions with guests while entertaining them. Dr John Oliver, an Oxford don who is sycophantically eager to reassure Cromwell that he has accepted Protestant opinions, recalled in a letter how Cromwell had entertained him and how the conversation had turned to theological matters:

And then for my further comfort, you were contented to ... call me to your honourable board [for] divers [various] dinners and suppers, where in very deed, I heard such communication which were [sic] the very cause of the beginning of my conversion. For methought it were a stony heart and a blockish wit that could carry nothing away of such a colloquy as was at your honourable board [dining table], and that made me to note them well, and when I came home to mete [compare] them with my English Bible. And I found always the conclusion which you maintained at your board to be consonant with the holy Word of God; and then I thought good to confer [compare] the English with the Latin through the whole Testament, and so I did ... but for a further trial I went and conferred [compared] Erasmus's translation with the Vulgar [Vulgate] which they call St Jerome's translation, and did interline Erasmus's translation through the whole Testament in the other translation with my own hand ... and then was I surely corroborate [persuaded to be] an adversary to all papists at all communications and ever hath been since.[77]

The obsequious tone reveals that Oliver is keen to demonstrate himself a true Protestant in Cromwell's eyes (the letter was written when the latter was at his most powerful), but it still gives a picture of how those wishing to discuss the pros and cons of Reformation ideas might do so in congenial circumstances, yet also in discreet privacy. Cromwell was clearly using these 'divers dinners and suppers' to proselytise, and although there is no conclusive evidence that this was what Hooftman was doing, it seems quite possible his dinners followed along similar lines.

What both Ruytinck's proposals and the passage above reveal is how central a careful reading of reliable biblical texts was to the Reformers' thinking. The themes chosen by Radermacher for de Vos's pictures provide a visual text free of any errors that might be in the Vulgate (St Jerome's late fourth-century translation into Latin), which the Roman Catholic Church at the Council of Trent insisted should be the only version of the Bible used, despite Erasmus's ground-breaking scholarship in producing a new edition of the original Greek texts of the New Testament.

A less complicated story is told by the second surviving picture, *St Paul on Malta* (ill. 13). Paul, as a Roman citizen, has argued that the case brought against him by some hostile Jews should be heard by Caesar, and so is on his way to Rome under guard. The ship carrying him and his guards has been wrecked off the coast of Malta, and those who rescued them have lit a fire to warm the wet and cold travellers. As Paul picks up a bundle of sticks to put on the fire, a viper emerges from it and fastens on his hand before he shakes it off into the fire. The islanders expect him to die, thinking this must be divine punishment for some wicked crime, but when he doesn't die, they start to consider him to be a god. Once again, the issue of true worship is raised: saints are not to be venerated, even though Paul's writings and the example of his life are to be respected. The picture also illustrates the axiom 'If God be for us, who can be against us?' – since Paul has survived both shipwreck and snake bite, it becomes a reassuring message for Protestants under threat of persecution, as was the case after the arrival of Alba to enforce conformity to Catholicism or execute those who refused.

The third picture identified by some as part of the same series, *St Paul and St Barnabas at Lystra*, shows Paul and Barnabas refusing to be worshipped as gods at Lystra after Paul has healed a crippled man, which raises the same issue again.[78]

In his letter to Ortelianus dated 25 July 1603 (long after the pictures were painted), Radermacher says that the series of five paintings for Hooftman's dining room featured about forty portraits of his servants, friends and relatives. However, in claiming this, he uses the Latin word *puto* ('I think', or 'I estimate'), and it should be noted that he had returned to London by the time de Vos had begun to paint and so the number may well be inaccurate.[79] Unfortunately, he does not say in which pictures these forty portraits appear. In the painting of the disturbance at Ephesus, there are only a few faces that might qualify as Hooftman's associates, and one assumes that few of Hooftman's friends would have been gratified to be portrayed as pagan silversmiths working up to a riot (although since their ringleader is called Demetrius, it is not inconceivable that he might be based on Emanuel van Meteren, whose Latinized name was Demetrius). The people burning books in the background are generally too distant to have distinguishable faces. This only leaves Paul and his companions: the city clerk trying to restore order and perhaps the youth on his knees at the front, who appears to be engaged in tearing out the pages of a book. Again, it is impossible to identify any of these with confidence, which does raise the question of whether this is genuinely a *portrait historié*. Zondervan agrees that there are hardly any portraits here, but does suggest that on the far right we can see the partially obscured face of Nicolaas Malapert, whose son, another Nicolaas, would later marry Margaretha van Panhuys, the younger girl on the right of the *Paneel*, whose head can be seen just above that of her elder sister kneeling in front of her. There is less doubt about the presence of some portraits in *St Paul on Malta*. The second head from the right with receding hair and looking at the viewer may well be Ortelius, who, in the absence of Radermacher, had given advice as to how de Vos should proceed with the paintings. On the right of the picture, a number of other people look out, rather than responding to the central drama. Zondervan suggests that the three older people on the left are Hooftman (furthest to the left), Jacob della Faille de Oude, and his wife, Maria Gamel, with their children seated below. Zweite, however, provisionally identifies the other bearded man on the left as Hooftman.[80] Finally, in the painting of Paul and Barnabas at Lystra, there is a seated woman at the front right surrounded by children and with an older woman behind her. In the absence of any other similar portraits to compare to these figures, there seems little point in speculating whether they are some of the forty that Radermacher mentions. What is worth noting, however, is that despite the Calvinist suspicion of images and violent destruction of images in the *Beeldenstorm* just two years earlier, these paintings are themselves images, albeit of episodes that lend themselves to a Protestant interpretation, a pictorial equivalent to biblical passages that might serve to stimulate discussion by guests around Hooftman's dinner table, safely away from any spies who might report them to the authorities.

Painting the castle chapel at Celle

The date of the St Paul paintings can be established by the fact that Radermacher returned to London in 1567 and that, consequently, when de Vos wanted advice about Radermacher's programme for the paintings, he had to turn instead to Ortelius. It must therefore have been at about the time that he was completing this cycle for Hooftman that de Vos received a major commission to decorate the Celle Castle chapel from the Lutheran Duke of Brunswick-Lüneburg, William the Younger. Zweite suggests that this work may have started as early as 1565 and continued until 1576, but not all the paintings are by de Vos. Furthermore, although most of the paintings are on wood panels, the largest ones are painted on canvas, which would have been easier to transport if de Vos was painting them in Antwerp.[81] The chapel paintings are almost unaltered, a unique survival of a complete sixteenth-century programme of Lutheran decoration combining the princely desire for grandeur with a Lutheran agenda.[82]

Celle Castle began as a moated medieval fortress, before gradually being enlarged and eventually converted into a palace. The last structural alterations to the chapel were in the late fifteenth century, but any internal regularity in the essentially Gothic interior was obliterated by the subsequent building of galleries on the north and west walls, with an organ placed high up to the north-east on the immediate left of the high altar and with a projecting pulpit on the south side. Subsequently, almost every surface was covered with a total of seventy-six paintings, including a triptych at the high altar and a very big canvas on a south-eastern wall in an ogival shape where a window might have been expected (**ill. 14**). Of these paintings, approximately one third were by de Vos. Art historians are not in complete accord about the attribution of some paintings either to de Vos or to members of his studio, but all I wish to do here is refer briefly to a few paintings which suggest a way of thinking about the *Paneel*.[83]

The fact that de Vos accepted a commission from the Lutheran Duke and Duchess strongly suggests that he was Lutheran at this time. It also seems reasonable to assume that they would not have chosen him if they had known him to be out of sympathy with the proposed scheme, which is clearly related to Lutheran theology. This can be seen first of all in the choice of subject for the triptych that serves as a reredos behind the high altar. The central panel, which is perhaps the focal point of the whole decorative system (or it would be if there were not quite so many other paintings to catch the eye), shows the Crucifixion, whereas a typical Catholic altar painting might well show the Nativity. In both cases, Christ is at the centre, but the Protestant stress on the importance of Christ's death on the cross as a saving sacrifice for the salvation of humanity is apparent (a Nativity scene would place the Virgin Mary at the centre as Christ's mother). It has to be acknowledged, however, that when the side panels of the triptych were closed (as they would be except during major church festivals), the congregation would see painted on the back of them the Annunciation (left side) and Nativity (right side), both of which, of course, do show Mary.

Another sign that this is a Protestant-inspired scheme is that the two sacraments represented are the only ones accepted by Protestants because they are the only ones to have biblical precedent: Baptism, after the baptism of Jesus in the River Jordan; and Holy Communion, following Jesus' command at the Last Supper to 'do this in remembrance of me'. There is a painting of the Last Supper to the left of the altar at a lower level, and of the baptism of Jesus on the wall to the right of the altar (partly obscured by a screen). This latter work follows all three synoptic gospels in portraying the dove descending to represent the Spirit of God and placing on a scroll in German (not Latin) the words heard from heaven: 'You are my beloved son on whom my favour rests.'

Perhaps of more significance than this rather general evidence that de Vos is following the requirements of a Lutheran theology is his treatment of the theme of the Transfiguration, in which, as in the Baptism picture, an image and a German text are combined. At the bottom, beneath the three disciples who accompanied Jesus up the mountain, are the words of Peter, saying that it was good to be there and asking if Jesus wished them to make three tabernacles: one for Jesus, one for Moses, and one for Elijah. Once again, there are words spoken from heaven, and these are within the elaborately painted 'frame' of the picture in the arch: 'This is my beloved son on whom my favour rests; listen to him.' Here, there is not only the use of the vernacular, but the placing of a biblical quotation in the margin of the picture.

The frame of the *Panhuys Paneel* is painted similarly, with a quotation from Exodus, this time in Dutch. In fact, every picture in the chapel is accompanied by some kind of text. Similarly, biblical quotations are clearly part of the overall conception of the *Paneel*, especially the Dutch translation of the Ten Commandments themselves.[84]

There is one further group of paintings in the Celle chapel that is especially relevant to a consideration of the *Paneel*. Above and behind the third set of stalls, under the gallery on the north side, is a picture of a father (possibly the Duke himself, judging by his fur-trimmed gown and receding hairline) who is reading the Bible to his children. Above the image is a scroll with words from Deuteronomy 6:6–7: 'These words which I give to you today, you must keep in your heart and repeat to your children' (**ill. 15**). On the panel below, behind the seating, is a bigger painting of Jesus blessing children, while on the narrow walls at either end are St Peter and St Paul accompanied by words from their epistles that, as Zweite points out, stress just how important it is for parents to repeat Christ's words to their children.[85] St Peter's First Epistle tells them that they were bought with the blood of Christ (the offering that is shown on the altarpiece), and St Paul tells them that if they acknowledge Jesus as Lord and believe that he was raised from the dead, they will be saved (1 Peter 1:18–19 and Romans 10:9, respectively). In Luther's *To the Christian Nobility of the German Nation*, the author sets out the principles on which he considers a Christian society should be based. Apart from such headline-grabbing ideas as that vows of celibacy should be abolished, and that monks and nuns be allowed to marry, Luther makes it very clear that literacy is the basis for a Christian life, since all should be able to study the Bible. As such, every town should have a school for girls as well as for boys; indeed here, just to the left of the adult, we see a girl who can obviously read, since she is helping her younger brother by pointing to each word as he reads it.[86]

Finally, on the theme of childhood, there is a series of paintings on the panels of the balustrade below, of which the first is Hannah offering her son, Samuel, to serve in the Temple under Eli, while the third is a painting of the twelve-year-old Jesus when he stayed behind in the Temple listening and asking questions of the religious teachers there. The theme running through this part of the decorative scheme is clearly the importance of children being brought up in faith. This, of course, is what by implication we see in the *Paneel*, in which the children of Peeter Panhuys and the younger children of Gillis Hooftman are placed in the presence of the Ten Commandments. With this, they would then be reminded of the Commandments' importance whenever they passed the picture in their home. Significantly, the *Paneel* also shows Moses pointing to the commandment that says, 'Honour thy father and thy mother.' It would have been from about the time that this picture was painted that paintings of Moses as he gives the Law would start to appear in Dutch

Reformed churches above the translated text of the Ten Commandments themselves. In Chapter 8, I shall consider what we know about the children of Peeter Panhuys, this father who attached such importance to biblical teaching that he wished his children to be reminded of the Ten Commandments not just when they were in church, but at home also.

De Vos's painting of black subjects

We know from Johan Radermacher's letter to Ortelianus about the painting of the five *portraits histories* for Hooftman's dining room that up to forty family members and servants were represented. Consequently, it is not unreasonable to speculate that servants as well as members of Panhuys's extended family and friends were also shown in the panel. In the back row of faces on the *Paneel* are two black servants or slaves (L3 and L5) who appear to be carrying further offerings to add to the collection in the foreground of the picture. There are no black faces in the other de Vos paintings made for Hooftman and his family, but before speculating about their circumstances, I want to consider the European context.

Portugal started trading in slaves from about the middle of the fifteenth century, and because of its small population, it had soon become economically dependent on slave labour. Joaquin Romero Magalhães estimates that by the middle of the sixteenth century, between 1,600 and 1,700 slaves were being imported annually. It was this increased population that made possible the building of a widespread empire across Africa, Asia and America.[87] The Portuguese were one of the trading *naties* established in Antwerp, and so it is not unlikely that any black people in Antwerp at this time would have originally been brought there by Portuguese slave owners.

The Spanish attitude to slavery varied over time. In 1542, Charles V had signed 'New Laws' decreeing that no natives of his South American empire should be enslaved. The response of the Spanish settlers was armed rebellion led by Francisco Pizarro, and in 1546 the Viceroy of Peru was killed in battle. Philip II, who was now ruling Spain under his father's authority, decided that it was impracticable to send an army to crush the rebels. Instead, he sent a priest, Pedro de la Gasca, as a 'pacifier'. Remarkably, by 1548 de la Gasca had raised an army, defeated Pizarro and executed him. In two formal debates in 1550 and 1551, a Spanish Dominican friar called Bartolomé de las Casas claimed that all native South Americans were equal spiritually to Europeans. De las Casas would go on to claim in his will that this spiritual equality was also true of black Africans; however, this final admission was not published until a quarter of a century after the friar's death. Although his arguments were accepted in Spain, they made no practical difference in her colonies.[88] The economic difficulties that Spain faced in maintaining an empire in the face of threats from the Ottoman Empire and France, along with trying to deal with Dutch rebellion, meant that high principles were gradually abandoned in favour of raising money to pay and equip troops. In 1556, Philip conceded the right of the still rebellious Spanish settlers to use native slave labour in exchange for five million gold ducats. Soon after this, he agreed to the import of African slaves to the Caribbean, even though he had suspended a licence for this trade just a year before. In the end, economic and political imperatives were allowed to override moral principles.[89] And almost nobody in Spain or elsewhere shared the insight of Dürer who, on seeing the Aztec treasures sent back by Cortés, recognised the artistic inspiration that underlay such precious artefacts: 'All the days of my life I have seen nothing that rejoiced my heart so much as these things, for I saw amongst them wonderful works of art and I marvelled at the subtle *ingenia* [talents] of men in foreign lands.'[90]

By contrast, in the countries of northern Europe, where the business of Panhuys and Hooftman was based, slavery had not been normalised. This does not mean that there were no black people, however, nor that they were quite as invisible as subsequent history has made them. David Olusoga records details of John Blanke, the black trumpeter who served in England under both Henry VII and Henry VIII. He suggests that John Blanke may have come to England in the train of Katherine of Aragon (where there were slaves, as in Portugal). If so, he was clearly no longer a slave when he applied to Henry VIII for formal appointment to the position and the wages of a deceased fellow trumpeter, and since he received a gift from the king to mark the occasion of his wedding, we know that he was able to marry, presumably to a white woman. Happily, therefore, he is not a 'blank' to us, since not only does his name appear in court records, but we can see his actual image in the Westminster Tournament Roll, which commemorates the tournament held to celebrate the birth of Queen Katherine's short-lived son.[91] Recent DNA research of skeletons found in the Mary Rose also suggests that a number of Tudor sailors were black and evidently trusted to fight in battle alongside their white companions. All of this suggests that slavery within England was not considered normal.[92]

Supporting evidence in the Elizabethan era can be found in the case of Dr Hector Nunes, a Jewish convert to Christianity who had escaped from Portugal. He bought a slave in England who then refused to 'tarry and serve' him. Nunes made a petition to the Court of Requests in 1587 claiming that when he had bought the slave, he had thought that it was a legal transaction as it would have been in Portugal. Although not all the records of this case have survived, his suit to have either the slave or his purchase price returned to him appears unlikely to have been successful. In an earlier case, a certain Cartwright was taken to court in 1569 for cruelly whipping a slave he had bought in Russia. The slave was set free after a much-quoted judgment that asserted that 'the air of England is too pure an air for slaves to breathe in'. That same year, William Harrison writes in his *Description of England*:

> As for slaves and bondmen, we have none; nay such is the privilege of our country by the especial grace of God and the bounty of our princes, that if any come hither from other realms, so soon as they set foot on land they become as free in condition as their masters, whereby all note of servile bondage is utterly removed from them.[93]

Smug English exceptionalism would appear to have deep roots. Although this claim was partially true at the time – in that there was no open slave trade within England – it was already being undermined morally by the first English engagement in overseas slave trading by Sir John Hawkins in the mid-sixteenth century.

A similarly ambiguous moral position was to be seen a few years later in the port of Middelburg in Zeeland in the Low Countries, to which many of the Reformed refugees from Antwerp moved, when over one hundred African men, women and children were unexpectedly landed in 1596. The local authorities decreed that they should be set free and that they could be employed as long as they were taught to be Christians. Yet when the Dutch captain appealed against the loss of his lucrative cargo, he was given permission to take them elsewhere for sale, after which he probably took them to the West Indies. Thus, as in England, there was no slavery within the borders, but no objection to continuing the trade overseas.[94] (For the little that it is worth, both responses are slightly better than that of the Portuguese back in 1444, when the first large group of African slaves was landed there: the sea captain who brought them was rewarded for his enterprise with a knighthood by Prince Henrique, and slavery in Portugal was sanctioned from then on.)

All this evidence is circumstantial, but it does suggest that although the two black women in the *Paneel* were almost certainly of slave origin, they were probably servants rather than slaves. Another kind of circumstantial evidence is also available, and that is the representation of blacks in contemporary art. There are two drawings of black Africans in Dürer's sketchbook: the first dates from 1508 and is of an unnamed African man, the second is from 1521 and is of a black woman named Katharina (**ill. 16**), the twenty-year-old servant of João Brandão, the Portuguese royal agent in Antwerp with whom Dürer was staying at the time, as we know from his diary. There is no hint of caricature in either sketch: Dürer's interest is in recording the personality of his subject, and he draws them with sensitivity; they are individual human beings, not mere types. Later in the same decade (1525–30), Jan Mostaert painted the first oil portrait of an individual black man (as opposed to the generally stylised depictions of Balthazar, the black king of the three that worshipped the baby Jesus). Mostaert's picture is not especially large (approximately 31 x 21 cm) but is painted with careful attention to detail. It is unusual in that such a finely finished portrait would normally be of a nobleman, but recent research suggests that he may well have been a certain Christofle le Mor, an archer in the entourage of Charles V.[95] Here again, we see an African subject being treated seriously and with dignity. The man's confident look suggests that this is a man respected for who he is, without any racial prejudice.

Similarly, there is a painting of about 1560 by Hans van der Elburcht of the *Baptism of the Eunuch by St Philip*.[96] Acts 8 tells how the eunuch, a high-ranking official of the Ethiopian court, was returning home from Jerusalem and puzzling over a passage from Isaiah when Philip met him and explained the passage, whereupon the eunuch asked to be baptised straight away. This story of an early conversion is presented with absolute dignity and no hint of stereotyping. It might be thought, by contrast, that little help would be provided by the conventional paintings of the adoration of the Magi (traditionally shown as three kings from Africa, Asia and Europe, the three continents known in the Middle Ages), but there are several striking portraits of Balthazar, including one by Joos van Cleve, an earlier Antwerp painter, and a second by de Vos himself. The van Cleve portrait is the surviving left panel from a triptych, and shows a sensitive and thoughtful face, which looks like an actual portrait (**ill. 17**).[97] In de Vos's painting of the same subject, the European king is shown as usual as the first to pay homage, but Balthazar stands prominently in the left foreground, magnificently robed, and de Vos clearly delights in the beauty of the black arm and skin contrasting with the white cloak with its pink attachments and gold braid and sceptre (**ill. 18**). The picture as a whole is very large, and the figure of Balthazar is almost life-size. In this case, the subject is not only treated with respect but with magnificence. On this admittedly scanty evidence, it would be difficult to accuse either painter of any racism.

So, what of the two black figures in our picture? Both of them are clearly meant to represent some of the Jews bringing offerings for making the tabernacle as commanded by Moses in Exodus 35. Nevertheless, they are both looking straight out from the canvas just as the other contemporary figures do. The Jews were known to have slaves, since Exodus 21 sets out the law about their treatment (repugnant to us, but relatively enlightened for the time). Did de Vos simply assume that slaves would be black, or was he 'colour-blind' to the extent that any black servants in the Hooftman/Panhuys household were simply given equivalent roles in the picture? We have no way of knowing, but there is one last piece of contemporary evidence which tells us something about likely attitudes.

The frontispiece of Ortelius's atlas, the *Theatrum Orbis Terrarum*, almost certainly engraved by Frans Hogenberg, who was responsible for the other engravings in the book, shows the four continents known at the time personified by four female figures grouped around an architectural monument (ill. 19). Europa is definitely very different from the helpless female of Greek legend, who was carried off through the waves by Jove in the form of a white bull while her maidens cried unavailingly from the shore. Rather, she sits enthroned on the top of the monument, carrying a sceptre and giving the reader a pretty hard stare. As John Hale memorably put it, she has become 'a sterner, more *dirigiste* figure, keeping her breasts but losing her poetry'.[98] Below her on either side are Asia with downcast eyes and Africa averting her gaze, while below them lies America with bow and arrows and a severed head, evidence, so the accompanying verses tell us, of her cannibalism. (Perhaps America had to be guilty of such unnatural behaviour to justify the ruthless destruction of her civilisations by the European invaders.) The key point here, however, is that the black women in the *Paneel*, and especially the one immediately to the left of Hooftman, are looking directly at the viewer with keen glances that do not seem at all intimidated. In other words, they are presented quite differently to the portrayals of Asia and Africa in the frontispiece.

It is a source of considerable regret that we can know no more about these two self-possessed women who confidently scrutinise the viewer from the back of the crowd around the Tablets of the Law.

CHAPTER 4

Three 'learned merchants':
Johan Radermacher, Abraham Ortelius and Emanuel van Meteren

'The Dutchman by his policy hath gotten trading
with all the world into his hands.'
– Sir Walter Raleigh speaking
in Parliament in 1593[99]

There is general agreement that the figure on the *Panhuys Paneel* between Moses and Aaron is Johan Radermacher (see, for example, the picture of him as a much older man by an unknown artist in 1607 [**ill. 20**]). Abraham Ortelius, on the other hand, is almost certainly not shown in the picture. The distinctive way in which his hair has receded is captured in Ruben's posthumous painting based on Philips Galle's print. Ortelius can also be seen one in from the right in the background of *St Paul on Malta*, one of the five paintings commissioned by Gillis Hooftman for his dining room (**ill. 13**). He merits discussion here, however, both because it was he who first suggested Maerten de Vos as a painter to Hooftman, and also because the many letters that he kept and which were passed on to the Dutch stranger church at Austin Friars in London for safekeeping throw so much light on the characters and period under discussion.

If Radermacher is almost certainly in the picture, and Ortelius is certainly not, my suggestion that the third of this group of close friends is the figure immediately to the right of Gillis Hooftman is a great deal more contentious.

Zondervan suggested that this figure might be the wealthy merchant Maerten della Faille, who at the time that the picture was painted had helped to secure the release of van Meteren after he was arrested by the Spanish authorities. This idea is dismissed by Rudie van Leeuwen, who points out that the portrait used as a comparator by Zondervan is in fact of a different member of the della Faille family. Van Leeuwen argues that this figure is the composer Jean de Castro, who is known to have taught some of Hooftman's younger children and who later dedicated two publications to their mother, Margaretha van Nispen. To support this suggestion, he refers to a picture by Pourbus of the Hoefnagel wedding, in which one of the musicians is thought to have been de Castro and looks very like the figure in the *Panhuys Paneel*. My own suggestion that this figure is Emanuel van Meteren, a close friend of Radermacher, is based on another comparison that cannot be definitive. The late Iain Buchanan recently drew attention to van Meteren's *memorieboek* (hereafter *Comentarius*), which is a record of key family events and includes miniature full-length portraits of van Meteren and his second wife, Hester van den Corput, which he attributes to Joris Hoefnagel (ill. 21; although Helmer J. Helmers attributes them to Lucas d'Heere).[100] Regardless of whether or not I am correct, van Meteren is worthy of discussion here both in his own right as the first historian of the Dutch Revolt, and also because it was through him that Radermacher first became a friend of Ortelius, who recommended de Vos's services as a painter.

* * *

Almost at the centre of the *Paneel* is a tall man. His hair is starting to recede, and his beard is tinged with grey. He is turned away slightly to give us an intimidating stare over Aaron's shoulder. This is Johan Radermacher (R13). He is placed between Moses and Aaron, but why is he here at the heart of the picture? We might have expected Peeter Panhuys, the man who actually commissioned the painting, to be in the centre, or even his wife's uncle, Gillis Hooftman, who was Radermacher's former master and quite possibly the richest man in Antwerp, yet they are placed away from the centre on either side. The most likely answer is that it was a natural way to organise the overall picture, as it makes sense to balance the families of Panhuys and Hooftman on either side and therefore to place the two men opposite each other. Once that had been decided, it may well have seemed natural to give the central place to Radermacher as a pivot between them. After all, he had worked in the firm with the two partners and had also, like Panhuys, married a niece of Hooftman, Johanna Racket.

It may, however, be more than a matter of compositional balance. It was Radermacher who had first introduced de Vos to Hooftman at Ortelius's suggestion and devised the scheme for the five *portraits historiés* that de Vos would paint for Hooftman's dining room. In de Vos's eyes, therefore, Radermacher was a man of learning as well as someone who had introduced him to a valuable patron. Apart from these matter-of-fact explanations, there is also the fact that Radermacher looks out at us with undeniable authority; it is not difficult to imagine why this impressive-looking figure was first appointed a deacon of the Dutch stranger church at Austin Friars in London at the age of twenty-three. (Calvinist deacons were not ordained clergy but rather lay members of the congregation whose job it was to assist the minister in such matters as distributing aid to the poor. Such people would be recognised as having sound theological views and being of unimpeachable moral character.) Later, in 1571, when he was still only thirty-three, he was elected an elder there, a further sign of the strength of his character, as well as of his religious commitment.[101]

Apart from Peeter Panhuys and Radermacher himself, there is one other prominent figure on the *Paneel* who may have been associated with Gillis Hooftman's business: his elder brother, Bartholomaeus Hooftman (R6), who is dressed in striking red like his brother Gillis on the opposite side. Bartholomaeus was the father of Margaretha, the wife of Panhuys. However, Bartholomaeus is unlikely to have been closely involved in his brother's firm, since records show that he was an alderman of Trier in 1562 and he was mayor there in 1574–5, which implies that his business activities were centred there and not in Antwerp. At most, then, he may have engaged in mutually advantageous business with his brother's and son-in-law's firm, or may perhaps have invested in it.[102] By contrast, however, we know that Radermacher was very much involved in the business, first as an apprentice and then as Hooftman's London agent.

Much later, in 1603, Radermacher was asked by Ortelianus, the nephew of his recently deceased friend Abraham Ortelius, for some information about the circumstances that had led to the latter's ground-breaking atlas, probably to include as part of the introductory material in a reprint. Radermacher, by now an old man himself, was delighted to honour his old friend, to write at some length about his own early life and involvement with Hooftman, and of how that led to his getting to know Ortelius.

Radermacher tells how he was destined for university and an academic life until the death of his father. Consequently, at the age of sixteen, he was apprenticed 'in ministerium celeberrimi mercatoris Aegidij Hooftmanni ab Eupen' ('to the service of the very well-known Antwerp merchant, Gillis Hooftman of Eupen').[103] It was whilst in Antwerp that he became acquainted with the young Emanuel van Meteren, who, like Radermacher, had recently been apprenticed to an Antwerp merchant named Sebastien Danckaerts, and who also chafed at the demands of a merchant career and yearned for an academic life.[104] The two young men consoled themselves by discussing their 'furtive studies' ('furtivorum studiorum communicatione leniebamus')[105] and by encouraging one another. Although Radermacher describes their studies as 'furtive', not many lines later he acknowledges that his master, although not a man of learning, valued academic pursuits and showed great generosity in allowing him to buy many of the books that he wanted,[106] and so it is hard to believe that his studies were all that clandestine. Indeed, when Radermacher goes on to describe how he finally met van Meteren's cousin Ortelius, it was because he wanted to buy some theological books from the library of John Rogers, the sale of which had been entrusted to Ortelius by another of Ortelius's first cousins, Adriana van Weyden, the Dutch widow of John Rogers, the first English Protestant to be burnt at the stake under Queen Mary.[107]

Radermacher's academic bent was soon apparent when, in 1568, while he was in London, he started to write what is the earliest known book on Dutch grammar. It only survives in manuscript, and the grammar section itself is incomplete and very brief, but it reveals the humanist's desire to promote his own language as one worthy to be treated with care and with real expressive value. Karel Bostoen argues that the discussion of translation in the preface shows his thinking to be far in advance of that of his contemporaries. Interestingly, he writes about the special language skills of merchants (he is, of course, a merchant himself working amongst foreigners). He also shows himself to be quite advanced in his thinking when he argues that language rules should be derived from the living language and not imposed upon it.[108]

In 1634, some seventeen years after his death, Radermacher's library was auctioned, and because a sale catalogue was printed, we know that he had at least 1,500 volumes comprising over 2,000 titles. (For comparison, Montaigne had 1,000 books in his library.) We don't know whether his children might have bought further books after his death or indeed have chosen to retain some of their father's books for their own use, but there can be no doubt that the wide range of interests and of languages in which the books are written[109] reveal Radermacher as a true humanist.

The relationship between Emanuel van Meteren and Abraham Ortelius must have been more like that of brothers than of cousins, for when Ortelius's father died in 1537, when Ortelius was only ten years old, it was Emanuel's father Jacob who helped his widowed sister-in-law to look after Abraham and his two younger sisters. Given this, Emanuel, who was eight years younger, must have regarded Abraham very much in the light of an elder brother. By this point, Jacob van Meteren had returned from London, where he had gone to avoid persecution for his Reformation sympathies (London was, of course, also an important business centre).

Like Emanuel, Ortelius also formed a strong friendship with Radermacher. It seems to have been one of those rare friendships in which interests, understanding and the whole approach to life coincide so closely that on any meeting the two are immediately in tune with each other. In the same letter of reminiscences, Radermacher writes of this exceptional sharing of interests, describing how Ortelius wondered at 'haec animorum praeter causas externas arcana coniunctio' ('this remarkable union of their minds'); *arcana*, with its hint of mystery, almost suggests a sacred union.[110] If these sentiments seem unduly extravagant, perhaps we should remember that this letter was written after Ortelius's death and in the expectation that it might be published as part of the prefatory matter in a reprint of the famous atlas. Nevertheless, there undoubtedly was a strong bond between the two. Indeed, Ortelius's talent for friendship is apparent throughout the remarkable collection of letters to him that has survived. Unfortunately, fewer of Ortelius's own letters survive, but the warm feelings so often expressed in the letters that he received are unlikely to be solely the fruits of polite intercourse. It is precisely because Ortelius is at the centre of this network of correspondents that the letters throw such helpful light on the group who are shown gathered together in the *Paneel*. Moreover, the range of the network does not seem to have been limited by religious differences. Despite its slightly hagiographical tone, I think we may take at face value the brief account of Ortelius's life by Francis Sweerts in the editions of his atlas published after his death, the *Theatrum Orbis Terrarum*. It is given here in the translation of an editor known only as W.B. in the first English edition of 1606, with my clarifications in square brackets:

In company he was of an excellent discreet carriage, passing [extremely] courteous, merry and pleasant. Such was his singular humanity, that it was strange to see how he did win and retain the love and favour of all men wheresoever he became [wherever he went]. His enemies he chose rather to overcome with kindness, or to contemn them then [than] to revenge himself of their malice. He did so much hate vice, even in his own kindred, that he rather reverenced virtue in his enemies and strangers. Vain questions, and subtle disputations of divinity, or matters of religion, as dangerous and pernicious, he did always greatly detest and abhor.[111]

* * *

A Protestant family: The religious background of Ortelius and van Meteren

Ortelius was clearly appalled by religious violence but does not otherwise appear to have allowed religious differences ('Vain questions, and subtle disputations of divinity') to affect his friendships. He himself remained Catholic (at least outwardly), but he came from a family with strongly Reformed connections. Adriana, the daughter of his father's sister, Ann Ortels, had married John Rogers. Rogers had gone to Antwerp in 1534 to serve as chaplain to the English merchant community there, the so-called English *natie*.[112] While he was there, he met William Tyndale, whose English translations of the New Testament and Pentateuch (from the original Greek and Hebrew, respectively) were becoming well known. In 1548, Tyndale had also published *The Obedience of a Christian Man*, which stressed the absolute authority of the Bible, and although it also stressed the authority of the king in secular matters, it was a book which attracted the fury of the Catholic authorities in England. When Tyndale was arrested the following year and subsequently executed, Rogers managed to rescue the manuscripts of his translation of the next quarter of the Old Testament. Rogers went on to combine Tyndale's translations with a revised version of Miles Coverdale's earlier translation of the second half of the Old Testament and Tyndale's own New Testament, thus producing an English translation of the whole Bible, which he had published in Antwerp under the fictitious name of 'Thomas Matthew', so as to protect himself and all those involved.

It was whilst Rogers was in Antwerp that he married Adriana van Weyden, described in Foxe's *Acts and Monuments* (commonly known as the *Book of Martyrs*) as 'more richly endowed with virtue and soberness of life, than with worldly treasures'. She was a first cousin of both Abraham Ortelius and Emanuel van Meteren, whose father, perhaps in association with Abraham's father, had helped with the expenses of printing Coverdale's slightly earlier translation of the Bible (made from various intermediate translations, including Luther's German and the Latin of the Vulgate). All this, certainly, would have been more than enough to establish Rogers's Protestant credentials, but then, back in London, where he had been made a prebendary of St Paul's Cathedral, he was arrested almost immediately after the accession of Mary I. Since he steadfastly refused to recant his Protestant beliefs, he was burnt at the stake on 4 February 1554, becoming the first Protestant martyr to be executed under the monarch.[113]

With a cousin who had edited a translation of the Bible into English and subsequently been burnt at the stake, and an uncle by marriage who had contributed to the cost of publishing the earlier Coverdale Bible (and who had also helped to bring him up), Ortelius's Protestant credentials could hardly have been more impressive. Nevertheless, he appears to have been reluctant to take sides in religious controversy. Perhaps this was merely habitual caution, dating back to the time when, at the age of eight, he had seen his own house searched by officers of the Inquisition who suspected that his father, who was abroad at the time, might possess heretical, Protestant material. In any case, he remained close friends with Johan Radermacher, who was unmistakably Reformed, being an elder in succession of the Dutch stranger church in London and then of the Reformed churches of Antwerp, Aachen and Middelburg. Despite these links, Ortelius accepted the title of His Majesty's Geographer from the devoutly Catholic Philip II. Several letters that he wrote to the cousin with whom he was brought up, van Meteren, reveal his detachment from religious partisanship and especially his disapproval of the use of violence to enforce conformity.

The first letter, written to van Meteren in London in July 1559 (by which time it may be assumed that Philip's attitude to heretics had hardened), describes a Spanish *auto-da-fé*, reporting on 'de solemniteijt *della sancta Inquisitione*'. Here, his sudden switch into Italian from the Dutch in which he normally and naturally writes to a close family member suggests a mock respect for 'the solemn ceremonies of the Holy Inquisition'. Those who were condemned for heresy, he reports, were given as much time to repent (so as to avoid being burnt alive) as it took for a candle to burn down. Those who recanted immediately were branded and forfeited all their property, but the *mede* (reward) of the fifteen who waited until the candle had almost burnt down before recanting was to be strangled before their bodies were burnt. Preferable though it may be to be strangled rather than burnt alive, the word 'reward' is surely used ironically here.[114]

Irony, of course, is difficult to prove (and usefully deniable), but there can be no doubt of Ortelius's forthright criticism of the damage caused by Reformed image-breakers in the *Beeldenstorm*. This iconoclasm, which had taken place in Antwerp the previous year, had seen the destruction of much church art. He describes how the trouble began when a woman paying her devotions before a statue of Our Lady in the Church of Our Lady (which is now the cathedral) was mocked by some boys. The woman became so annoyed that she threw water at them, whereupon a disturbance began and people started to sing psalms in Dutch, at which point the Catholic priests hastily withdrew. Shortly afterwards, the destruction of statues and paintings ensued and then spread to every other church in the city. The next day, he observed, all the churches looked as though 'de duijuel sommyge hondert iaeren huijs gehouden hadde' ('the devil had been at work there for a hundred years').[115]

These two letters suggest that Ortelius is critical of all extreme positions, and this seems to be confirmed in a further letter at the end of 1567, in which he does not distinguish between the harms caused by the supporters of various political and religious parties. After the *Beeldenstorm*, the Duke of Alba had arrived with 10,000 Spanish soldiers to impose control. The special tribunal that Alba established, the Council of Troubles, soon became known as the 'Council of Blood' as it led to widespread executions. In a letter Ortelius writes to van Meteren, he foresaw the devastation that lay ahead, but does not distinguish between Catholic and Reformed as sources of trouble. He describes the country as a sick patient, suffering from the 'Catholic evil, Geuzen fever and Huguenot dysentery'. *Geuzen* (beggars) was the scornfully dismissive term used when a petition of 400 of the lesser nobles calling for an end to the persecution of Protestants was dismissed by Margaret of Parma, Regent of the Netherlands. It was, however, defiantly taken by the Protestants as a proud title from then on by those who resisted Catholic, Spanish authority (Huguenot was a general term for all French Protestants). After this description of the diseases affecting the Low Countries, Ortelius observes drily that at the end of all the robbing and murdering, the country will probably long for the peace that it had formerly had but failed to appreciate.[116] Many years later, in 1592, he writes to Ortelianus that he doesn't know whether the scholar Justus Lipsius is Catholic or Calvinist, but 'si aures ad audiendum habeat, neuter erit. Peccatur intus et extra' ('if he has ears to hear, he will be neither; both sides are guilty of sins'). Whether this even-handed detachment is evidence of his being a member of the Family of Love will be discussed later (see p. 160), but it certainly shows that despite his family's Protestant credentials, he was certainly not a committed Calvinist.[117]

* * *

Ortelius's dislike of 'subtle disputations of divinity', his reluctance to take sides, and the warmth of his character all help to explain how he maintained his links with so many across Europe. Many of these friendships are recorded in his *album amicorum* (friendship album), in which friends were invited to inscribe a poem, motto, or even a painting to affirm both their mutual affection and to share their mutual interests. Nor could Ortelius have maintained this network of friends who so much relished exchanging new discoveries and ideas had he himself not been both knowledgeable and eager to increase his knowledge. He had still been young when his father died in 1537, and once his uncle by marriage, Jacob van Meteren, was no longer looking after him, he needed to find a way to support his mother and two younger sisters. What he chose to do was to become an illustrator and seller of maps. His sisters helped him in this endeavour with their colouring, as the printing technology of the time could not produce coloured maps, and so careful colouring by hand was the way to make maps easier to understand. This colouring required not merely basic artistic skill but also the knowledge required to interpret the map correctly and, indeed, the initiative and knowledge to find good maps in the first place.

Ortelius's skill had been recognised when he was admitted as an illustrator of maps to the Guild of St Luke (the artists' guild in Antwerp) in 1547 when he was only nineteen.[118] In addition to selling maps, he soon began to sell books and prints and to visit the Frankfurt Book Fair, where he met the cartographer Gerard Mercator. His business was evidently successful, since he was soon able to collect books, prints, coins, medals, and natural history specimens. The humanist passion for collecting such material was not merely an indulgence of that acquisitive instinct shared by humans with magpies, but also an important means by which scholars fleshed out their understanding of ancient history and the natural world. The study of inscriptions on coins helped to elucidate early attempts at archaeology, while the collecting and exchange of seeds, plants and such things as animals' teeth and bones paved the way for a better understanding of biology. It is noteworthy, too, that the learned circles of correspondents who searched for such material exchanged information freely, generously swapping or lending specimens without hesitation.

In Radermacher's letter to Ortelianus detailing how the latter's uncle came to produce the first atlas (see Chapter 2), Radermacher describes how his master, Gillis Hooftman, an international merchant and shipowner, liked to have his maps with him wherever he happened to be, so that he could immediately consult them when he heard the latest reports of wars across Europe. Despite this proclivity, he often lacked the space to unroll them without great inconvenience. As a result, Radermacher had suggested acquiring maps of such a size that they could be bound together as a book. Hooftman then told Radermacher to find appropriate maps printed on a single sheet of paper so that this could be done, a task that he then passed on to Ortelius. Ortelius then travelled to France and Italy in search of these articles, eventually producing a book of about thirty maps. In a follow-up letter written the following year, Radermacher says that he has now seen this early precursor of Ortelius's atlas and that it actually contained thirty-eight maps, mainly printed by Tramezini in Rome, but with eight or nine printed in 'Belgium' (i.e. the Low Countries) and that it was 'multo usu valde tritum ac lacerum' ('much worn and torn by hard use'). Most of the maps, he says, were of European territories, but also included maps of Asia, Africa, Egypt and Tartary, this last name being a rather vague term used at the time to describe a part of central and eastern Asia.[119]

Radermacher makes clear that he does not think that Ortelius had thought of publishing such a collection in book form before he suggested that it could be done for Hooftman, and claims that he was the first to be consulted about publishing a map of the world 'in forma quaso cordis' ('in heart shape'). Nonetheless, he goes on to say that Ortelius then consulted other friends and especially the 'clarissimum geographorum Gerardum Mercatorem' ('very famous geographer Gerard Mercator').[120] If Radermacher can claim to have first suggested the idea, it was Ortelius himself who made the decision to publish such a work, and his vision was of something that went far beyond simply being a convenient aid for international merchants.

The term 'atlas', however, was not the one that Ortelius chose to use. An image of the Titan Atlas carrying the heavens (or the world) on his shoulder appeared on the title page of a collection of maps brought together by various map-makers and assembled by Antonio Lafreri, a print-seller who, although Burgundian by birth, worked in Rome. Lafreri's collections of maps were individually commissioned, and so their contents varied depending on the interests of the commissioner. The maps also varied in scale, and unlike Ortelius's work, had no consistent typography or symbols. The term 'atlas' more properly belongs to Ortelius's contemporary, Gerard Mercator, who confusingly had in mind a different mythical figure: not the Titan, but a king of Mauretania after whom the Atlas mountains were named. He used the term for his own atlas of Europe which, rather like Hooftman's, was first put together in response to a personal request, on this occasion for the tutor of the heir of the Duchy of Cleves, who was planning a tour of Europe in the 1570s.[121] In this case also, an individual commission led to a significant development, Mercator's world atlas, *Atlas Sive Cosmographicae Meditationes de Fabrica Mundi et Fabricati Figura*. If the reference in Mercator's title to 'cosmographical meditations' makes clear that he has much more in mind than simply a handy collection of route maps for travellers, so too does Ortelius's choice of a title, *Theatrum Orbis Terrarum* ('Theatre of the Lands of the Globe'). Both have in mind what Paul Binding calls an 'organic book': for a start, each map was to the same scale, and the world map at the front made it possible to envisage the world as a whole.[122]

The Latin word *theatrum* comes from the Greek *theatron*, which in turn is derived from a word meaning to see or view. It had already been used by Theodor Zwingler, a Swiss professor, when he edited his encyclopaedia, *Theatrum Humanae Vitae* ('The Theatre of Human Life'), which was published in Basel in 1565, five years before Ortelius's atlas. Just as Zwingler's work was to put on display a great range of knowledge, so Ortelius's atlas was to display the whole known world before the eyes of its users. As Pietro Bizzari, an Italian protestant who taught at Cambridge, put it when he wrote in Ortelius's *album amicorum*: 'orbem plurimis ignotu[m], ita illustravis, ut ia[m] omnibus innotescat Album' ('You have thrown such light on a world previously unknown to many, that now it is known to all').[123]

The world had become a theatre on which Europeans could not only see the world laid out for them, giving them some sense of their place in it and of their own identity, but also a stage on which they felt entitled, alas, to play out their role as masters. Significantly, a dispute between what were then the two principal colonising powers of Europe – Portugal and Spain – all depended on how many degrees to the east or west the Moluccas were from a line of longitude through the Atlantic agreed in an earlier negotiation and backed with the Pope's authority in a papal bull. Modestly, each country had claimed only half the globe. The dispute between Portugal and Spain hinged on where the two halves of the globe met 'on the other side'. Needless to say, the maps produced by the two sides were markedly different and very difficult to prove or refute.[124] As François I of France observed drily, 'I should be very happy to see the clause in Adam's will which excluded me from my share when the world was being divided.'[125]

Ortelius himself had nothing to do with this dispute and would, one might hope, have been disturbed by the entitled sense of European superiority that led to competing empires claiming the right to despoil distant lands, exploiting their wealth and, in the case of the Portuguese, just starting to engage in the slave trade. Nevertheless, the frontispiece of the *Theatrum* suggests that Ortelius himself is not free of this sense of European superiority: the figure of Europa is clearly dominant (see **ill. 19**), but he modifies his position significantly by the choice of quotations from Cicero and Seneca that he places at the four corners of one edition. A quotation from Book 2 of Cicero's *De Natura Deorum*, observes that a horse exists to drag things, an ox to plough, and a dog to hunt and guard, but a man is raised for the purpose of contemplating of the world (an idea taken up in Mercator's title). Contemplation of the world laid out as if on a theatre's stage for us to view as a whole within the universe gives a sense of

71

proportion that shows the folly of human ambition. In one of his quotations from Seneca, a rhetorical question is asked about the world: 'Is this the small point that nations divide with sword and fire? Oh, how ridiculous are the boundaries that humans set up' (Book 1 of *Quaestiones Naturales*, 8). On the page before his world map, in 'A Description of the Whole World', Ortelius quotes from Pliny, for whom the 'small point' of the world is no more than a mere pinprick:

> And these so manifold portions of earth (saith Pliny in the 11. Book of his Natural History) yea rather, as some have termed them, the prick or centre of the world (for so small is the earth in comparison of the whole frame of the world [i.e. the universe]) this is the matter, this is the seat of our glory. Here we enjoy honours, here we exercise authority, here we hunt after riches, here men turmoil and tire themselves, here we move and maintain civil dissensions, and by mutual slaughter make more room upon the earth. And to let pass the public tumults of the world, this in which we force the borderers to give place and remove further off, and where we encroach by stealth upon our neighbour's lands: as he that extends his lands & lordships farthest, and cannot abide that any should seat themselves too near his nose, How great, or rather how small a portion of earth doth he enjoy? Or when he hath glutted his avarice to the full, how little shall his deadcarcasepossess?[126]

These words seem to underlie the final scene of the second part of *Tamburlaine*, a play by the English playwright Christopher Marlowe, in which the ruthless conqueror Tamburlaine, recognising that death is inevitable, calls for a map so that he may find some consolation in recalling his many conquests, even while regretting that so much remained to conquer.[127]

How far Ortelius was aware of the use of maps to justify territorial aggrandisement is uncertain, but the above quotations suggest that he would not have approved. Another thing is also clear: he understood that no map can be completely objective, since only so much can be shown on any map, and therefore each decision to include one thing meant that another had to be omitted. However, his choice of the title *Theatrum* suggests that his vision would still be as all-inclusive as possible. As a humanist, he turns to Cicero, Seneca and Pliny for guidance, but this does not exclude a Christian understanding of creation. Did he have these words of Philip Melanchthon, the theologian who developed some of Luther's ideas, in mind?

This magnificent theatre – the sky, lights, stars, earth – is proof of God the Ruler and Former of the world. Whoever casts his eyes around will recognise in the order of things God the architect who is permanently at work, preserving and protecting everything. In accordance with God's will we may trace His footprints in this world by studying the sciences.[128]

'Sciences' here does not have quite the same meaning that it has today. Here, it refers to all branches of knowledge, and Ortelius and his many correspondents would not have separated the natural sciences from other areas of learning. Their interests ranged from ancient history to what we might now categorise as natural history. A key example of the former is his investigation of the *Arx Britannica*, the ruins of a Roman fortress that had become visible off the coast near Leiden in the aftermath of an exceptionally high tide. Ortelius does not simply measure, draw and then engrave the outline of the building, but also discusses its place in history with two fellow antiquarians, one of whom, Laurinus, reports back to him that he has come across the record of an inscription on an altar stone that confirms that the Emperor Claudius had dedicated it there. This in turn seemed to confirm their supposition that Claudius had passed through the *Arx* on his way to and from Britain. The inscription is recorded on the print, and it is this use of the evidence on the ground together with that of inscriptions and coins that was typical of Ortelius's approach to early history and was precisely the approach that he commended in William Camden's work *Britannia* when he visited England in 1577 (see p. 159).[129]

CHAPTER 5

Van Meteren's Comentarius:

A trade dispute and its consequences

Emanuel van Meteren, the man who had first brought together his cousin Ortelius and his close friend Radermacher, was a key figure in the exchange of information and material. After his apprenticeship, he set up as an independent merchant based in London, where he soon established himself as a member of the expatriate community. Later, he became consul for the Dutch merchants based there and would use his international links to serve as postmaster for the community, ensuring through his trading and political contacts that letters reached their destination together with such things as specimen plants and unusual insects, as well as coins and copies of classical inscriptions.[130] One other thing that he began to circulate as consul of the Netherlands merchants in London was the latest information about political and diplomatic affairs. As is still the case, information had a monetary value in this period, and we have already seen in Radermacher's account how anxiously Gillis Hooftman would seize upon the latest news and refer to his maps to see how it might affect his own projects.

We know quite a lot about van Meteren at this time because a later friend, Simon Ruytinck, a minister of the Dutch stranger church at Austin Friars in London, wrote a brief account of van Meteren's life which was appended to the latter's history of the Eighty Years' War. Some very close verbal echoes

74

suggest that Ruytinck was also familiar with van Meteren's recently identified *Comentarius* (or *memorieboek*), in which the portraits of him and his wife are to be found. This includes a series of entries year by year, many of which record the birth of one or more of his thirteen children by Hester van den Corput. He also considers his occasional visits overseas and various political events to be worthy of mention. This mixture of family matters, trading concerns and momentous political events provides a good idea of how national and international events came to influence private lives. However, first I wish to look at his account of his early life, before going on to consider his entries for the years up to 1575, when the *Paneel* was painted.

In the introduction, I suggested that civilisation could hardly develop without the wealth generated by merchants, but nor could it have developed if these merchants had not themselves highly valued another requisite: learning. Neither Radermacher, Ortelius nor van Meteren attended a university and yet all three truly deserve to be called 'learned merchants'. After his father's death, Ortelius needed to make a living to support his mother and sisters; similarly, Radermacher, who might have otherwise been destined for an academic career, was apprenticed to Gillis Hooftman at the age of fifteen after the death of his father. Van Meteren alone would have been able to go to university, but it was decided that he should be apprenticed to another merchant to learn the necessary skills to continue with the family business. Nevertheless, we discover that his education up to the age of fifteen (the age when he was apprenticed) provided a very solid base on which to build his subsequent academic interests. His account of his early years also gives us a good idea of the cultural and political milieu in which all three friends grew up, and so I shall summarise what he has to say.

Van Meteren starts by telling us the facts of his birth and baptism in 1535 (ever the future historian, he cannot refrain from pointing out that this was the noteworthy year in which the Anabaptists briefly controlled Munster, and Charles V captured Tunis from the Turks). He follows this with a brief account of his father and mother, who had moved to England (then ruled by Edward VI and his strongly Protestant council) to escape persecution for their Protestant beliefs. They were both killed in 1552 when the ship on which they were travelling from Antwerp to England was attacked by a French warship.[131] (There was a war at the time between the Habsburg emperor, Charles V, and Henri II of France. A contributory factor to this conflict was the French concern about being surrounded on almost every border by Habsburg territories, since the Low Countries were ruled by Charles.) Van Meteren then turns back to his childhood and mentions that he spent two of his earliest years with his paternal grandmother just outside Breda, while his parents and elder sister were in London. He moved to Antwerp in 1546, where his schoolmaster was his godfather, Gheleijn —— (van Meteren had presumably forgotten his second name, leaving a blank to be filled in later, simply calling him 'Master Gheleijn the schoolmaster' in the later account of his schooling).

After noting that he was in Antwerp at the time of the siege by Maarten van Rossum (a particularly ruthless general who was doing his best to prevent the annexation of the Duchy of Guelderland by the Habsburgs), he writes that he learnt Latin at the church schools there, before going on to Tournai (Doornik in Dutch) to learn French. Whilst there, he stayed in the house of a Jan de la Rue, whose own son was staying in van Meteren's father's house in exchange. (This was presumably in London, enabling the other boy to learn English while van Meteren was learning French, which gives us some insight into the care that the merchant classes took to ensure that their sons were equipped with the necessary language skills and knowledge of other places to carry on their businesses.) He also continued his Latin studies there, albeit 'with little fruit', and so he was sent to Duffel to study Latin there. He praises this school's care and discipline, and says that Latin grammar was well taught along with music. He adds that by the age of fifteen he was familiar with the plays of Terence and the like. Schools were starting to teach using genuine classical texts at about this time, and the Roman playwright Terence's comedies were accessible to schoolboy minds. More importantly, in a world where Latin was still used for ordinary communications, Terence wrote in a relatively simple style which provided a useful model of clear, 'functional' Latin, as opposed to the elaborate prose of writers like Cicero. It was while he was at Duffel that he witnessed one of the 'Joyous Entries' of Prince Philip (the future Philip II); these were the formal first visits of the rulers of Brabant to its cities, at each of which they promised to uphold the freedoms and charters given by their predecessors.

It was in 1550 that his only sister, Sara, married Troylus de Critz.[132] It was after Sara's wedding that Emanuel's father brought him back to England, where they were able to live safe from persecution during the reign of the strongly Protestant Edward VI. It was at this point that he studied briefly with Immanuel Tremellius, a Jew from Italy, who had been converted to Christianity and baptised by Cardinal Pole. He had subsequently turned Protestant and had taught Hebrew in Strasbourg, before being driven to England by the Schmalkaldic War, in which the Protestant German princes were defeated by the Catholic Charles V. On arriving in England, he was welcomed by Thomas Cranmer, along with other Protestant refugees from the continent. In 1549, he was appointed Professor of Hebrew at Cambridge, before fleeing back to Europe when the Catholic Mary came to the throne. Tremellius would go on to play a major part in a new translation of the Old Testament into Latin, a version preferred by Protestants to the Vulgate. In the early 1580s, Philip Sidney was to refer to him as 'the learned Tremellius', and the translation would be used by John Milton in the seventeenth century.[133] Although van Meteren says little about Tremellius except that he was 'seer gheleert ende godsalich' ('very learned and godly'),[134] contact with a man of such varied experience and significant learning must have played its part in whetting van Meteren's intellectual curiosity. Nevertheless, a decision was made soon after this that he should pursue a mercantile career rather than an academic one, and he was apprenticed to another Antwerp merchant, Sebastiaan Dankaerts.

Van Meteren starts writing the *Comentarius* in 1570, but his regular entries for each year start in 1565 (although what he writes for this first year starts earlier still by recording his marriage on 7 August 1564 to his second wife, Hester van den Corput, at Breda, and how they moved to London a month later). The winter of 1564/65 was particularly harsh, and van Meteren reports both his recovery from a worrying illness (helped, he claims, by bloodletting and a purge) and the fact that the Thames was frozen over (as was the Scheldt at Antwerp). Finally, he reports the birth of his eldest daughter, Lucretia.

Had he started his record a little earlier, he might have recorded a dispute within the Dutch stranger church at Austin Friars. When the church was allowed to resume worship on the accession of Elizabeth I, one of its first pastors was Adriaan van Haemstede, who was accused of Anabaptist tendencies. Van Haemstede not only argued that Anabaptists (the quiet followers of Menno Simons, not the revolutionaries of the kind who had seized Munster) should be treated kindly as fellow Christians, but he also revealed that he was not in favour of infant baptism and did not regard the virgin birth as an essential dogma. Following a meeting with the Bishop of London, Haemstede was excommunicated and given one month to leave the country.[135] As a supporter of Haemstede, van Meteren was expelled from the Dutch stranger church and so worshipped at the smaller Italian stranger church instead, where he was joined by Radermacher, who had only just recently helped its Dutch equivalent to regain use of the Austin Friars site and where he had just been elected a deacon. It is not clear whether van Meteren's support for Haemstede was doctrinal, or merely support for greater tolerance regardless of doctrine, but Radermacher's decision to follow him was probably motivated by friendship. Certainly, once van Meteren was reconciled with the Dutch stranger church in 1571, Radermacher returned as well and was elected an elder in the same year.[136] Van Meteren shared his opinion of Haemstede, we may assume, with the third person to be expelled from the Dutch church in this controversy, who was Acontius, an Italian humanist who had shared lodgings with him in London. Acontius had written earlier on the principles of scientific investigation, and in 1565 wrote *Satanae Strategemata*, which asserted that the division of Christians into different denominations was a stratagem of the devil. Moreover, Acontius was sceptical about the validity of elaborate human theories about religion, let alone their use as a reason for condemning others who disagreed. If van Meteren and Ortelius shared this scepticism, it may well provide a better explanation than Familism of their ability to make and keep friends across confessional divides.[137]

Daniel Rogers, van Meteren's first cousin once removed, provides another surprising example of tolerance; surprising because his father, John Rogers, had been the first Protestant martyr to be burnt at the stake under Mary I. John Rogers had married Adriana van Weyden, a first cousin of both van Meteren and Ortelius, while he was in Wittenberg, and it was here that Daniel, their eldest son, was born. After his father's death, Daniel returned to Wittenberg where he studied under Philip Melanchthon, the Lutheran theologian. After continuing his studies at Oxford, he went to Paris, where he came to know several of the poets of La Pléiade and developed his skills as a Latin poet, as well as pursuing his antiquarian interests while serving as steward to Sir Henry Norris, the English ambassador, and tutor to his children. His wider circle of literary friends included Justus Lipsius, George Buchanan (the Scottish humanist who was a noted Latin poet and tutor of James VI) and Jan Dousa, who was to be the first 'curator' of Leiden University when it was founded shortly after the Spanish besiegers had been driven away. In Daniel Rogers's correspondence with Dousa, he reveals his hope for religious reconciliation, betraying no bitterness about his father's death, and his verses praising John Jewel also seem to support this. Jewel had written a defence of the newly founded Church of England, *Apologia Ecclesiae Anglicanae*, which was based not so much on attacking Catholic errors as on appealing to the authority of the Bible and the early church, claiming that the Church of England followed Christianity's first teachings and practice: it was 'no innovator, but a renovator'.[138]

In *Comentarius*, van Meteren describes 1566 as a 'merckelijck iaer' ('noteworthy year') due to a rather different form of religious tolerance. He describes how in a show of force, 400 of the minor nobility, led by Hendrick van Brederode, presented a formal request to Margaret of Parma that the government's decrees against Protestantism should be revoked (the so-called 'placards') and recording that the suitors were dismissed as *Geuzen* (beggars). With this dismissal, he writes, the rebellion of the *Geuzen* started that was to cost so much blood. Next, he turns to family matters, describing a visit in June that year to Antwerp and on to Breda with his wife and his baby daughter, Lucretia, to visit his wife's seventy-five-year-old grandfather (a former mayor of Breda) so that he could see his great-grandchild, 'syn kints kint, kint' ('his child's child's child') as he puts it. At this point, Lucretia was still less than a year old, and the fact that they were travelling when Hester was already pregnant with their second daughter, who was born the following January, not only says something about her toughness (she went on to have thirteen children in total) but also about how much travel between London and Antwerp took place as a matter of course. Van Meteren then went on to Bruges, where trade talks between England and the Netherlands were taking place, revealing the future historian's appetite for the latest news, as well as the merchant's eagerness to spot what advantage might be taken of any new agreement. Despite his travels there, the talks, already adjourned from the previous year, remained deadlocked and were postponed indefinitely.[139] Next, he records that in July the Reformed religion was preached openly across the Netherlands for the first time, and that the *Beeldenstorm* began in August, although he and his family were already safely back in London by this time. His final entry for 1566 records that he received a commission for silk trading.

Although 1567 was a momentous year, van Meteren says comparatively little about it. He records the birth of his second daughter on 4 January, but also that she only lived one year. The slightly matter-of-fact way in which he records this is a reminder of the high rates of infant mortality that were, if not exactly taken for granted, nevertheless considered inevitable. He had a young wife, and by the time he was summing up the year in this account, he would have known that his 'tweede Susanna' ('second Susanna') was to be born in early March of the following year.

He then observes that the year was noteworthy for the Battle of Oosterweel, just outside Antwerp, at which the premature Calvinist rebellion led by van Brederode was crushed; William of Orange had fortunately persuaded the Calvinists of Antwerp not to go to an unnecessary death by joining them. Next, he records the siege and capture of Valenciennes by forces loyal to Margaret of Parma, the departure of William of Orange from the Netherlands, and the arrival of the Duke of Alba with his army to punish the provinces. All of this was bad news for any Protestant hoping for freedom of worship, but provokes no further comment, although it is followed by a sign which may be some sort of abbreviation, or simply a discreet way of avoiding any comment on Alba's ruthless actions (some of which might be called war crimes today).

Then, somewhat surprisingly, he finishes his account of the year by saying that he had enjoyed good health and that it had been a good year for trade. This serves as a reminder to those who read into history the knowledge derived from hindsight: that good health and prosperity for oneself and one's family were most people's priority, rather than engaging in what must have seemed a hopeless cause of fighting for freedom of conscience against the overwhelming force that Alba was using to compel acceptance of the authority of Philip II and the Catholic Church. The restoration of order, no matter how brutally done, must have been a source of relief to many merchants at that time. Nevertheless, Antwerp merchants must have been deeply shocked when their Roman Catholic mayor, Antoon van Stralen, was arrested, tortured and executed; he had, after all, tried to restrain the iconoclasts and had intervened to protect Dominican friars from the mob, but he was also a moderate who had been in touch with William of Orange.[140] Even so, the benefit of restored stability in the markets could be appreciated, while the wider political impact caused by alarm in Protestant countries at the return of a disciplined and effective Spanish fighting force to northern Europe was yet to manifest itself.

Van Meteren starts his entries for 1568 by recording the birth of his 'second Susanna' and then describes a visit in May to see friends in Antwerp and Breda, where his father-in-law lived. It is at this point that he records in his account that his own interests are involved in the developing conflict, when he notes that he returned before the troubles began. Next, he tells us that what is sometimes described as the first battle of the Eighty Years' War took place on 24 May. Here, the brothers of William the Silent, Louis and Adolphe of Nassau, decisively defeated a small Spanish force commanded by the Count of Arenberg, who was killed along with many of his troops. It did not gain the rebels any significant advantage, though, and Adolphe was killed; Louis was to be crushingly defeated soon afterwards at Jemmingen. It did, however, probably lead to Alba's decision to press ahead with the public execution of the Counts of Egmont and Hoorn, neither of whom was Protestant, but who had shared William the Silent's concerns about Philip's overriding of the independent governance of cities in the Netherlands. Other nobles and a range of people across the country were also executed. Van Meteren concludes by saying that the family had had a healthy year.

Up to this point in van Meteren's year-by-year account of his personal affairs, wider political issues are mentioned, but seem to be of secondary importance. However, in 1569, political matters force themselves to the front: his opening words are that on 3 January there was a 'general arrest' in England – a seizure of the property of all subjects of Philip II.

A trade dispute and its consequences

In order to understand the context for this abrupt interruption to the normal trading life of an Antwerp merchant based in London, it is necessary to go back to the period just before van Meteren's annual entries in the *Comentarius* start. The entries began in 1565, but the year before had seen an earlier threat to trade between England and Antwerp, when Philip II's Regent in Brussels, Margaret of Parma, encouraged by her chief adviser, Cardinal Granvelle, had sought to exploit the English vulnerability caused by the unavoidable surrender of Le Havre to the French when the English garrison supporting the Huguenots had been fatally weakened by an outbreak of plague. This had coincided with plague in London and a period of difficulties in raising loans. Using the risk of plague infection as an excuse, Margaret had banned the Merchant Adventurers of London, the authorised body for English cloth exports, from importing cloth into Antwerp. Plague was used as an excuse, since the hostility of France meant that she did not want to give Elizabeth I any cause for similar hostility on the north side of the English Channel, which was a key transport link between Spain and the Habsburg Low Countries. This was intended to force trading concessions from Elizabeth I's government, whose main source of income was an export tax on woollen cloth, and to remind her that it was risky to offend Habsburg power. Moreover, Granvelle seems also to have hoped that the subsequent unrest caused by unemployment in the wool industry would force Elizabeth to return to the Catholic fold. The fact that the ban caused equally great hardship in Antwerp does not seem to have troubled the Brussels government. The lords of Antwerp were very clear that they wished to keep the Inquisition out and keep control of their own courts, which in practice meant that they did not pursue the heretical merchants who brought prosperity to the city. From Margaret's point of view, a little hardship might help to bring them to heel and would be no bad thing.

This severance of trade certainly caused economic damage on both sides, but it eventually backfired badly when the English in turn banned all trade with Antwerp, again using plague as the excuse. The Regent did not know that Elizabeth had already been in negotiations with the Lutheran ruler of East Friesland, the 'Lady of Emden'. Emden was not only Protestant, but was also a port only a little further east than Antwerp and relatively easily reached. It did not have the market facilities or comforts of Antwerp, but the cloth fleet that was sent there discovered that there was sufficient trade to justify the voyage. Moreover, although they could not find enough purchasers for all their goods, some of the merchants were able to go on to Cologne, where their cloths could be 'improved' and dyed, before travelling to Frankfurt, where they could sell their wares and also buy German linens to import back to England. This may have been less convenient than going to Antwerp, but it opened up a new and not unprofitable line of business. Antwerp remained the preferred option, but it was no longer seen as essential to England's mercantile prosperity. Nevertheless, after an eighteen-month stand-off, both sides agreed to appoint a team of three to negotiate a new settlement. Crucially from the English point of view, they agreed in the meantime to revert to the arrangements as they had been in 1558, just after the death of Queen Mary; this included the much increased tax rate that Mary had introduced shortly before her death when, as the English liked to point out to forestall Habsburg objections, she was married to Philip II, the ruler of the Netherlands as well as King of Spain. Although both sides were willing to resume trade, certain difficulties meant that they failed to reach an agreement, not least due to the intervention of Gillis Hooftman, whose objections were supported by d'Assonleville, one of the Netherlands' negotiators, yet dismissed by both the Regent's council in Brussels and the Privy Council in London (see Chapter 2). Consequently, negotiations were adjourned until the following year, when again, no final agreement was reached. Thereafter, things continued as before until the events of 1568. Meanwhile, England had entered into quiet negotiations with the city and port of Hamburg, coming to an agreement in 1567 brought about after the disruption caused by the iconoclasm of 1566.

In 1567, the skilful and emollient Spanish ambassador to Elizabeth, Guzman de Silva, was replaced by Don Guerau de Espés, a man who had no experience of North European and Netherlands affairs, but with a militant desire to bring England back under Catholic control.[141] His role was important because in the absence of an English ambassador in Spain, he was the only diplomatic link between Elizabeth and Philip, as well as being the nearest channel of Philip's authority to Alba in the Netherlands. This was because Elizabeth had withdrawn the English ambassador to Spain after Philip had effectively prevented him from doing his job by excluding him from Madrid for protesting against not being allowed to have private Protestant services, just as the Spanish ambassador was allowed to have Roman Catholic services at his embassy in London. The failure of de Espés to realise the full significance of the links between trade and diplomatic interests might not have mattered, since everything seemed to be stable in Antwerp: Alba and his troops had crushed Protestant resistance relatively easily, and the danger of Huguenots crossing the border from France to support their co-religionists had ended after they had suffered heavy defeats in France. Catholic dominance may have been upsetting news for English Protestants, but it was reassuring for merchants of other religious persuasions, since it brought stability and meant that the kind of disruption to trade caused by the Protestant iconoclasm of 1566 was no longer an issue. Alba, however, still had problems. Having chosen to treat the Netherlands as a conquered territory rather than as an integral part of Philip's patrimony, he found raising taxes from resentful cities, each with their own legal traditions, more difficult than he had expected, despite his complete military control. Philip, like other early modern rulers, was handicapped by the lack of regular tax revenue, and had to raise most of the monies he needed from Castille.[142] The Low Countries, however, although wealthy, were naturally reluctant to raise taxes on a similar scale for a standing army that was in effect occupying their own lands. Alba also discovered that the channels for financial support from Spain to pay his troops were less secure than he had hoped. This occurred when two barges on the Rhine bringing a considerable sum of silver borrowed by Spain from Genoese bankers were detained and the money unloaded on the orders of the Calvinist Elector Palatine on the grounds that transporting foreign coins in this way was against the currency regulations of the German Empire. Therefore, the alternative sea route from Spain via the English Channel was even more important to Alba. It was this practical consideration that explained Spanish tolerance of Protestant England for so long: given that France was often at war with Spain, it would have been folly to have provoked hostility on the opposite side of the Channel as well, a point that de Espés does not appear to have understood.

Although Netherlandish and French Protestants had been defeated on land, they still posed a threat at sea. The Prince of Orange and the Protestant Queen of Navarre both had the right as sovereign rulers to issue letters of marque to privateers. Privateering was a kind of licensed piracy, permitting those who held these letters of marque to attack any merchant vessel that might be deemed to be trading to the advantage of a hostile state. When actual pirates were added to the mix, any kind of trade either across or through the Channel proved extremely hazardous, and it was this that was to trigger the next crisis. Rather than escorting ships carrying silver bullion to Alba with warships, Philip relied on using fast vessels to evade pirates and privateers, knowing that if the worst came to the worst, they could seek shelter in friendly English ports. In late 1568, a combination of Huguenot privateers and bad weather meant that one group of Spanish vessels had to do just this, with one vessel docking in Southampton Water, where the captain asked for protection; four more of the fleet took shelter further west at Saltash and Fowey. When it became known that these ships were carrying treasure, there was naturally curiosity as to its owner. If it belonged to the King of Spain, Elizabeth was certainly not going to risk a major breach by interfering with the valuable cargo, but Benedict Spinola, a Genoese merchant based in London, revealed that it actually belonged to Genoese bankers, and that although the intention was to lend it to Alba to pay his troops, it had not yet changed hands. Furthermore, the five ships were prevented from putting to sea again because the Huguenot privateers were waiting offshore to attack them. Indeed, following a night-time raid by the Huguenots on the ship at Southampton, the Spanish captain asked for English help in protecting his precious cargo (the English had already helped fight off the French attack and the mayor of Southampton himself had been wounded in the action). The English replied that this would be difficult as long as he was moored off the coast, and that the best thing that he could do would be to land the cargo so that it could not be stolen in a further night raid. The captain agreed, albeit with some misgivings. Instructions were then given that the other ships should also be unloaded whether they wished it or not.

At this point, there may well have been some ambiguity about English intentions. Although Genoa was technically independent of Spain, and its bankers were therefore not Spanish subjects, those dependent on trade with the Spanish Netherlands were appalled by the damage that could be done to their businesses by illegally seizing what was virtually Spanish money. Some Protestants, on the other hand, felt that the money could be taken as a loan on which Elizabeth would agree to pay interest to the Genoese, thus preventing it being used by a Catholic commander to pay a powerful and potentially threatening army just the other side of the Channel.

At this point, de Espés, who does not seem to have been alarmed at first by the unloading of the bullion, suddenly became suspicious and decided to take pre-emptive action. He had been briefed in Brussels on his way to England by d'Assonleville, the most ardent advocate of the previous unsuccessful attempt to use a trade embargo to put pressure on the English, and he now believed that he could kill two birds with one stone, forcing the English to give up the money and also bringing the government under such financial pressure that it would collapse, thus obliging Elizabeth to give way to her Catholic subjects and sack her Protestant advisers, Cecil and Walsingham. De Espés thus sent clandestine instructions that all English merchants and their goods in the Spanish Low Countries should be seized (his messenger even insisted on the arrest of the crew and seizure of the ship which had taken him back). The furious and predictable response of the English was, of course, to order the general arrest, which was recorded by van Meteren. It soon became clear that English debts in Antwerp were significantly greater than their assets, and because of the slowness of communications, unsuspecting Spanish ships kept arriving in English ports, where they were promptly seized. Since de Espés was the Spanish king's representative, Alba felt obliged to follow his instructions in Antwerp, albeit as tactfully as he could, but English merchants elsewhere were treated a great deal more roughly. For tactical reasons, Alba did not want to damage Anglo-Spanish relations, and so he sent d'Assonleville to England to try to quell matters. Unfortunately, he had not yet assessed the latter's character and had also failed to take into account that he had been the strongest advocate of the previous interruption to trade in 1563 and the biggest obstacle to reaching an agreement in the subsequent negotiations. He was, however, the acknowledged expert on Anglo-Netherlands trade relations, and so he was sent by Alba. Shocked and angry at his extremely hostile reception in England (what did he expect, one wonders), d'Assonleville was not the man to take the heat out of the situation. In the end, convinced that he was at some personal risk, he fled back to Antwerp. In the meantime, de Espés had been conclusively shown to be the source of the initial order for the arrest of English merchants (which he had originally denied), and he therefore lost any influence that he might have had at Elizabeth's court. In these circumstances, Elizabeth could claim with entire justification that her actions were 'for the indemnity of her majesty's subjects already without any just cause detained'. The treasure – some 155 chests of silver coins worth approximately £85,000 – was transported from the ports to the Tower of London.

One of the things which one assumes de Espés had not appreciated was that Hamburg, to which the Merchant Adventurers had already started sending some of their exports, was, unlike Emden, sufficiently far from the reach of Alba to be a safe alternative to Antwerp. After three successful early voyages in 1569 and 1570, Hamburg was to become the normal port for cloth exports for the next few years, and so all that de Espés had achieved was to destroy Antwerp's pre-eminence as the preferred destination of the English trade that was the major source of its wealth. No wonder that the great Antwerp merchant, Gillis Hooftman, looks so care-worn in the *Paneel*.

No wonder also that in 1569, for the first time, van Meteren's entry in the *Comentarius* focuses primarily on affairs of state and their effect on his trading position rather than on his family. His entry for the year begins by recording the 'general arrest' in England of the persons and property of all subjects of Philip II. However, he thanks God that his own affairs were entrusted to his landlord, Sir Christopher Draper, an alderman of the City of London who had recently been Lord Mayor and who allowed him to stay in his house on parole (van Meteren goes on to report that his goods were soon released to him without great trouble). This light-touch treatment is not surprising, especially given that the City of London did not wish to upset trading relationships with Antwerp, and because van Meteren had lived a good while in London and had impeccable Protestant family associations. It is only after this that he records the birth of his first son, Jacob, before mentioning the heavy Huguenot defeat in France at Moncontour. He finishes by recording that at Michaelmas he had moved to a house in Lime Street (where Ortelianus also lived) and that he had passed the year in good health.

Domestic matters are very much to the fore again in the entry for 1570, where we are first told at some length that Jacob was weaned before he was seven months old because his mother had found breast-feeding very painful. In a time of high infant mortality, this was a not insignificant matter, and van Meteren's concern for the welfare of mother and baby is very understandable, and shows time has not had a softening effect on his memory of his wife's and baby's distress. Next, we hear of a family visit to Salisbury where Elizabeth, the daughter of Adriana van Weyden and John Rogers, had married James Proctor, who was a residentiary canon at Salisbury Cathedral from 1561.[143] Perhaps unsurprisingly, van Meteren's wife was very ill on arrival. She recovers, however, and in November she gives birth to a second son, Carolus. The only political matter recorded for this year is the peace agreed in France at St Germain that brought to an end the third French War of Religion.

In 1571, van Meteren records a visit to Antwerp to 'speak to his friends', including Anna Ortels, the unmarried sister of Ortelius and a first cousin (he mentions in passing that her sister, Elizabeth, the mother of Ortelianus and wife of Jacob Coels Snr, lived near them in Lime Street in London). Subsequently, he went up the Rhine to Arnhem, and then through Nijmegen to Breda.

The affairs of the outside world force themselves upon his attention once more in 1572 when he mentions what was to prove a turning point in the struggle for independence: the capture of Brill by the rebel *Watergeuzen* (Sea Beggars), who had continued to resist Philip II despite Alba's victories on land. The capture of an undefended fishing port would not have been especially important had it not provoked a domino effect, with Flushing (Vlissingen) rebelling six days later and others shortly after that, including a third port, Enkhuizen. Possession of these three ports meant that a strategically important stretch of coast, including the approach to Antwerp up the Scheldt estuary, was controlled by the rebels. In addition, a large part of the provinces of Zeeland and Holland was suddenly in rebel hands. Van Meteren then records the marriage of the Protestant King of Navarre (the future Henri IV of France) in Paris, which became the occasion of the St Bartholomew's Day massacre of thousands of Huguenots. This massacre gave the Pope great satisfaction (he had a medal struck to mark the occasion), but it and the copy-cat murders across France unsurprisingly hardened Protestant determination to resist the Inquisition both in the Netherlands and in England. The Pope's decision two years earlier to excommunicate Elizabeth I and deny her right to the crown – something that van Meteren had not thought to record – had already put great pressure on the loyalty of English Catholics and made Jesuit priests traitors by definition in the eyes of the government. Philip, who had tried to block the excommunication of Elizabeth, describing it as a move that would be 'futile', nevertheless expressed great satisfaction at the massacre.[144] Certainly, like the Pope, he will have been very pleased by the ending of the threat posed by William's brother, Louis of Nassau, who had invaded Flanders and captured Mons, the capital of Hainault, with Huguenot support. Once this support was withdrawn, Louis was unable to defend Mons and Alba soon recaptured it. Alba was then able to turn his attention to recapturing many of the rebel towns in the north, and van Meteren gives a long list of these, culminating with a mention of the siege of Haarlem. Although Alba recaptured the city, it would take six months, during which time other towns were able to strengthen their fortifications and the Spanish counter-attack lost its momentum. Finally, van Meteren records a naval clash with a 'rich' Spanish flotilla, which offers a reminder of the vulnerability of Spanish supply routes and explains Alba's failure to pay his troops.[145] It is easy to see why van Meteren considers all these matters too important to omit, but at the end of his entry for 1572 he returns to domestic matters, noting the marriage of his wife's second sister and thanking God for his good health.

In 1573, van Meteren reports the birth of another daughter in January and the marriage of another of his sisters-in-law, this time to an Italian. He also mentions that after five years, the 'general arrest' of trade between the Netherlands and England had come to an end. Once again, he then turns to war issues. He notes how Haarlem was finally starved into submission after a six-month siege and surrendered after being given assurances, yet he doesn't record the subsequent savagery of the Spanish troops who had then executed every member of the garrison (over 1,000 men). This shocked many at the Spanish Court and also Cardinal Granvelle, who was by then Viceroy of Naples. Granvelle subsequently wrote to Zúñiga, the Spanish ambassador in Paris, of the hatred that had been stirred up, concluding that Alba's time as Governor of the Low Countries amounted to 'many millions ill-spent, and the complete ruin of those provinces'.[146] The savagery at Haarlem probably explained the desperate and heroic repulse of the Spanish siege of Alkmaar, where citizens joined in hand-to-hand fighting alongside the garrison, knowing that surrender almost certainly meant death and the destruction of their homes. The Spanish finally withdrew when the dykes were breached and their camp was flooded. Further good news for the Protestant cause came from France, where the Royalist siege of La Rochelle was abandoned (many Huguenots had taken refuge there after the St Bartholomew's Day massacre). Sancerre, another Huguenot stronghold that had held out heroically, only finally negotiated surrender after the Royalist army had withdrawn from La Rochelle and agreed a truce. Long sieges cost lives and money, and damage morale, especially when unsuccessful. Although van Meteren does little more than mention these events in passing, these successful resistances reduced the pressure on Protestants in both France and the Netherlands, and provided time for reorganisation before the next phase of the war began.

Van Meteren describes 1574 as a 'wonderbaer iaer' ('extraordinary year'); 'extraordinary' perhaps, but certainly not 'wonderful' in the modern English sense of that word. For the first time in his entries, the summary of events in the outside world of war and political conflict demands more space than his personal affairs, although he has much to tell us about the latter as well, recording another visit to Zeeland and Holland, two provinces on the west coast of the modern Netherlands, both of which had rebelled against Alba. He travels via Middelburg to Delft, where he visits an uncle of his wife. He then records the sickness and recovery of two of his daughters, and his fear that it might be the plague. Next, we learn of the birth of another daughter, Othilia, before we are told of the death of his second sister in childbirth. From here, however, he moves on to list the emphatic victory of the Sea Beggars over a Spanish fleet attempting to relieve the siege of Middelburg (the Battle of Reimerswaal), and the subsequent surrender of the city by its Spanish garrison; he then notes the relief of Leiden from a lengthy Spanish siege after the dykes were breached and the relieving forces came by barges across the fields, and the complete defeat and death of William the Silent's brothers, Louis and Henry, at the Battle of Mookerheyde. Further afield, he mentions the recapture of Tunis by the Turks, which ensured Ottoman control of North Africa. Tunis had been taken by Don Juan of Austria for the Spanish the previous year, and its loss provides a reminder that Philip II was trying to prevent Turkish domination of the Mediterranean at the same time as attempting to bring the Netherlands to heel. The financial pressures caused by these different conflicts helps to explain why the Spanish troops in the Netherlands had not been paid, and van Meteren tells us how after the

Spanish victory at Mookerheyde, the victorious troops had entered Antwerp and threatened to sack it unless they were given their back pay.[147]

Turning to France, van Meteren makes a brief reference to the complex affairs of the French court and the power struggle that developed after Henri III, a brother of Charles IX, who had been elected King of Poland the previous year, had returned to claim the French throne upon the death of Charles. This was of importance to anyone with family or business in the Netherlands because of the possibility of French incursions, whether in the guise of Huguenot support for their co-religionists in their rebellion against Philip, or as French policy to resist encirclement by the Habsburg armies.[148] Van Meteren finishes by noting that he has enjoyed reasonable health but done very little business.

If the entry for 1574 sees the personal outweighed by the political, the two would collide inescapably in 1575. First, van Meteren describes how he leaves London for Antwerp, sailing from Dover. They meet a French warship from La Rochelle, a centre of Protestant resistance in France, that was sailing from Flushing (Vlissingen), a port in control of the Protestant Sea Beggars. It would have been difficult, to say the least, for van Meteren not to remember the death of his parents after their ship was intercepted by a French warship while making the same cross-Channel passage. Nevertheless, they were allowed to continue on their voyage 'beleefdelijck' ('courteously'), for which he thanks God. He then visits Antwerp and Breda to become better acquainted with certain merchants and their agents. Back in Antwerp, on the morning of 2 May, he is returning from the Bourse to the house of his cousin Abraham Ortelius when he is arrested in the street by a Spanish officer with a military escort. He is then bound and marched off to a jail with a soldier holding each arm, as if, he writes indignantly, he were some 'straetschender' ('street hooligan'), and without being told the reason for his arrest. His keys, letters and notebooks were seized and Spanish troops confiscated his other writings from his lodgings. Up to this point, van Meteren makes no claim to bravery, saying that he was 'seer verslagen' ('absolutely terrified') that he would be tortured and might die. That evening, an old woman bringing alms asked him if his name was Emanuel and assured him that his friends Hoefnagel and Hooftman would be pressing for his release. The next morning, he had to justify himself after his failure to attend Mass by explaining to his jailer that as a denizen of England he would be fined 100 marks if he did.

He notes that he was in some perplexity as to whether he should defend himself as a citizen of Antwerp or as a 'ghenaturaliseert' ('naturalised') Englishman who had been living in London for the previous twenty-four years.[149] It was then that the daughter of the under-gaoler came to him, addressing him as 'Englishman, Englishman' and telling him that he should indeed answer his interrogation as a resident of his adopted nation. She also informed him that his interrogator would be a city councillor called Boone, a severe but decent man. At this point, van Meteren tells us that he thanked God and felt much encouraged to prepare for his examination. It seems clear from the ease with which messages were brought to him (and perhaps from the choice of interrogator) that the city authorities were unenthusiastic about enforcing what they saw as Spanish authority and a threat to their free trade status, but that they could not ignore the instructions to question van Meteren closely.

On 15 May, Councillor Boone summoned him to his house and examined him in his dining room (this sounds very informal, but the dining room was normally a room at the back of the house and therefore private). When Boone asks for his personal details, van Meteren describes himself as Antwerp-born and English by denization. Boone has all his confiscated papers and books in front of him, and questions him about religious and political matters, although primarily the latter. He asks him who his contacts were in Antwerp and London, and about him being in possession of a Latin translation of the Psalms by Eobanus Hessus (a German humanist and Lutheran) and a pamphlet in Dutch about free trade in Holland. There were obviously suspicions that he might be spying (especially given all the trade details in his notebooks), and so he was questioned about the Prince of Orange and about his contacts with Daniel Rogers (see p. 161). He defended himself by pointing out that he had put himself at the service of the Netherlands ambassadors trying to renegotiate the trade agreement (the *Intercursus*) that had been broken by the Duchess of Parma at the urging of d'Assonleville, and when attempts were being made to end the 'general arrest' (see pp. 81–6). He mentions by name François Halewijn, Lord of Zwevegem, and Jan Boischot, the envoys sent to London by Requesens to try to secure a new trade agreement.[150] After the interrogation, he gives thanks to God that he was able to give brief and cautious answers without incriminating himself.

In the meantime, news of van Meteren's arrest had got back to his friends in London, and Radermacher obtained letters of support from Walsingham, secretary of Queen Elizabeth's council, and from the Governor of the Merchant Adventurers' *natie* in Antwerp requesting that he be treated as an Englishman. Maerten della Faille, a friend of his brother-in-law's wife, asked that Boischot should also write on his behalf. Boischot had been in England for much of 1574 and was in London at the time of van Meteren's arrest, where

1. *Wedding portrait of Gillis Hooftman and
Margaretha van Nispen* by Maerten de Vos, 1570.

(*Rijksmuseum, Amsterdam*)

2. *Moses Showing the Tablets of the Law to the Israelites, with Portraits of Members of the Panhuys Family, their Relatives and Friends (Panhuys Paneel)* by Maerten de Vos, 1574–5. The commandments are translated into Dutch and divided in the Lutheran manner and not the Calvinist one.

(Catherijneconvent, Utrecht)

3. *The Kraanenhoofd and Werfpoort (Crane and Harbour gate) on the Scheldt in Antwerp* by Sebastiaan Vrancx, 1616–18.

(The Phoebus Foundation, Antwerp)

4. The Antwerp Bourse as it was in 1531, the predecessor of every bourse and stock exchange throughout the world. *(The Phoebus Foundation, Antwerp)*

5. *Antverpia*, a bird's eye view of Antwerp and the citadel by Joris Hoefnagel, before 1597. Daniel Rogers' Latin poems in praise of Antwerp and the great gathering of merchants in the Bourse are at the bottom left. *(University Library of Antwerp)*

6. Portrait medallion of Gillis Hooftman
attributed to Steven van Herwijk, 1559.

(Museum aan de Stroom, Antwerp)

7. Portrait medallion of Gillis Hooftman
by Jacob Jonghelinck, 1580.

(Museum aan de Stroom, Antwerp)

8. The companion of Jonghelinck's portrait medallion, 1580, sometimes made
separately and sometimes as the reverse of no.7. This shows a ship with rocks
and possibly thunder bolts falling on it surrounded by an anagram of Gylis
Hooftman, HA LOF SY MIN GOT ('Ah praise be to my God').

(De Nederlandsche Bank, Amsterdam)

9. *Septentrionalium Regionum Descrip. (Description of the Northern Regions)*
from Ortelius's *Theatrum Orbis Terrarum*, first printed 1570, showing not only
the Baltic, but also the sea route to the White Sea for trade with Russia.

(Harvard University)

10. *Portrait of Peeter Panhuys, Aged 34*, 1562. Formerly attributed to Pieter Pourbus, but now attributed to his son Frans I. This was painted a year after Panhuys had married Gillis Hooftman's niece, Margaretha.

(Galerie Lowet de Wotrenge, Antwerp)

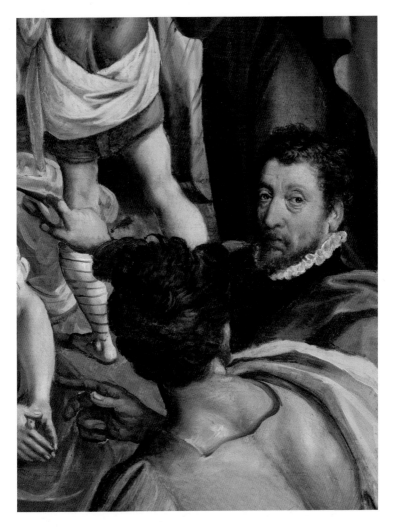

11. Detail of *Die Sintflut (The Flood)* in Celle Castle chapel by
Maerten de Vos, *c.* 1570, showing a self-portrait of the artist.

(Residenzmuseum im Celler Schloss, Celle)

12. *St Paul at Ephesus* by Maerten de Vos, 1568. St Paul is dragged away from the rioting silversmiths who make images of Diana, while in the middle ground to the right the magicians' books can be seen burning on a pyre. *(Musées Royaux des Beaux-Arts, Brussels)*

13. *St Paul on Malta* by Maerten de Vos, *c.* 1568. As St Paul bends to put wood on the fire the viper can be seen twisting round his arm before he shakes it into the fire. *(Louvre Museum, Paris)*

14. A view of the Castle chapel at Celle looking east.

(Residenzmuseum im Celler Schloss, Celle)

15. *Teaching the Children* by Maerten de Vos, 1565–1576.
A father (perhaps the Duke himself?) catechizes his children.

(Residenzmuseum im Celler Schloss, Celle)

16. *Katharina* by Albrecht Dürer, 1521. A silverpoint drawing of the
servant of the Portuguese royal agent in Antwerp.

(Galleria degli Uffizi, Florence)

17. *Balthazar* by Joos van Cleve, *c.* 1525. The surviving side panel of a triptych that would have shown the adoration of the Three Kings.

(Brighton & Hove Museums)

18. *The Adoration of the Kings* by Maerten de Vos, 1599.

(Musée des Beaux-Arts, Valenciennes)

19. The frontispiece of Ortelius's *Theatrum Orbis Terrarum* engraved by Frans Hogenberg, 1570. The four known continents are represented by four female figures; Europe sits enthroned at the top, Asia is on the left and Africa to the right and America is below. *(Library of Congress, Washington, DC)*

he was attempting to wrest some concessions from Elizabeth and persuade her to soften the uncompromising English response to the general arrest. Presumably, the last thing he would have wanted was for Elizabeth to be given further cause for complaint by the unnecessary ill-treatment of an English denizen. His Antwerp friends also presented a petition on his behalf to the Governor. There is no definite evidence of how influential these letters were, but after a further interview in which he was warned that the evidence of his papers and his possession of two forbidden books provided ample grounds for proceeding against him with rigour, he was released with the advice to return home as soon as possible. Van Meteren was released on 20 May and, having swiftly settled his accounts, he was safely back in London ten days later.

At this point, van Meteren's account of key moments in his life has brought us to the year that the *Paneel* was painted. We are given a picture of a man who was one of a company of learned merchants, with family and friends on both sides of the sea, who thought nothing of the short passage from London to Antwerp. Despite this ease of travel, there were plenty of dangers, not only from privateers and French warships, but also from arbitrary arrest on the streets of Antwerp. Van Meteren had clearly had good reason to think that his life was at risk. However, it would not be foreign warships but Philip's determination to stamp out heresy that would scatter the civilised and international group depicted on the *Paneel*.

CHAPTER 6

Christophe Plantin and his authors

There is little reason to doubt the generally agreed identification of Christophe Plantin (R9) and his wife, Jeanne Rivière (L8), which appears to be confirmed by a comparison with their posthumous portraits by Rubens. Although posthumous, they were based on earlier images and commissioned from Rubens by their son-in-law who knew them well, and so it seems reasonable to assume that they are fair likenesses. The identification of Peeter Heyns (R11) also appears to be confirmed beyond reasonable doubt by the laurel wreath that he is wearing, since he was the master of a famous school for girls attended by Hooftman's daughters, known as De Lauwerboom (The Laurel Tree). Zondervan is confident about the identification of Rembert Dodoens (R3) on the grounds of a similarity with another image, but this remains uncertain.

The next two suggested identifications are, however, extremely dubious. I would like to suggest that the man behind and just to the right of Moses, who is gesticulating (L14), might possibly be Justus Lipsius. Most pictures of Lipsius show him as an older man, but at the time of the painting he was in his late twenties, and the man shown here still has dark hair and a beard in a style that is arguably sixteenth century, as well as the sunken eyes that one sees in later images. A still wilder suggestion is based on the fact that by the time of the painting, we can be sure that Montano, in whom the Inquisition was taking an unhealthy interest following the publication of the *Biblia Regia* (see pp. 120–21) would not have wished to be publicly associated with some of his Antwerp friends whose religious beliefs were also under suspicion. Could the small, simply clad figure gesturing towards the text of the Ten Commandments (L14), lacking both his beard and his normal habit bearing the red cross of the Order of Santiago, really be a symbolic representation of Montano that reveals his philological interest in the biblical text that he is gesturing towards? The sceptical reader may well feel that this is just one more of the many rhetorical questions to which the answer is undoubtedly no. For what it is worth, however, we are told that he was 'a small slight man' who 'always wore the plain habit of his order'.[151] Whether or not these last two identifications are correct (and in neither case are the depicted men wearing sixteenth-century clothes), both scholars need to be mentioned, since they are probably the two most important authors that Plantin published.

* * *

A reminder of the relative unimportance of national boundaries to the merchant class is provided by the career of the printer and publisher Christophe Plantin (R9), who consensus generally agrees *is* depicted in the *Paneel*. Just as Emanuel van Meteren lived in London but would travel freely to the Netherlands to do business and visit friends and wider family until greater caution was forced on him by the events of May 1575, so Plantin was a Frenchman who chose to live and work in Antwerp but who still had property and business interests in Paris. Nevertheless, the conflicts of the Reformation played their part in prompting this mobility, as well as the demands of trade. We know very little about Plantin's early life, but we do know that in 1548 he moved from Paris to Antwerp, a city renowned for its welcome to foreign merchants since they contributed to its thriving commerce, and which reckoned that encouraging trade took priority over persecuting heretics. In France, however, publishing was becoming more dangerous. The Lyons publisher Etienne Dolet had been burnt at the stake the year before Plantin's departure, and by the end of the decade, two other French printers and booksellers had had to flee to Calvinist Geneva (namely Conrad Badius and Robert Estienne).[152]

Plantin came from a humble background in Touraine but was brought up in Lyons in the household of Antoine Porret, a canon obedientiary (one assigned financial or administrative duties) of the Church of Saint-Just in Lyons, which was a significant centre of the French book trade. Here, Plantin became the lifelong friend of one of the canon's nephews, Pierre Porret. He subsequently went to Paris, at which point his father appears to have disappeared from his life. After this, he went to Caen where he was apprenticed to Robert Macé II and learnt the trade of bookbinding. It was also here that he married Jeanne Rivière (L8), a woman of limited education (she signed her will with a cross), but a valuable support to Plantin throughout his life. He then set up as a bookseller in Paris, renting a house from the printer Jaques Bogard, and it was probably from him that Plantin learnt more about printing. In 1548, a year after the birth of his first daughter, he moved to Antwerp, yet he retained his links with Paris.

There is no reason to suppose that Plantin was not doing perfectly well in Paris, but apart from the possible religious motives mentioned above, there were also good commercial reasons for moving to Antwerp, which was rapidly becoming the most prosperous city in northern Europe. It was a place with a well-established banking system, where an ambitious trader could easily obtain credit, and had excellent trade links to the rest of the world. Plantin summarised it like this: 'No other town in the world could offer me more facilities for carrying on the trade I intended to begin. Antwerp can be easily reached; various nations meet in its market-place; there too can be found the raw materials indispensable for the practice of one's trade; craftsmen for all trades can easily be found and instructed in a short time.'[153] According to the Italian historian Lodovico Guicciardini in his *Description of all the Low Countries*, it was also a city of conspicuous consumption, where wealth was flaunted and the urban élite enjoyed themselves. (Life for the poor in an increasingly over-crowded city was, needless to say, a good deal less pleasant.) Guicciardini also describes its citizens as 'merchants to the whole universe'.[154] Like Plantin, Guicciardini was yet another foreigner who came to Antwerp and never went home: he arrived in 1542 as the agent of an Italian business and stayed there until his death in 1589.

Plantin started in trade selling books and prints, and also working in the complementary trade of bookbinding, while his wife traded in haberdashery. In 1550, he became a citizen of Antwerp. If the authorities felt that an applicant for citizenship was making a useful economic contribution, this simply required taking an oath and making the necessary payment. It was a year or two after this that he was attacked and wounded one evening as he made his way through the streets. There are two accounts of the consequences of this. The first suggests that the long-term effect of the wound prevented him from continuing with his work as bookbinder and leather-worker, and this led to his following the alternative trade of printing. The other story says that he recognised his assailant, who had mistaken him for someone else, and that the money paid to Plantin by his attacker's wealthy father to prevent his son facing trial enabled him to set up as a printer.[155] Another competing claim was that the capital he needed to set up as a printer came from a merchant called Henrik Niclaes, who wanted him to publish heretical material (see p. 96).

Whatever the precise facts, he was certainly printing by 1555. The books that he initially chose to publish reveal his desire to print works that would not only sell well enough for his business to prosper (a commercial necessity), but also volumes that were more academically ambitious. From 1558 he establishes a profitable line in selling almanacs in both French and Flemish. As well as such obvious money-spinners, he printed popular works such as *Les Secrets de reverend signeur Alexis Piemontois*, which contained remedies against sicknesses and trauma, and which was frequently reprinted. Other titles were more ambitious, such as André Thevet's *Les Singularitez de la France antarctique*, which was a study not only of South America but also (despite its title) of Canada, giving an account of its peoples and their customs. More specifically academic was his *Dictionarum Tetraglotton*, a dictionary printed in Greek, Latin, French and Flemish, with each language distinguished by the choice of type (the Latin was in roman, the French in italics, and the Flemish in gothic). This was not just a forerunner of his later dictionaries, but also an early use of different fonts in a single work that was to reach its pinnacle in the *Biblia Regia* (see Chapter 7).

The dictionary was published in 1562, the same year in which Philip II's Regent in the Netherlands, Margaret of Parma, sent instructions to the Margrave (chief magistrate) of Antwerp to confront Plantin about his workshop's publication of a Protestant work of devotion entitled *Briefve Instruction pour prier* ('Brief Guide to Prayer'). Antwerp might be safer than Paris for a printer suspected of heresy, but it was not that much safer. Ironically enough, Plantin was at this time in Paris, where he stayed for some time. Three of his workmen were found to be responsible for the book, but since all those responsible were non-nationals, they were probably just banished.[156] The Margrave declined to take further action against Plantin, since he had been abroad when the offending book was published, yet he may well have still felt insecure.

Shortly afterwards, Plantin's goods were seized and sold to pay off alleged debts. This was not an ordinary case of bankruptcy. For one thing, Plantin was repaid no less than 2,878 florins of excess profit from the sale of his goods. Furthermore, one of those who bought much of his printing equipment was a Cornelis van Bomberghen, who was to become Plantin's business partner only a year later. Plantin's biographer, Colin Clair, suggests very plausibly that the whole exercise was intended to put Plantin's possessions beyond the reach of a possible confiscation if he were found guilty of heresy. Clair also suggests that the fact that Plantin stayed away from Antwerp for two whole years points to his being seriously afraid that his life was at risk, and that although the *Briefve Instruction* had been printed by others, he might have been personally responsible for printing something more seriously heretical, namely the *Spegel der Gerechticheit* ('Mirror of Righteousness') by Henrik

Niclaes, founder of the *Huys der Liefde* (House of Love), a movement that became known in England as the Family of Love (in Latin, *Familia Caritatis*). Since Niclaes was a prosperous merchant, and had need of a discreet and competent printer, the claim that he helped fund Plantin to set up as a printer is certainly possible, especially as Plantin had joined the Family of Love in France before moving to Antwerp. Nevertheless, there is no supporting evidence for this, and in the end Clair expresses doubt on stylistic grounds as to whether the *Spegel der Gerechticheit* really was printed by Plantin.[157]

Plantin and the Family of Love

The Family of Love was a religious sect that stressed the importance of the inner spiritual life and taught that its members should continue their normal outward religious life as members of whatever church they already belonged to. They were definitely not in the business of becoming martyrs, and their secrecy makes it very hard to be sure who was, or was not, a member. However, there are two or three pieces of evidence that confirm that Plantin, despite his lifelong professions of loyalty to the Catholic Church, was in fact a member. The first is a manuscript history of the start of the Family, *Chronika des Hüsgesinnes de Lieften*. This records how Plantin was converted by Henrik Niclaes in about 1550. Niclaes saw Plantin's usefulness as a potential printer of his own writings, and so according to this account, Niclaes provided the money to set up Plantin's printing press and also paid for the type and paper. The account suggests that Plantin unscrupulously took advantage of this situation for his own profit, but the anonymous writer's account was probably prejudiced, for he will have considered Plantin an apostate. This was because the writer, unlike Plantin, had remained loyal to Niclaes when the latter seemingly succumbed to delusions of grandeur, trying to establish himself at the head of a much more hierarchical organisation. Plantin had at this point joined a splinter group, the *Liefhebbers der Warheyt* (Lovers of Truth), a group that had broken away from Niclaes under the leadership of Henrick Jansen van Barrefelt, who went under the name of Hiel.[158]

The other evidence for Plantin's membership is much more circumstantial and takes the form of an exchange of letters between Plantin and Guillaume Postel in Paris. Postel was renowned for his formidable knowledge of oriental languages (two of his pupils were to help Plantin with the preparation of the *Biblia Regia*), but at the time of this correspondence he was under house arrest in Paris for his unorthodox religious beliefs, which were of a mystical and Cabalistic nature, but not unappealing in their emphasis on love. Postel believed that the three monotheistic religions – Judaism, Christianity and

Islam – could be brought together, and argued the case for a universal world religion in *De orbis terrae Concordia* ('Concerning the Concord of the Whole World'). Postel's valuing of 'concord' between the religions explains why he might have been sympathetic towards the Family of Love. In the final paragraph of a letter to Ortelius, he asks for his greetings to be passed on to Plantin and notes that 'scholae charitatis summos alumnos mihi non esse ignotos' ('the distinguished pupils of the school of love were not unknown [to him]'). He adds that although he does not belong to any particular group, he knows and observes the 'consortii charitatis usum' ('practice of the society of love'). This seems to have provoked Plantin's curiosity, and so he writes cautiously to Postel, presumably to probe whether the latter actually is a member of the Family. He writes in French rather than Latin, except where he quotes the passages above and begs Postel to explain more fully what he means: 'je vous supplie de m'interpréter ce passage'. Plantin also makes reference to the 'aged father of the congregation of charity', which sounds like a guarded reference to Henrik Niclaes himself.[159] Postel writes back in French, but quotes from the Latin Vulgate translation of St Paul's first epistle to Timothy to make it clear that his references to *caritas* are not covert hints at membership of the Familia Caritatis, but a reference to the Christian belief that love is the fulfilment of the law: 'finis pracepti charitas, de corde puro, de conscientia bona, de fide non ficta' ('the end of the commandment is charity out of a pure heart, and of a good conscience, and of faith unfeigned', I Timothy 1:5). Plantin's acknowledgement of this letter is equally orthodox, although the way in which he says he praises God for Postel's steps being directed along the path of charity might be thought to offer a further opportunity for Postel to acknowledge membership. However, he does not do so.[160]

One final piece of possible evidence is a letter that Plantin wrote to a 'Monsieur Hncs'.[161] 'Hncs' may well be an abbreviation of Henrik Niclaes, the leader of the secretive Family of Love, which suggests that he did not wish others to know the true name of the intended recipient if the letter went astray. The latter part of the letter mentions that he has sold 200 Hebrew Bibles to Johan Radermacher for sale in Barbary, where there was a Jewish community, and that Gillis Hooftman has offered to pay cash for an even larger number (see pp. 112–13).[162] Since Niclaes wished the Family of Love to be open to Jews, Muslims and Christians, this evidence of the shared religious interests of Plantin and Niclaes, together with their cooperation in business affairs, may also point to Plantin's being a Familist.

Plantin had left Antwerp for Paris in January 1562, and he did not return until June 1563, when he set about advancing his printing business. For this, he needed finance, and so almost immediately entered into partnership with four people who were related to each other by family links and who were all Calvinists. This does not appear to have bothered Plantin, either because outward affiliation to a church was unimportant to him as a Familist, or because religious scruples took second place to pressing business needs. One fact that raises questions about both the nature of Plantin's bankruptcy and his religious and political loyalties, however, is that only a few years after being declared bankrupt, he could now afford to spend 500 florins on a printing press that he provided for Brederode, the then leader of the rebel *Gueux* (Beggars), which the latter installed in his castle of Vianen.[163]

Usefully, one of his four business associates was Cornelis van Bomberghen, who had bought up some of his printing equipment at the time of his alleged bankruptcy. Van Bomberghen was also able to let Plantin have the use of Hebrew fonts that he had inherited from his uncle, the printer Daniel van Bomberghen. The other partners were Karel van Bomberghen, who was Cornelis's cousin, Jan van Gorp, who was married to the sister of Karel's wife, and Jacopo Scotti, who was a brother-in-law of Cornelis. Just as Gillis Hooftman's trusted partners and agents were linked to him by marriage, so here family links provided reassurance about the trustworthiness of one's partners.

Thus supplied with the necessary capital, Plantin began the greatest period of his career, with a remarkable range of books published up to the time of the painting of the *Paneel*. Included in his output were many editions of classical authors, not only the well-known ones such as Caesar, Cicero, Aristotle and Euripides, which would have been sure of steady sales, but also the first printed editions of more obscure authors such as Hesychius, compiler of a fifth-/sixth-century lexicon, and Stobaeus (John of Stobi), compiler of an early fifth-century anthology, which were surely printed out of an interest in learning rather than from any expectation of easy profit. One work that he published at this time was a philological work, the *Variae Lectiones* ('Variant Readings'). This book of 1569 was the first of the classical scholar and philosopher Justus Lipsius (Joost Lips), who was to become a lifelong friend and to whom Plantin's last known letter was written.

Lipsius was born in Overijse, a town between Brussels and Leuven. He was educated by the Jesuits in Cologne before returning to Leuven to study law at the university there, while also attending lectures at the Collegium Trilingue. This latter was a college founded on principles laid down by Erasmus (the three languages of the college's title were Hebrew, Greek and Latin), and would be the subject of much suspicion from the religious authorities since Erasmus was thought to favour the Lutherans, while the philological study of biblical texts in their original languages that he advocated was feared to open the way to individual and heretical interpretations. Nevertheless, in 1569, Lipsius became private secretary to Cardinal Granvelle and travelled to Rome. From there, he was able to further his studies in the Vatican Library, and was allowed to examine manuscripts and rare books in the collections of various eminent humanists to whom Granvelle introduced him. It was almost certainly here that his lifelong love of Tacitus and Seneca had its roots. Then, in 1570, he returned to Leuven to resume his law studies. A year later, he visited his friend Carolus Langius, who was to appear as a character in his most popular book, *De Constantia* ('On Constancy'), which is written in the form of a dialogue in which Langius is an advocate of Stoicism. (*De Constantia* and many of his other writings had not been published at the time that the *Paneel* was painted.)

In 1572, Lipsius went first to Vienna and then, after Spanish soldiers had looted his property at home, to the Lutheran university at Jena, where he took up the professorship of history. At this time, he was working on his first edition of the works of the Roman historian Tacitus, which was published in 1574 by Plantin. Realising that the commentary on textual readings and proposed emendations in this book was insufficient by itself to help a student appreciate the work, he then devoted much time to providing a fuller commentary, inspired by the humanist hope that a careful study of the past could lead to wiser decisions being made in the present. His ground-breaking work was still being referred to by scholars in the nineteenth century.

One less weighty book that Plantin published at this time was a slim volume of Latin verses in praise of Antwerp entitled *De laudibus Antverpiae oda sapphica* ('A Sapphic Ode in Praise of Antwerp') by the first cousin once removed of Ortelius and van Meteren, Daniel Rogers. (The poem quoted at the start of Chapter 2 in this volume comes from this.) Rogers was a skilled poet, but this was the only volume of poetry that he published, although individual poems were published from time to time as dedications and others remained in manuscript, such as the ode written in Ortelius's *album amicorum* (see p. 193). It may be that, as someone pursuing a career as a diplomat, he decided to conform to the English reluctance to do anything so supposedly vulgar as promote one's own works by publishing them. The convention is best expressed by the English poet John Donne when he writes: 'The fault which I acknowledge in myself is to have descended to print anything in verse.'[164]

The challenges of being a printer at this time are best exemplified by Plantin's printing of *Les Pseaumes de David mis en Rime Françoise*, referred to today as the *Genevan Psalter*. This was a translation of the Psalms into metrically regular verses that could be sung to a repeated simple tune (like the verses of a hymn) and had been begun by the French poet Clément Marot, who then versified more Psalms at the request of Calvin while he was in Geneva. However, Marot was not comfortable in Calvin's theocratic Geneva and so he moved to Turin, leaving the task unfinished. Théodore de Bèze, a French Calvinist theologian, was then asked to complete the work, which he gradually did, the complete *Psalter* finally appearing in 1562. Not only was this obviously a Calvinist production (Marot's versions of the psalms had been sung with vigour by Huguenots during the French civil wars between Reformed and Catholic, as well as by Calvinist congregations in Geneva), but its translation could also be seen as justifying and encouraging those who were persecuted by the Catholics. The practice of attributing modern contexts within which to understand them can be seen in Marot's *argument* (or summary) for Psalm 137 ('By the waters of Babylon we sat down and wept'), which makes no reference at all to its historical, biblical context (the Jewish exile in Babylon), but is said to be appropriate for Christian prisoners of the Ottoman Empire. That, of course, would have been unexceptionable in Christian Europe, but the claim that Psalm 7 is appropriate for a prince going to war who has right on his side, and Psalm 3 for a general whose forces are outnumbered, points to the kind of use that was to be made of them during the French Wars of Religion (just as in the next century Cromwell's troops would sing English metrical Psalms before going into battle with the Royalists). Similarly, de Bèze's *argument* for Psalm 20 says that it is appropriate for a church assailed on all sides by faithless princes, which, from the point of view of the Catholic authorities, was incendiary stuff.[165] The president of Margaret of Parma's privy council, Viglius de Zuichem, was clearly astonished and outraged that the printing of this subversive work had been authorised by the Council of Brabant, and gave orders for the withdrawal and burning of all copies. Margaret herself even writes to Philip that she has sent instructions to the faculty of theology at Leuven to visit the rash priest who had assured the Council that there was nothing heretical in the translation.[166] This strong reaction is not surprising: public psalm-singing had become the hallmark of Calvinist gatherings and had been forbidden only a few months earlier by Philip II in a placard of 18 December 1561.[167] Unsurprising, maybe, but after going through the proper channels to get permission and spending money on printing the *Psalter*, Plantin must have been upset, to say the least, to see his entire investment literally going up in flames.

Difficulties were not reserved for Protestant books. In a letter of 21 August 1568, Plantin explains to his patron, Cardinal Granvelle, why he has not yet printed copies of the new breviary (prayer book) authorised by Rome; this was because the Chancellor was unwilling to authorise the printing of any book before it has been approved by the Duchess of Parma's privy council. Next, he reports that while waiting, he has been told that a rival printer has secured a copy of the new breviary printed by Paulus Manutius, the Italian printer favoured by the Pope, and has approached the Council of Brabant for permission to print it despite knowing that Plantin himself had been given the Pope's authorisation and Manutius's agreement. Clearly, a rival edition would undermine the financial case for printing the breviary, and he asks for reassurance that his right to be the sole printer will be protected and then he will press on and observe the commitment made to Manutius to give him a tenth of the sales.[168] Another letter two months later reveals that Plantin had decided to use three presses to speed up the printing of the breviary, but that the copy text that he had been given contained errors. While they waited for an accurate text, the presses were devoted to another book, but no sooner had this begun than the corrected copy arrived.[169]

In these kinds of situations, the patronage that Plantin had found from Cardinal Granvelle was very important to him. However, it was not simply that, as a prince of the Church and an influential statesman, he could help to iron out issues with both secular and religious authorities. Nor was he just an eager and wealthy customer.[170] As a learned humanist he could also offer comment and advice on Plantin's work in progress, as we shall see was the case when the *Biblia Regia* was being printed.[171]

Sometimes, the publishing problems were more logistical than theological. The mixture of hyperbole and flattery in the opening of this letter to Guillaume Vaillant explaining the delays in publishing his commentaries on Virgil's *Eclogues* suggests that the irate author had been complaining indignantly about the non-appearance of his book: 'Combien il m'a despleu, desplaist et desplaira tousjours que je n'ay peu satisfaire à vostre désir et au mien d'imprimer vos tant doctes commentaires sur le Virgile...' ('How much it has displeased, displeases and will always displease me that I have not been able to satisfy your desire and mine to print your extremely learned commentaries on Virgil...').[172]

What follows is a list of excuses that he hopes will 'adoucira la cholère' ('soften his anger'). As soon as he had received the manuscript, he had it sent to the censors for approval, but their poor knowledge of Greek had delayed their decision. He had then finally obtained the necessary Consent and Privilege from the Court, which had, he points out, cost him twenty crowns. Following this, his paper merchant had been unable to provide him with the right paper;

eventually, shamed by the delays, he had resolved to use a superior and much more expensive paper which had cost him twice as much. He had then sent the manuscript to the compositor, who had started to lay out the work in a different manner from that agreed. After this had been resolved, the compositor disobligingly died, and the compositor that he wished to use after this was working on his polyglot Bible, work under royal command that he could not possibly interrupt. Distressed and embarrassed by this further delay, he had then sent the work to be printed in Paris (along with the bridal clothes that he was sending ahead for his daughter's wedding), and owing to the dishonesty of the carters or for some other reason, everything had disappeared en route. All in all, he reckons that he was 300 crowns out of pocket, and he finishes by regretting that there is nothing he can do for the next eight months until the polyglot Bible was finished. What Guillaume Vaillant thought about all this is not recorded.[173] It is easy to imagine Plantin's own frustration, especially as he is so obviously eager to satisfy his clients' requests. Indeed, the word which he uses most often in his correspondence when writing about fulfilling an order or printing a new book is 'incontinent' ('straightaway'), although he frequently qualifies any promise with 'Dieu aidant' ('God willing').

Apart from religious and classical texts, Plantin also printed some major scientific books in the years running up to the painting of the *Paneel*. One was a key medical work, *Valerii Cordi Dispensatorium* ('The Pharmacopeia of Valerius Cordus'), which was revised and edited by Pieter Coudenberg and published in 1568. Cordus (1515–44) studied botany, pharmacy and medicine at Marburg under his father, Euricius Cordus, who was professor of medicine there. His *Dispensatorium* was published posthumously in 1546, and Coudenberg's revised version was to remain a standard reference work until the nineteenth century.

Not all the books that Plantin publishes in this period are as obviously scientific as this, but there was no clear-cut division at the time between philosophy (abstract or 'natural'), or between different branches of knowledge and the arts. One example of this kind of overlap can be seen in the long poem, 'L'Encyclie des secrets de l'éternité' ('The gathering-together of the secrets of eternity') by Guy Lefèvre de la Boderie, published by Plantin in 1571. The literal meaning of *l'encyclie* from the Greek is something like 'within the circle'. An encyclopaedia aims to gather together everything needed for education (*paideia* in Greek); hence, Lefèvre calls each section of his all-inclusive poem a circle. He had studied oriental languages in Paris under the scholar Guillaume Postel and, together with his brother Nicolas, was part of the group of five specialists who would help Montano with correcting the polyglot Bible for Plantin. 'L'Encyclie', however, does not draw on Lefèvre's knowledge as an orientalist, but is an attempt to summarise his knowledge of the universe in a lengthy poem in rhyming alexandrines. His ambition can be compared with that of Ortelius, whose atlas covers the whole known world. Lefèvre uses his poetic skills in what might be described as an essay poem, following the Roman poet Horace's dictum that poetry should instruct by pleasing. Nor does he see any disconnect between his religious beliefs and his knowledge of the physical world. As such, in his dedicatory epistle, which serves as an introduction, he makes clear that he sees 'le bel ordre' ('beautiful order') of the universe as evidence of 'une grand Raison'; that is, of the mind of a creator God, the *Moteur* (prime mover or first cause).[174] It is also clear that for Lefèvre, the universe is still geocentric, with Aristotle's spheres carrying the sun, moon and stars around the earth. To the modern mind, this has little to do with the universe as it is, but with Ptolemy's 'improvements' to the scheme, it provided a plausible explanation at the time for the observed phenomena (although the more that was observed, the more complicated the explanations had to become). Despite these difficulties, the poem is not unlike the work of botanists like Coudenberg in its recording of significant data, which paves the way for later analysis.

Lefèvre records biological information about fish, animals and humans, describing, for example, the behaviour of tuna fish, their response to the seasons, and their formation when swimming in a shoal.[175] He also describes the five senses, partly using imagery that would seem very out of place in a modern scientific journal – the head and brain that receive perceptions through the nervous system are likened to an *échauguette* or watch-tower. Nevertheless, he also recognises that there must be some kind of nervous system to convey what is seen or sensed to the brain, even if he describes the nerves with a double-image as spreading like the roots of a plant and being like narrow passages leading to 'les racines des antres' ('the roots of the caves'), or describes the optic nerves as 'Canaus de ceste pure flame' ('channels of pure flame') and the eyes as the 'Verrieres de l'Ame' ('windows of the soul').[176] The reader is not only pleased by the imagery, but also given some idea of the complexity of the nervous system. With this, the poet has achieved Horace's aim of both doing us good and delighting us.[177]

More significant for the historian of science was Plantin's work with the botanist Rembert Dodoens (sometimes referred to as Rembertus Dodonaeus; R3), which began in 1565 when he reprinted his *Historia frumentorum, leguminum, etc* ('Account of Cereals, Pulses, etc.'), the first part of his multi-volume *Cruijdeboek* (later spelled *Cruydeboek*). Dodoens studied medicine at Leuven and first practised it in his home town of Mechelen. Later, he was offered a professorship in medicine at Leuven University and the post of royal physician to Philip II in Madrid. He turned both these offers down, however, and instead accepted the post of physician at the imperial court in Vienna. Despite his wider medical commitments, he must have devoted an increasing amount of time to his botanical investigations, and his initial interest in the medicinal properties of plants widened to include every type of plant. The *Cruijdeboek* in its first edition, published by another Antwerp printer, Jan van der Loe, described over 1,000 plants and had 715 plates of illustrations.[178] Since this had sold out before the expiry of its ten-year privilege, it was obviously a financial success, and van der Loe printed a revised edition which now described 1,406 plants and had 841 illustrations. It was after this that Dodoens turned in 1566 to Plantin to print his future books. Plantin for his part agreed to have the illustrations engraved at his own expense by artists chosen by Dodoens and copied from specimens that the latter would provide.[179] A second volume appeared in 1568, and we know from one of Plantin's letters, dated 7 May 1568, that he sent a copy to one of his most important patrons, Cardinal Granvelle.[180] After this, however, there was a delay caused by the sacking of Mechelen by Spanish soldiers wanting their back pay, who destroyed Dodoens's house. Nevertheless, the third and final part was published in 1574, shortly before the painting of the *Paneel* and his decision to leave the Netherlands and accept the post of physician at the imperial court in Vienna.

The close description of plant life (and also its classification by similarities, rather than just listing them alphabetically) was an essential preliminary to further scientific advance, and there is no doubt that Dodoens was one of the most important and ground-breaking scientists of the period. His appearance on the *Paneel* is a reminder of Plantin's central role in facilitating the growth and spread of knowledge in the sixteenth century. Furthermore, it was a growth that depended on the free exchange of specimens and knowledge, enabled by people like Emanuel van Meteren, who acted as the 'postmaster' for the Dutch Lime Street community in London that included such distinguished botanists as Matthias de l'Obel (after whom the lobelia is named), who was to be the future father-in-law of Ortelius's nephew Jacob Coels (Ortelianus).[181] Both these distinguished botanists were published by Plantin, and although Deborah E. Harkness argues that the Dutch scientific community was cut out of many scientific records by their failure to publish in England (unlike Gerard, who used their work in his *Herbal* without acknowledgement), this was only true in English circles and not in European ones, where the work of de l'Obel and Dodoens was well known.[182]

Plantin's press concerned itself with other areas beside cutting-edge science. As one would expect in a prosperous city, the citizens of Antwerp clearly set a high value on education, with about one in every 200 men being a teacher. This is what Guicciardini has to say about education in Antwerp in his description of the Low Countries: 'Here [in Antwerp] there are many learned masters to instruct youth in all kinds of skill in letters ... In this city, as in many other cities of the country, there are also several schools where both girls and boys learn the French language.'[183] It is not surprising, therefore, that one of Plantin's books in 1567/68 was the *A.B.C.* of Peeter Heyns (R11), first printed in French and then in Dutch. Each page of this book had an elaborately decorated capital letter and an improving proverb followed by a few lines of verse expanding the idea; it also contained letters of the alphabet in five styles and then a little more verse. The aim is clearly to combine teaching children to write and read with some elementary moral instruction, and its author owned and ran De Lauwerboom (The Laurel Tree), a well-known girls' boarding school. Thanks to the provision of boarding, the girls came from across the Low Countries, but also from across a wide social range, including both the upper and mercantile classes.[184] Education at this level may seem a far cry from the scientific research of Dodoens, but both civilisation and prosperity depend on a base of educated citizens, and that requires educated mothers. No society is truly civilised unless it educates its women.

Women in sixteenth-century Antwerp had only limited independence, as was the case in most other places, where unmarried women were usually subject to their fathers, and those that were married were largely subject to their husbands. Nevertheless, Guicciardini comments on the confidence with which women spoke publicly in Antwerp, and there are also instances of married women running a business alongside their husband, just as Jeanne Rivière did with her haberdashery alongside Plantin's printing press. Guicciardini also notes the particular financial advantage that women in Antwerp have by comparison with other jurisdictions in the Netherlands; for instance, although husbands were liable for the debts of their wives, wives were not liable for their husbands' debts.[185]

If I have said very little about Plantin's wife, it reflects the sad fact that relatively little is known about her. It seems inconceivable, however, that he could have lived such a busily productive, but often highly stressful, life without his wife's support in running the large home and workplace where his many printing presses were situated and where many of his employees had board and lodging. The scale of what she had to do is revealed when

Plantin, asking to be excused having to billet Spanish soldiers, writes to Alba's secretary explaining that the house is so full of workers and the work being done for His Majesty (i.e. the printing of the polyglot Bible) that he is obliged to find 'trois licts [beds] hors de ma dicte maison pour y coucher aucuns de nos correcteurs' ('accommodation elsewhere for three of my proof readers').[186] The words of Lipsius, who had stayed so often in her house, provide a fitting epitaph: 'She was a woman of the highest integrity, without pretence and without vanity, who loved her husband and who, with a perfect understanding of all that concerns good family management, gave to her household all the care to which she felt in duty bound; that should suffice any woman.'[187]

Jeanne Rivière's illiteracy is surprising and perhaps reflects her French upbringing. When Philip II made his first visit to the Netherlands in 1549, one of his entourage noted with interest that 'almost everyone' was literate.[188] Certainly, Antwerp's Dutch-speaking, middle-class citizens expected their daughters to be well educated, at least in French, the language of the Walloon areas of the Spanish Low Countries, as well as in basic arithmetic.[189] We know that several, and possibly all, of Gillis Hooftman's daughters were educated by Heyns, whose influential book on French grammar, *Cort onderwijs van de acht deelen der Fransoischer talen*, was published by Plantin in 1571.[190]

In addition to teaching French, Heyns helped develop what was to become the standard form of Dutch in the verse that he wrote. For example, the poems that he wrote to describe the maps in a cut-down version of Ortelius's *Theatrum Orbis Terrarum*, called the *Spieghel der Werelt* ('Mirror of the World'), were in Dutch. Each of the reduced-size maps was accompanied by a sixteen-line poem linked by a very simple rhyme-scheme[191] that offers some basic information about the territory being described. For the French edition, he translated his verse into French prose. Later editions of this book were called *Epitome* and, indeed, as this later title suggests, the verses offer no more than bare summaries; thus, the poem about England tells us little more than that the northern border is formed by the River Tweed, that the principal trading city is London, and that the country is 'schaep-ryck' ('rich in sheep'). Once again, we see the schoolmaster at work here, wanting to present key information in an easily absorbed form.[192]

One of Heyns's teaching methods was to use his literary skills to write plays for the girls to perform. This was more or less contemporary with the Jesuit use of didactic drama. The Jesuits founded a college in Antwerp in 1575, but it was closed only a year later, and any direct influence seems extremely unlikely. There were, in any case, two much more likely reasons for his educational use of drama. Most obviously, Heyns's own involvement as a writer of plays for his *rederijkerskamer* (chamber of rhetoric), called *de Bloejende Wijngaert* (Flowering Vineyard), suggests that writing plays would have seemed a natural educational ploy.[193] Secondly, educational drama develops naturally from Erasmus's well-known *Colloquies* (dialogues written so that students could practise their Latin as well as learn from the content). Writing about these, Erasmus notes: 'I am not sure anything is learned better than what is learned as a game.'[194]

Chambers of rhetoric were not only drama clubs, but also provided forums in which new ideas could be debated. Unsurprisingly, this led to ideas being voiced in their plays that tested the bounds of what was acceptable in the eyes of the authorities. Two of Heyns's French prose plays for the girls of De Lauwerboom might appear to be challenging the authorities in a similar way were it not for the fact that they were not written until after the Pacification of Ghent, when the Protestants had briefly taken control. Both of these tackle religious subjects: *Le miroir des meres* ('The Mirror of Mothers'[195]) is about how Moses' mother hides him in the floating basket amongst the bulrushes to protect him from the Egyptian command that all baby Hebrew boys should be killed; the other, *Le miroir de vefves* ('The Mirror of Widows'), is based on the story of how the widow Judith seduces and kills Holofernes, the commander of an army oppressing the Jews. It is not difficult to see how Pharaoh's persecution of the Jews could be compared to Philip II's persecution of Protestants, or the invading Assyrian general Holofernes compared to the Duke of Alba, the commander of the Spanish army, and his successors. Heyns was indeed Protestant and withdrew to Cologne on the arrival of Alba in 1567. He would only return to Antwerp to re-establish De Lauwerboom after a general pardon was issued in 1571. His many literary activities make it clear that Heyns was not 'just a teacher', but a highly learned man whose pedagogical theories were influential in shaping Antwerp's civilisation.

Just as the biblical plays of Heyns could be given a contemporary interpretation, so the sharply epigrammatic comments of Tacitus to be found in Lipsius's critical edition of Tacitus's *Historiarum et Annalium Libri* (books from the *Annals* and *Histories*, i.e. the surviving parts of a history of Rome from the reign of Tiberius in 14 CE up to the conflict-ridden Year of the Four Emperors in 69 CE) could be applied to the Spanish Netherlands under Philip II.[196] One of the best-known epigrams must have rung sourly true for many of his contemporaries as a comment on Alba and his Spanish army: 'Auferre, trucidare, rapere, falsis nominibus imperium, ubi solitudinem faciunt, pacem appellant' ('Plunder, murder and theft they falsely call empire, and where they make a desert, they call it peace').[197]

CHAPTER 7

Plantin's great challenge:
Printing Biblia Regia

A humanist desire shared by Lipsius to get back to the accurate original texts also lies behind the huge project that Plantin was working on alongside all these many books: the printing of the polyglot Bible that was to become known as the *Biblia Regia*. Plantin's original intention had been to re-print the Complutensian Polyglot, the Bible financed by Cardinal Francisco Jiménez de Cisneros at the Complutense University in Alcalá de Henares in Spain, which was finished in 1517 but not published until 1520. Reprinting this six-volume work in Hebrew, Greek, Aramaic and Latin would in itself would have been an enormous task, but the ambitions of Plantin himself and those who were sponsoring the work led to something even more challenging.

Polyglot Bibles

A polyglot Bible has the original Hebrew and Greek texts of the Old and New Testaments, respectively, together with various translations and commentaries.[198] The first polyglot was the Complutensian Polyglot, which contained the Old Testament in the original Hebrew with Greek and Latin translations and the New Testament in the original Greek with a Latin translation. This was completed in 1517 and published in 1520. The Latin translation used and given priority was the Vulgate, a translation dating back to the fourth century and attributed to St Jerome. By the later Middle Ages, the Vulgate had become the standard translation used by the western Church, although centuries of copying in handwritten books meant that a number of variations had crept in. In addition to the original Greek of the New Testament, the much earlier translation of the Old Testament into Greek supposedly made simultaneously by seventy-two Jewish scholars in the third and second centuries BCE in Alexandria and known as the Septuagint was included with a separate interlinear translation into Latin. Further elucidation of the first part of the Old Testament text was offered by including the Targum Onkelos, an explanatory Jewish paraphrase of the Pentateuch into Aramaic (the language of Jesus' time that had evolved from Hebrew); this also had its own Latin translation. Not only was a high level of linguistic knowledge required to complete such an enormous project, but also remarkable typographical skill (ill. 22).

By the time that Plantin's polyglot was finalised, it contained two more Targums, which, combined with the Targum Onkelos, covered almost the entire Old Testament, as well as including early Syriac translations of the New Testament.[199] The purpose of including all these different translations was to throw as much light as possible on the original Hebrew and Greek texts and to facilitate interpretation. When the Complutensian was being prepared, the desire to have a fuller understanding of sacred texts was seen as admirable, although any new interpretations had to be checked carefully to ensure that they were not heretical. By the time that Plantin gathered his team of scholars some time later, however, Protestants were putting forward interpretations that challenged the Catholic authorities, and so anything new was regarded with extreme suspicion. Thus, Plantin needed to tread very carefully.

One of the things that had been decided at the fourth session of the Council of Trent in 1546[200] was that to avoid disputes over the meaning of Scripture, an accurate text of the Vulgate translation should be established and that it should thenceforth be the only acceptable version of the Bible to be used in the Church; in other words, its authority overruled the original Hebrew and Greek texts.

By this time, Luther's German translation was widely available. Catholics saw his translation as biased, not least by his use of the word 'alone' in translating 'Man is not saved by good works but by faith alone' (Romans 3:28), which does not appear in the original Greek and, although arguably reasonable in context, was seen as an unjustifiable insertion and a tendentious challenge to the Catholic emphasis on the importance of good works (including giving money to buy pardons).

The Council of Trent was held after the publication of the Complutensian, but before Plantin's polyglot. There were two more great polyglots in the following century: the Paris Polyglot of 1645 (otherwise known as the Lejay Bible) and the London Polyglot of 1657. They were all ruinously expensive to produce – Cardinal Jiménez is thought to have spent about half a million ducats on the Complutensian – and unsurprisingly no further ones were published in the early modern era.

* * *

When Plantin decided to go ahead with printing his polyglot, he was well aware of the great expense involved. After all, he had already had experience of printing a work in different languages and alphabets, his *Dictionarum Tetraglotton*, which was printed in Greek, Latin, French and Flemish (see p. 95). That had been a far smaller work, but must have still been relatively expensive to produce, as well as providing useful preliminary experience, not least in using four different typefaces alongside each other. Financial support for printing the polyglot was highly desirable, if not essential, and various German princes were willing to provide it, as was the Emperor himself. Plantin's preference, however, was to gain the support and approval of Philip II. Not only would this cover the necessary expenditure, he hoped, but it would also provide impeccable cover against any accusation of heresy. After all, what could be more obviously orthodox than to be providing an accurate text of the Bible at the behest of His Most Catholic Majesty, Philip II of Spain?[201] To this end, towards the end of 1566, he began writing to Philip's secretary, Gabriel de Çayas (Zayas). The first letter that we have, dated 19 December 1566 and in French, is responding to a request for clarification of what Plantin is proposing for his polyglot. He explains that there would be versions of the Bible in Hebrew, Syriac and Greek, each accompanied by its own translation into Latin, and that it would appear in six volumes and be printed within three years.[202] He proposes to obtain paper of a high enough quality from Troyes and La Rochelle, which he estimates will cost about 12,000 florins, and he suggests that wages and other printing expenses will come to another 12,000. To this he adds that he has already spent 'a good sum of money' securing the services of those with the necessary linguistic skills, and on correcting a dictionary of biblical Hebrew that he intends to add to the work and which will 'décoreroit grandement' ('much enhance') it. Even with good linguists at his disposal, he writes, he would not venture on such a project, with its heavy burden of proof-correcting, if he did not have the services of his son-in-law, a young man learned in Hebrew, Syriac, Greek and Latin. This was François Raphelenghien (Raphelengius), who had married his eldest daughter. He also draws attention to the fact that he has assembled a fine collection of types at a cost which is beyond calculation, and says that he has received compliments on their high quality from knowledgeable people at the previous Lent's Frankfurt Fair, where he had taken some specimen pages of the proposed work. So high was the standard that Duke Augustus, the Elector of Saxony, had given up his own rival plans to publish a polyglot, despite already having spent a lot of money on the project. The lords of Frankfurt had offered to fund him if he would move to Frankfurt and likewise the Constable of France if he would move to Paris, but after pointing out that there was competition to sponsor this prestigious project, Plantin finishes by saying that he wishes to print it nowhere else than in 'ceste noble et renommée ville d'Anvers' ('this noble and renowned city of Antwerp') in the territories and under the patronage of his Most Catholic Majesty.[203]

A second letter of the same date in Spanish has enclosed with it a further note about the costly enterprise. He wishes to assure the king that he is not being dragged into 'a labyrinth of expenses without end' and that he is prepared to print the polyglot in the name of Philip if he will let him have six or eight thousand crowns, for which he is sure he can find security in Antwerp. He stresses that he will do everything possible for the advancement of the Catholic religion and the honour of his majesty. For further reassurance about the orthodoxy of the work, he mentions various distinguished theologians who are willing to advise him.[204]

At this point, having already laid out a very considerable sum of money, Plantin begins to worry that he may not receive financial aid from Philip and that the whole project may be sunk if he is accused of heresy. In a letter dated 27 July 1567, he starts by pointing out that he has twice written to Çayas about a proposal to include a Syriac translation of a section of the Old Testament, as well as sending several other letters, but that he has heard nothing in reply since the previous Easter. In the record of the letter that he keeps, Plantin expresses concern that Çayas may have heard 'false reports and rumours from malicious and envious detractors'. This does not appear in the minute of the correspondence kept in the Habsburg archives at Simancas, which suggests that Plantin may have had second thoughts when he copied out the letter that he actually sent because he was afraid of putting suspicions into Çayas's mind.[205] Whether or not this was the case, by 30 August he is voicing his fear openly, writing that he is in doubt whether his previous five letters have reached Çayas, or whether the 'envy of certain hostile and slanderous people' has alienated him.[206] Plantin certainly had good reason to be afraid that his unorthodox beliefs might be exposed and punished, since it had been in May and June that year that he had been writing cautiously probing letters to Guillaume Postel to establish whether he was a member of the Family of Love, and since he had also written to the Family's founder, Henrik Niclaes, discussing negotiations with Jan Radermacher about sending Hebrew Bibles out to North Africa (see p. 97).[207]

His relief is apparent when, in a letter of 1 October, he writes to Çayas 'rejoicing' that two of the latter's letters had reached him. He assures him that he still has the skilled team necessary to print the polyglot, while wasting no time in pointing out that he has had to sell 'a lot of things' to make up the shortfall in his income as he waits for the go-ahead. Nevertheless, he treads cautiously in asking for money, explaining that he doesn't need the 6,000 ducats that he asked for straightaway, but that 1,000 will be sufficient for the meantime. He also spells out his expenses in buying paper of the high quality necessary for such an important work.[208]

With this letter, he encloses a copy of a letter from Postel as evidence of the fact that learned scholars are supportive of his scheme to publish a polyglot.[209] Apart from adding strength to his request for support, the potentially risky decision to send a copy of a letter from the unorthodox Postel may have been a way of forestalling any accusation of heresy by making it clear that he has indeed been corresponding with a man of suspect religious beliefs, but only as a distinguished scholar of eastern languages and not to discuss heretical ideas. In a later letter to Çayas, he describes Postel as 'a very learnèd man with a good knowledge of Greek, Latin, Hebrew, Syriac, Arabic, Turkish and other languages' who has recently offered to make available a Syriac New Testament transliterated into Hebrew characters together with a literal Latin translation, which, he says, will 'enrichera merveilleusement l'ouvrage' ('much enhance the work').[210]

Finally, Plantin hears the news that he has been waiting for. In a letter dated 1 May to Cardinal Granvelle, the other patron through whom he has been hoping to get a favourable verdict from Philip II, he tells how, on his return from the Frankfurt Book Fair, he had found a letter from Albernoz, the Duke of Alba's secretary, summoning him to Brussels. In it, he learns that Philip was sending him a learned doctor, Benito Arias Montano, both to act as a corrector of the proofs and to bring him money. The royal message included a command that he should have six sets of copies printed on parchment, and instructed him to prepare the parchment (by no means a cheap option for the forty-eight volumes that would be required) and everything else necessary. At this request, Plantin protested that he could not proceed without an advance, to which the reply was that the money would arrive with Montano. On his return from Brussels, he found a letter from Çayas telling him that Montano had left Madrid on the last day of March.[211] And with that, he had to be content, although he does record in a letter of 11/12 June that Philip's agent in Antwerp, Curiel, had lent him one hundred pounds to continue his preparatory purchases.

When Montano finally arrives (after suffering shipwreck on the way), Plantin sets on record his pleasure at meeting him, describing him as being both gifted and full of grace. This same letter also reveals Plantin's ongoing financial difficulties. Philip demanded security for his loan, something that Plantin had thought easy to organise in Antwerp a year earlier. Now, however, it had become almost impossible to arrange after the arrival of Alba and the setting up of the so-called 'Council of Blood', which had understandably created an atmosphere of doubt, undermining confidence and provoking many merchants to flee, including Plantin's Protestant partners and Gillis Hooftman's brother, Hendrik. As a compromise alternative, Plantin suggested that he would give each sheet to Curiel as it came off the press, and also offer his own home and place of business as security. After some hesitation, the offer was finally accepted.

It is not surprising that, as an ambitious and careful businessman, Plantin kept careful records of his correspondence. What we learn above all from his letters is his persistence in the seemingly endless stream of letters that he wrote to Çayas, which I have drawn upon above. These letters to Çayas, however, are not just to do with his polyglot Bible. Although he writes to Çayas as the king's secretary to obtain royal support, it becomes clear that the latter has intellectual interests of his own and is eager to use his contact with the foremost printer and publisher in Philip's dominions to acquire books that interest him. Plantin's first letter to Montano, the royal chaplain that Philip is going to send to supervise the project, is in response to a letter forwarded by Çayas that must have asked about his ability to provide maps, astrolabes and globes. In a letter of 15 February, he thanks Çayas for having put him in contact with Montano and tells him what books to expect in a package that he fears has been delayed, which included some theological texts and an edition ofCicero.[212]

Plantin's feelings must have been mixed when Philip finally gave his response. The good news, of course, was that the long-planned project on which he had already spent so much money and time was given the go-ahead. On the other hand, working so closely with a number of scholars of varying religious beliefs, he must have been a little uneasy about Philip's decision to send his chaplain, Montano, to keep an eye on his work and ensure that nothing heretical was published. Here was a theologian, renowned not only for his learning but also for having been selected as a member of the Spanish delegation to the Council of Trent, which had been summoned to determine the direction of the Counter-Reformation and re-establish orthodoxy in the Church. Plantin may have found some reassurance in the fact that he had already been in touch with Montano and knew that his interests were wide-ranging. Despite this, all was to be well: the shared passion to complete the demanding project and their similar work ethic led to Montano and Plantin becoming lifelong friends. Montano was not only impressed by Plantin's energetic commitment, but also by the scholarly group of co-workers that he had assembled (and who evidently disguised any religious unorthodoxy). He writes to Çayas: 'God has brought together in this city five men who are assisting me in this work, and who are knowledgeable about the corrections ... Without hesitation I dare to assert that in no land and at no time have been brought together men with greater fervour for the Catholic faith, and with more sustained labour and diligence...'[213] For his part, Plantin was immediately impressed by Montano, writing in the month of his arrival to Philip's chaplain, Jean Mofflin, describing how he was 'transported with love and respect for his rare virtues' and to Çayas about his 'singular gifts'.[214]

Benito Arias Montano was to be a key member of the group that produced the *Biblia Regia*. Born in 1527, he had been educated at the universities of Seville and Alcalá de Henares, both of which must have played an important part in his intellectual formation. Seville was a university where a tradition of Erasmian scholarship flourished. Erasmus had stressed the importance of going back *ad fontes* (i.e. to the earliest texts). In terms of biblical scholarship, this involved looking past the officially approved translation of the Vulgate and establishing reliable texts of the Hebrew Old Testament and Greek New Testament. Erasmus's own edition of the latter was published in 1516 and drew on all the available Greek texts. It was to be the first edition of the Greek New Testament to be published and the first serious attempt to provide a reliable and authoritative text. Moreover, it was also accompanied by a revision of the Vulgate translation. The second university that Montano attended, Alcalá de Henares, was where the Complutensian Polyglot had been produced and was an important centre of Hebrew studies. His time here, combined with the stress on the importance of philological rigour in his earlier education, will have prepared him admirably for working on the Old Testament parts of Plantin's polyglot.

Although Plantin and Montano appear to have rapidly come to admire each other's skills and energy, and formed a long-lasting friendship, there is no doubt that Montano would definitely not have approved of Plantin's unorthodox religious beliefs had he been aware of them initially. After all, despite his Erasmian education, this was a man who had chosen to join the military Order of Santiago as a priest. Although this order was originally founded to protect pilgrims travelling to the shrine of St James at Santiago, by Montano's time it was an aristocratic order, membership of which conferred status and it was essentially conservative in nature. When he first arrived in Antwerp, it is clear that Montano thoroughly approved of Alba's ruthless suppression of all heretical opposition. And as a scholar who valued libraries, and the peace and quiet needed to work in them, he naturally disapproved of the iconoclasm of 1566 and appreciated anyone who could restore order. Shortly after his arrival, he wrote to Philip II:

> During the beginning of the rebellion these miserable people set fire to an abbey called Dunes, which was reputed to be the most richly endowed with fine old books. ... My bowels were torn with compassion when I saw the misery that had befallen these regions through the fault of a few, who were the authors of their own misfortune as well as of the common damage and disturbance.[215]

Significantly, he got on well with Alba, who frequently discussed with him the measures that he was planning to 'pacify' the Netherlands. In October 1569, Alba asked him to compile a new index of forbidden books (the *Index Librorum Prohibitorum*), an invitation that would only have been made to someone thought to be of impeccable orthodoxy.[216] Montano also had the approval of Philip II, as this letter from Çayas to Montano shows: 'Your letter of December 28 contains such excellent matters that I decided to show it to His Majesty. After the King had read it with close attention, he ordered me in his name to express to you his thanks for the contents, especially for the details concerning the Duke of Alba and the administration of those lands.'[217]

Montano's support for Alba is seen in its most public and rather surprising form in his proposal and design of a statue to celebrate his crushing of revolt. This was to be cast from bronze cannons captured at the defeat of the Netherlandish rebels at Jemmingen and shows Alba triumphantly standing on his vanquished foes and with an outstretched arm possibly offering peace (albeit very clearly on his own terms). The statue was placed in the marketplace at Antwerp, but later withdrawn to the citadel in an unsuccessful effort to placate the outraged citizens, shortly after Philip had replaced Alba with a new Governor.

Montano's instigation of this monumentally tactless statue, which appears designed to rub salt into the wounds of Alba's opponents, makes it seem improbable that he would fit well into the humanist circle around

Plantin. Nevertheless, working on the great project with a shared Erasmian passion for textual accuracy led not only to a personal friendship with Plantin, but also to an understanding of how his Netherlandish co-workers felt about the presence of Spanish soldiers over-ruling their own traditions and laws. The change in his attitude can be seen in his subsequent letters to Çayas, the king's secretary. Prior to his change of heart, in a letter of February 1571, he whole-heartedly supports Alba's ruthless approach to suppressing not just heretics, but also any Netherlanders who wish to defend their ancient civic privileges against Philip II's encroachments. But by August of the same year, he is warning against the damaging effect on prosperity of Alba's ten-percent tax, the so-called Tenth Penny. The following December, after the harsh winter of 1571 had caused more hardship and damaged the country's prosperity, he writes 'me rompe el corazon de ver tanta mudanza' ('it breaks my heart to see so much change').[218]

By the end of 1571, the *Biblia Regia* had been printed and bound. Quite apart from the weight of sheer scholarship behind it, the volumes are exceptionally impressive even today, with a generous use of space that makes them very easy to read. If you look at a double-page spread in one of the Old Testament volumes, the Hebrew is in a column on the left-hand side of the *verso* with the Vulgate Latin translation in a column alongside it, while printed across the bottom of the page in its own special type is the Chaldaic paraphrase of the same passage. On the opposite (*recto*) page is the Greek Septuagint text in a column on the far right, while in a column to the left of it is a Latin translation of the Greek; below this, opposite the Chaldaic paraphrase, is Montano's own translation of the Chaldaic. To aid comparison, each verse is carefully numbered in each version (ill. 23). In the New Testament volume, no Hebrew is needed, but there is a version in Syriac (the language used in many early translations).

Once the *Biblia Regia* was completed, Philip II naturally wanted this magnificent product of his patronage to receive Papal approval, for which Montano was dispatched to Rome. Not much more than a month later, however, in February 1572, Montano and Philip received an unpleasant shock when approval was withheld. In particular, Montano's treatise in the final volume, *De Arcano Sermone*, had provoked suspicion. In it, Montano had pointed out that since written Hebrew does not include the vowels, the same word could have more than one meaning depending on which vowels were inserted. One reason that the Council of Trent had insisted that the Vulgate was the correct and only authoritative translation permitted was to stamp out the kind of alternative interpretations that had led to the start of the

Reformation. Montano's decision to prioritise philology at the expense of an agreed translation on which a unified theology could be based was seen as dangerously subversive.

This was a problem that might have been forestalled if Plantin had given more thought to the postscript of a letter from Cardinal Granvelle, in which the latter says that he has received the *ternion* (a gathering of three sheets which, when folded, would produce twelve pages) that Plantin has sent as an early specimen of the work in progress. This had been shown to various learned scholars, who pointed out that the Complutensian translation had avoided ambiguity by printing the Hebrew verbs in their preferred form in the margins (see **ill. 22**). Granvelle explains that he has defended Plantin and Montano by pointing out that when the Complutensian was printed, knowledge of Hebrew was less widespread, but he might have done better to stress the potential difficulties that did, in fact, arise. He also passes on that some of the scholars had complained that the *poinson* (*poinçon* or matrix used to stamp the letter on to an individual piece of type) for the Chaldaic letter *tau* was defective. (That Granvelle concerns himself with such a minor detail shows how supportive his patronage was.)

The Papal commission's concern that there should be no room for alternative interpretations was not the end of Plantin's problems. It also thoroughly disapproved of Montano's use of Jewish authorities when dealing with the text of the Tanakh (the Jewish scriptures that form what Christians call the Old Testament). This might appear ridiculous to the modern reader since Jesus was a Jew and would have read the Tanakh from a Jewish viewpoint, but to many sixteenth-century Europeans, it would have seemed axiomatic that since the Jewish authorities of Jesus' time had rejected his teaching, they could have nothing to say that would be helpful and much that would be heretical. Montano had been warned of possible difficulties but had brushed them aside. This must have been a rude shock, which was further intensified by the news that three of the most learned Old Testament scholars in Spain had been arrested in Salamanca accused of heresy for not dissimilar reasons.

One can't help feeling that quite apart from the warnings he was given, Montano should have realised that what he was doing was unlikely to meet with approval. Even before the Council of Trent's decree that the only permissible text of the Bible was the Vulgate, Cardinal Jiménez had insisted that no Jewish scholars should be consulted in the preparation of the Complutensian Polyglot (although his team did include converted Jewish scholars who were familiar with both the language and culture of the Old Testament). The Complutensian preface, *Prologus. Ad Lectorem*,[219] states that the printing of the Vulgate between the Hebrew and Greek texts was symbolic of Christ on the cross between the two thieves; in other words, the Hebrew text was equated with the errors of the Jews and the Greek with the errors of the Orthodox church (the two thieves), whereas the Vulgate text (Christ) was beyond criticism. This symbolism doesn't really work when you examine the Complutensian. If you open the book and look at a double-page spread, the Greek text of the Septuagint is on the right of the *verso* pages and the left of the *recto* ones: therefore, there is a double-column of Greek in the centre flanked by the Vulgate in two separate columns (albeit each of those columns is in the centre of an individual page) and the original Hebrew is on the outside of both *verso* and *recto* pages (see **ill. 22**). As such, it may be that the claim of symbolism was simply a sop intended to pacify reactionary suspicion of anything different from the generally accepted Vulgate. Even if this is the case, it is still evidence of a deeply engrained prejudice and suspicion that would not easily be overcome. The theologically and academically reactionary nature of the Church which Alba was trying to force on the Low Countries with a Spanish army must now have been sharply highlighted for Montano. His own feelings can probably be deduced from the *Biblia*'s first title page, which he had proposed. The design, drawn by Pieter van der Borcht and engraved by Pieter van der Heyden,[220] is based on Isaiah's vision of a world at peace after the coming of the Messiah (Isaiah 11), a chapter read by Christians as foretelling the birth of Jesus (**ill. 24**). It shows a lamb resting on top of a wolf (verse 6), while an ox and a lion eat hay together from the same manger (verse 7). It will be a reign of 'godliness' and 'concord' (PIETATIS and CONCORDIAE as it says below the picture). For Montano, 'godliness' is associated with 'concord' and not persecution.

Montano had initially approved of the order that Alba had imposed on the Low Countries through the sheer size of his army, but that order then began to disintegrate rapidly. At first, the Sea Beggars' capture of Brill, a small undefended seaport, had seemed insignificant, but the rapid spread of rebellion and the loss of control of his sea communications soon magnified Alba's difficulties. His response was the use of terror – no longer just against individuals through the 'Council of Blood', but by killing virtually all the inhabitants of any town that resisted his army. Alba must have preferred Machiavelli's advice rather than that of Seneca in *De Clementia* ('On Mercy'), the latter having already been edited by Erasmus and commentated on by Calvin (it would later be edited by Lipsius). In it, Seneca argues that clemency towards the defenders of a city brought more advantages than revenge.[221] Under Alba, however, Zutphen and Mechelen were both thoroughly looted, with considerable loss of civilian life and much wanton destruction. When Naarden, after a good deal of hesitation, finally agreed to surrender, its 'reward' was that virtually every inhabitant was killed (it is suggested that out of a population of over 3,000 only about sixty survived). The knowledge that surrender was likely to lead to nothing better than pillage, rape and murder probably explained the desperate defence of Haarlem during a siege that ran from December 1572 to July 1573.[222] When the town finally surrendered, the Spanish, under the command of Alba's son, Don Frederick, followed a new policy of being 'merciful'. The town was not totally destroyed, but the entire garrison was executed along with a significant part of the male population. In a letter to Çayas afterwards, Montano shows how he was slowly moving to a more tolerant position:

> By the example of mercy shown to the conquered, and of liberality and honour shown to the faithful and constant, the virtuous will find the courage and the spirit to persevere, and many others will surrender confessing that they have been deceived and seduced, as several of them declare even now. I am certain that in this manner a large number of lost souls will be recovered ... We have seen what has been gained through the example of Naarden and Zutphen, which in my opinion acted as a thorn in the flesh of the inhabitants of Haarlem and the whole of Holland.[223]

To describe the massacres at Naarden and Zutphen as being simply the 'thorn' (literally the 'nail', el clavo) that provoked the resistance of Haarlem may seem to us a monstrous understatement of the moral obliquity of what happened, but we need to remember that Montano is writing to Philip's secretary. At risk of prosecution by the Inquisition, he can hardly afford to be quoted as sympathising with heretics. And in any case, if his advocacy of a more moderate approach was to be successful, he needed to avoid an unduly direct criticism of Alba's implementation of Philip's policy. Montano may strike us here as morally pusillanimous, but he is being realistic in working to achieve a peaceful resolution. He goes on in the same letter to argue the need both for a general pardon and to appoint local people to positions of authority, as had always been done before. He also points out that in mixing with Netherlanders as an equal rather than as a government official, he is much more conscious than the Spaniards at Alba's court in Brussels are of how bitterly the locals resent the heavy-handed and arrogant behaviour of Spanish officials, not to mention their appointment to positions previously held by Netherlanders.

Montano's unheroic but pragmatic response to Spanish cruelty is not unlike the policy of the Family of Love, who thought it folly to court martyrdom and urged followers to conform outwardly to whichever church had power where they lived. It is impossible to know whether Montano himself had become a disciple of the Family of Love at this point, but it is easy to see that the attacks on his work might have disillusioned him with the Roman Catholic Church, while the threat of arrest by the Spanish Inquisition, which made him reluctant to return to Spain, would have strengthened his criticism of violent Spanish attempts to enforce religious conformity in the Netherlands.

In any case, he was certainly willing to cooperate with people of different religious beliefs, including Familists such as Plantin, and it was this tolerance that made possible his important contribution to textual scholarship. This same tolerant cooperation may be taken to epitomise the civilisation of Antwerp, which ranged across boundaries. After all, Plantin's team for the *Biblia Regia* was an international one: Montano came from Spain, Plantin himself came from France, as did a key member of his academic team, Guy Lefèvre de la Boderie, while Raphelengius came from the Habsburg Netherlands. In a similar way, the wide range of authors that Plantin published came from across Europe, as is made apparent in his letters. Of the ones mentioned in the last two chapters, de la Boderie, Marot and de Bèze all came from France, Dodoens and Lipsius from the Netherlands, Cordus was German, while Montano, of course, was Spanish. Peeter Heyns alone was actually a native of Antwerp, and his works were published in French as well as Dutch.

CHAPTER 8

The nature of art:

Copying well and the 'forging' of two artists and poets, Lucas d'Heere and Joris Hoefnagel

While there is general agreement about the identification of Joris Hoefnagel (L1, 1542–1601) and Lucas d'Heere (R5, 1534–84), it is impossible to be absolutely sure that these two figures are they. What is certain, however, is that both had connections with Johan Radermacher and were part of the circle of learned merchants that included both Radermacher and Ortelius. Hoefnagel dedicated his emblem book, *Patientia*, to Radermacher, and d'Heere drew an elaborately emblematic picture in Ortelius's *album amicorum* together with an accompanying inscription.

* * *

So far, our picture of civilisation has included the generation of the mercantile wealth needed to pay for it and some of the things paid for, such as the textual scholarship that established reliable texts for its religious and philosophical underpinnings, and the study of the world both geographically and botanically through the work of people such as Ortelius and Dodoens. Yet I have said little so far about the important role played by art in these endeavours.

Art did not just provide tasteful decorations for the wealthy. The paintings that Hooftman commissioned from de Vos for his dining room, for example, provided talking points for his guests, just as they do in Erasmus's colloquium, *The Godly Feast* (see p. 50). Art can also have a more utilitarian purpose, though, as in the woodblock engravings made to illustrate Dodoens's *Cruijdeboek*.[224] Of similarly practical purpose was the hand-colouring of maps by Ortelius and his sisters and the consistent use of different fonts for different types of place names, which did not simply make them more attractive, but enabled them to be read more easily. Pragmatic as the motivation for such work may have been, it still produced works that used beauty to convey meaning. It was entirely appropriate that Ortelius's skill as a *afsetter van Karten* (map-colourer) was recognised and that he was enrolled in the influential artists' guild, the Guild of St Luke, at the age of nineteen.

The art historian Kenneth Clark sums up this broad understanding of art when he says:

> The first artist, in the modern sense, was by inclination a scientist. ... And he made no distinction between the various forms of knowledge. He believed that what we call science and what we call art are one. Art was a branch of knowledge, in which a permanent record of natural appearances was valuable, both for its own sake, and because it would furnish man's imagination with credible images of important things.[225]

Amongst the 'important things' that art reveals is truth as well as facts. Dürer's portrait of an African woman (see **ill. 16**) does not just tell us what she looks like, it gives us an insight into her personality. Similarly, in the *Paneel,* de Vos's depiction of the way in which Panhuys holds his son's hand while gently resting his other hand on his shoulder tells us much about the paternally protective affection shown to the rather nervous-looking boy. To reveal such truths, however, requires being *een goed Contrefaicter* (a good copyist).

Just as the work of the artist and engraver contributes to civilisation, so also does the work of the poet, and not just when describing the emotional heights and depths of love and war. In fact, in a sonnet to the Scots humanist and Latin poet George Buchanan, d'Heere rejects the kind of poetry that depicts the 'doulceur' ('sweetness') and 'peine' ('pain') of love, not to mention 'Mars tout sanglant' ('the bloodshed of war').[226] Much of the poetry of the period, including d'Heere's own, is, in fact, more down-to-earth or even prosaic (paradoxical though that adjective may seem when used to describe verse). Guy Lefèvre de la Boderie's poem 'L'Encyclie' is an example of this (see pp. 102–3), providing an effective vehicle for expounding and debating ideas. Following classical models such as the verse epistles of Horace and the epigrams of Martial, poets of the Renaissance could use poetic forms to express ideas in such a way as to 'put prose in a nutshell'.[227] It was the Roman poet Horace who makes the famous comparison between the two arts: 'ut pictura poesis' ('as painting is, so is art').[228] D'Heere and Hoefnagel were two such artists whose poetry combined with their art to make significant contributions to sixteenth-century civilisation.

Lucas d'Heere

D'Heere has much to say about the nature and purpose of art, both poetry and portrait painting. He was born in Ghent, the second son of two artists, Jan, a sculptor, and his wife, Anna Smijters, a miniaturist. The latter was described as a truly gifted and great illuminator by Guicciardini in his *Description of the Low Countries*, and Karel van Mander praises the astonishing delicacy of her brushwork in his life of d'Heere.[229] After he had been taught to draw passably by his parents, he was sent as an apprentice to work in the studio of his father's friend, Frans Floris, the principal painter in Antwerp at that time. Such was his rapid progress that he was soon drawing cartoons (designs) for glass painters and tapestry-makers. According to van Mander, some of this work was so skilfully drawn that it was mistaken for Floris's own work, and when he was still a young man, he had such a good reputation that he was commissioned by the Dutch statesman and scholar Viglius to paint a picture of the Queen of Sheba's visit to King Solomon to be hung in the choir of St Bavo's Cathedral in Ghent in preparation for the celebration of the twenty-third chapter of the Order of the Golden Fleece. The painting was an allegory of the Spanish Low Countries (represented by the Queen of Sheba) paying tribute to Philip II (portrayed as Solomon, but with an unmistakable Habsburg chin; see p. 23). It was at about this time that d'Heere went to Fontainebleau, where he drew cartoons for tapestries being made for the French Queen Mother, Catherine de Medici.[230]

D'Heere was also a ground-breaking poet. His first collection of poetry, *Den hof en boomgaerd der poësien* ('The Garden and Orchard of Poetry'), was published in 1565,[231] and includes home-grown, vernacular styles of poetry, notably in his *refreinen* (poems with a refrain, usually a complete line repeated at the end of a quite lengthy stanza). He also translated a number of poems by the French Protestant poet Clément Marot and some prose tracts. The *refreinen* in vernacular style are very different in feel from English ballads, which also often have refrains, but are typically written in quatrains with much shorter lines. Given that he had just spent about two years in France, it is not surprising that he includes some translations of French poetry. It was through such translation and imitation that more sophisticated Renaissance poetry gradually spread northwards from Italy to France and then on to the

Low Countries and England. A similar process can be seen at work in the poetry of his almost exact contemporary, Jan van der Noot, whose collection, *Het Theater oft Toon-neel* ('The Theatre of Worldlings'), illustrated by d'Heere with twenty etchings, was published in 1568 in London (like d'Heere and Hoefnagel, van der Noot had fled there to escape Alba's persecution). Van der Noot's epigrams from this volume would subsequently be translated into English by Edmund Spenser, and his work included translations from the Italian of Petrarch and the French of Du Bellay.[232] It is open to debate whether d'Heere or van der Noot wrote the first sonnet in Dutch, but together they played a major part in establishing poetry written in the vernacular rather than in Latin, as it more often had been up to that time. In the dedicatory preface of *Den hof en boomgaerd der poësien*, d'Heere says that he is 'not in the least ashamed' to have copied others. He continues, 'I would believe that I had received enough honour if I were simply to pass for "a good imitator" of those other excellent poets, for that [i.e. imitation] is what almost all writers and authors have done.'[233]

An illustration of the validity of this claim in English literature would be the way in which Thomas Wyatt translates and imitates Petrarch, producing nonetheless something new, a practice that helped to establish the sonnet form in English – a form that Shakespeare and Milton were to make their own so successfully in the following century. It is just this form of copying in art that d'Heere praises in his poem, paying tribute to his great forerunner, Jan van Eyck, the fifteenth-century painter who, with his brother Hubert, painted one of the masterpieces of European art, *The Adoration of the Mystic Lamb* in St Bavo's Cathedral in Ghent. Philip II had wanted this for his own collection and had commissioned a *contrefaiten* (copy) by Michiel Coxcie, a task that took him two years. What Coxcie produced, however, was not an exact facsimile but a version with some deliberate changes that he signs as his own work, replacing the images of the original donors and their patron saints with images of the four evangelists and adding images of Charles V and Philip II among the Christian knights shown on the lower wings to the left of the central panel. In essence, he has used the work of the earlier artist as a means to express his own understanding.[234]

It is important to note that although *contrefaicter* and counterfeiter are cognate, they do not have the same meaning, the former being a complimentary name for a skilled artist who copies well from nature and not for a clever forger. D'Heere tells us that Coxcie's copy of the Ghent altarpiece brought 'glorie groot' ('great honour') not only to van Eyck but also to Coxcie himself. This understanding of what it is to be 'een goed Contrefaicter' is well illustrated in the emblem of de Vos that is shown at the top of a portrait of him by the Swiss painter Joseph Heintz I (1564–1609), engraved by Aegidius Sadeler (1570–1629). The emblem shows the fox (the literal translation of de Vos) with a paw on a spade to represent hard work. On the fox's back is a dove to represent purity of motive, and above is the motto 'puro astu et labore' ('by pure/sheer cunning and hard work'; ill. 25). The Latin word *puro*, like the English word 'pure', has a double meaning: both 'untainted' and also 'sheer' (as in 'He succeeded by sheer effort'). The *astu* (ingenuity or cunning) by which de Vos intends to succeed is not only 'sheer', but also 'pure' in motive, and is the means by which a *contrefaicter* becomes a good artist. The aim is to deceive us into accepting the inner reality of what we see and not just its outward appearance.

Karel van Mander, d'Heere's pupil, was another painter and poet. He wrote a long didactic poem on how to paint called 'Den Grondt der edel vry Schilder-const' ('The Foundation of the Noble, Free Art of Painting') at the start of his major work about painting and painters, *Het Schilder-boeck*. Here, he makes clear that being 'een goed Contrefaicter' is not just a matter of achieving photographic accuracy, but also of revealing 'the concerns that move the heart':

> Here the Painter must diligently observe
> And thoroughly scrutinize the forms of Nature,
> Thereby to position the body's parts
> One against the other, such that they
> Make known the concerns that move the heart,
> Evincing them by means of Bodily gestures:
> For Nature reveals more about what induces affects [*inner feelings*]
> Than one can describe [*in words*].[235]

The same concern can be seen in Hoefnagel's work. One of his early pictures, *Allegory of the Struggle between Avarice and Ambition* (1571), carries a motto that he was to repeat, *natura magistra* ('nature, the mistress or teacher'). Accepting nature as one's teacher, however, is not just a matter of accurate copying: the painting itself is an allegory and far from anything to be seen in nature. In the painting, avarice and ambition are represented as two naked and headless wrestlers, and Hoefnagel's view of these traits is supported by a quotation adapted from Virgil about the evils of those vices. As is so often the case in Hoefnagel's work, image and words combine to reveal not a literal image of nature, but an understanding of truth. It is *human* nature that is being portrayed, not a literal wrestling match in the countryside.

Ortelius makes a similar point in the Latin epitaph that he writes for Bruegel in his *album amicorum* by referring to the classical painter Eupompius, who when asked what models he followed, replied that it was 'naturam ipse imitandam esse, non artificem' ('nature alone that should be copied, not anything artificial'). Certainly, Bruegel's paintings have virtually nothing artificial about them, but although they are 'minime artificiosas, at naturales' (that is, natural), they are open to interpretation. This can be seen, for example, in his painting of the slaughter of the Holy Innocents, in which Herod's murdering troops look remarkably like one of the *bandes*, the local troops of heavy cavalry who were occasionally mustered to enforce unpopular decrees and do the will of the Duke of Alba.[236] In the painting, the standard carried by the soldiers bears a distinct resemblance to the Habsburg double-headed eagle.[237]

Very early in the dedicatory preface of *Den hof en boomgaerd der poësien*, d'Heere refers to Horace's comparison of the arts of poetry and painting in *Ars Poetica*,[238] and so it is not surprising that in d'Heere's manifesto-like collection, there are not only poems illustrating a variety of poetic forms but also a number of poems about painters and painting. Indeed, the title page of d'Heere's book describes the poet as a 'Schilder van Ghend' ('*painter* of Ghent'). (D'Heere is very clear about this view of himself: at the front of his later collection of poems written in French, *Tableau Poetique*, he describes himself as a 'peintre gantois')

The poems in *Den hof en boomgaerd der poësien* reveal d'Heere's artistic principles, as well as his links with contemporary painters and his admiration for those who had preceded him, not least in his poem in memory of Jan van Eyck (see above). After acknowledging Jan's brother's contribution to *The Mystic Lamb*, he praises the clarity of Jan's draughtsmanship – literally its 'scherpicheit' ('sharpness'). He then pays tribute to his 'grooten gheest' ('great mind' or 'inventive spirit') that lies behind 'd'inventie, en de ordinancien' ('the invention and disposition') of his material. Coming from the Latin for 'finding', *inventie* (invention) is the term in classical rhetoric for discovering the necessary resources to persuade the listener or, as in this case, to move the beholder. *Ordinancien* (disposition) is another term from classical rhetoric and refers to the organisation of the arguments and material selected by 'invention', which itself draws upon 'memory'. Thus, we can see how d'Heere takes the traditional rules of classical rhetoric designed to teach how to persuade the listener and applies them to the technique of the artist trying to influence those who look at his paintings. It is made clear in the following stanza that in van Eyck's case, invention was more than just 'finding', when he is praised because he paints as if he had witnessed or 'gh'experimenteert' ('experienced') what he is painting (the 'Mystic Lamb'); if his painting is copying, then it is not so much copying nature as his vision.

Karel van Mander, d'Heere's pupil, also explores the links between poetry and painting in his *Het Schilder-boeck*. Not only does he write 'Den Grondt', a long poem about how to paint (referred to above), he also writes a commentary on *Metamorphoses*, Ovid's great poem, which describes in highly visual terms a variety of transformations, such as Daphne turning into a laurel to escape the unwanted attentions of Apollo, and Narcissus, the youth so obsessed by the beauty of his own face's reflection that he turns into the flower that bears the same name. At first sight, a commentary on Ovid might seem to have nothing to do with painting, but the enormously influential Venetian painter Titian would have disagreed. When he painted many of the scenes from *Metamorphoses* in the 1550s and early 1560s for Philip II, he called his cycle *poesie*: Ovid's paintings in poetry had become his poems in paint.

In another poem, d'Heere expresses his respect for contemporary painters, such as de Vos and also for his former master, Frans Floris. He makes the highly complimentary comparison of Floris to Apelles, the most famous painter of ancient Greece, just as he had done with Jan van Eyck. (When Charles V knighted Titian, he called him 'the Apelles of this century'.)

Most instructive of all is his *Invective, an eenen Quidam schilder: de welcke beschimpte de Schilders van Handwerpen* ('Invective against a certain painter, who was rude about the painters of Antwerp'), which is more direct and down-to-earth than his theorising in the Jan van Eyck poem. He indignantly rejects the suggestion that the paintings of his former master, Frans Floris, and his followers are mere 'suukerbeeldekens' ('sweeties'), since their works are decorated in a 'becamelic en rijke' ('becoming and rich') manner. They paint 'sonder bedrieghen' ('without deceiving'); in other words, they are true *contrefaicteren*, unlike their critic whose figures are like 'kaeremespoppen' ('kermis puppets'). The reference to kermis, a Netherlandish peasant carnival or fair, immediately makes one suspect that d'Heere's target here is Pieter Bruegel, whose pictures of peasant jollifications are full of lively but not especially life-like figures. (This is not to denigrate Bruegel, whose figures are particularly successful in expressing life, character and energy.) But if d'Heere is referring to Bruegel, then he clearly disagrees with Ortelius's judgement.

This kind of vigorous debate (admittedly only presenting one side of the argument here) helps to define what art should be. A gentler debate is presented in a delightful translation by his wife of a dialogue poem in the form of a sonnet that d'Heere had written about a picture by Willem Key.[239] The subject debated is whether the beautiful woman seen in the picture is real or not. After deciding that it is a painted image, the second speaker argues that they have not been tricked by the picture because it is 'soo wel is gheschildert naer d'leven' ('painted so accurately from life') that it is indistinguishable from the living woman. Given this, Key can be considered *'een goed Contrefaicter'*.

The final artistic debate in *Den hof en boomgaerd der poësien* is addressed to the Antwerp *rederijkerskamer* (chamber of rhetoric) known as De Violieren (the Gillyflower), and the topic is one that understandably concerns a painter who writes about his art in poetry and who was himself a member of a chamber of rhetoric in Ghent.[240] The debate is whether poetry or painting requires the greater artistry. Given that a *rederijkerskamer* was a literary and dramatic club that fostered the writing and performing of verse plays in the vernacular (see pp. 106–7), it might seem tactless that d'Heere's conclusion is that the art of painting is supreme, but since De Violieren was closely associated with the Guild of St Luke, the artists' guild, his conclusion is not so maladroit. Members of De Violieren included Maerten de Vos and d'Heere's own teacher, Frans Floris himself.[241] D'Heere's poem, a traditional *refrein*, starts with Apollo posing the question to the nine Muses, but Apollo soon starts to answer his own question, and each verse ends by stating that painting is 'de constichste conste der consten' ('the most artistic art of arts'). In the final verse, however, in a compliment to its readers, the poet tells them that 'Dit zijn de constichste van alle constenaren' ('They [i.e. the artists themselves] are the most artistic of all artists').[242]

In view of this, it is hardly surprising that according to van Mander, d'Heere did his best to rescue some of Frans Floris's works from the iconoclasts. Although opposed to the destruction of art, he was a Protestant, and in 1566, the year after *Den hof en boomgaerd der poësien* was published, d'Heere fled the Duke of Alba's persecution by going to London, where he met Emanuel van Meteren and Johan Radermacher and became an elder of the Dutch stranger church at Austin Friars in London. It may well have been at this point that he took some comfort from making an anagram of his names, *Schade leer u*, or 'May misfortune teach you'. Certainly, his response to misfortune was to find influential patrons in England and to continue both painting and writing. There is a good deal of controversy about the identification of his English paintings today; the waters were muddied when earlier scholars, including Horace Walpole, mistakenly attributed paintings by Hans Eworth to him. However, three of his illustrated manuscripts do survive. The first is his costume book, *Theatre de tous les peoples et nations de la terre avec leurs habits, et ornements divers, tant anciens que modernes* ('The theatre of all the peoples and nations of the world with their dress and ornaments, both ancient and modern'). This consists of a series of ninety-eight watercolours illustrating differing styles of dress across the world, both contemporary (i.e. sixteenth-century) and earlier. There are, for example, Turks, Persians, Ethiopians and Egyptians, as well as an Inuit, and even an English peer wearing the robes of the Order of the Garter. From the past there are ancient Britons, naked except for woad patterns drawn on their bodies, and a Roman tribune and captain. There are usually two figures on each page, and every picture is a life-like miniature portrait. What we see is the same desire to understand and encompass the whole world, past and present, that is also found in Ortelius's *Theatrum Orbis Terrarum*.

The second manuscript is the *Corte beschryvinghe van England, Scotland, ende Irland* ('Short Description of England, Scotland and Ireland'). Unfinished and dating from the period immediately before the painting of the *Paneel*, this was presumably prepared for his fellow refugees. Similar in intention to Guicciardini's *Description of the Low Countries*, yet smaller in scale, it contains a number of watercolours, which suggests that it was intended to be passed around in manuscript form rather than published. Among the illustrations is the earliest known picture of Stonehenge, a watercolour sketch probably painted on site (see **ill. 26**). It provides evidence of the antiquarian interests that he shared with Ortelius and another example of art being used to further knowledge.

The third manuscript that survives is *Tableau Poetique*, a collection of poems dedicated to Edward Seymour II, Earl of Hertford and son of Edward Seymour I, Duke of Somerset, who was the eldest surviving brother of Jane Seymour (Henry VIII's third queen). He had been Lord Protector during Edward VI's minority reign until he was overthrown and beheaded in 1552. Later, the younger Seymour was also to find himself in the Tower of London for the offence of marrying Lady Catherine Grey (she was a sister of Lady Jane Grey, the 'nine-days Queen') and a potential claimant to the throne once the childless Elizabeth I had died. Nevertheless, after Lady Catherine had died, he was released from the Tower, and an influential and strongly Protestant circle gathered around him when he withdrew to the family estate at Wolf Hall in Wiltshire. D'Heere's poems are addressed not only to Hertford, but to other prominent members of the Protestant ruling class. Amongst these was William Cecil, 1st Baron Burghley, whose early career had been spent in the service of Seymour's father and who later became Elizabeth I's principal adviser for most of her reign. It also included the Earl of Leicester, Robert Dudley, a favourite of Elizabeth and a patron of the Puritan movement, who was to lead the English expeditionary force in support of the Dutch rebellion against Philip II. D'Heere also writes a long poem on the motto of Sir Thomas Gresham, whose financial acumen enabled Elizabeth I to stay solvent even as Philip II, with all the resources of the Spanish empire at his disposal, repeatedly went bankrupt.

He also slips in a self-flattering poem written as if by his son, who supposedly tells how before his birth, his father had painted an imagined picture of him; after his birth, his father had painted him as he actually was, and both paintings were so life-like that when he stood beside them, 'Qu'on ne peut discerner sinon par coniecture, Silz sont troix enfants peints ou bien troix naturelz' ('no one could tell except by guessing whether they saw three painted or three living boys').[243]

Despite the insertion of this little puff for his wares (claiming to be a 'goed Contrefaicter'), most of this poetry is written for the purpose of cementing his position as a member of Seymour's household and to demonstrate his political and religious loyalties. Nevertheless, it is not devoid of feeling, not least when he describes what it feels like to be an exile. In a sonnet to Radermacher, a fellow elder of the Dutch stranger church, he writes of his sadness:

> Veu que nostre patrie a lors si florissante
> Sert ores de Theatre auquel iouent ces trois
> La cruaulte, rapine & faulcete des loix
> Leur triste Tragedie inhumaine & sanglante.[244]
> ('Since our once flourishing homeland has become a theatre on the stage
> of which cruelty, rapine and false laws perform an inhuman and bloody
> tragedy')

Another way of looking at this collection of poems dedicated to many different people is to see it as the verbal equivalent of a whole gallery of paintings (the word *tableau* can mean 'picture' in French), a kind of reversal of Titian's description of his Ovid paintings as *poesie*. D'Heere's metaphorical use of 'theatre' in the poem above raises the question of d'Heere's lost English paintings. Van Mander reports that d'Heere was commissioned by Edward Clinton, Earl of Lincoln and Lord High Admiral under Edward VI and again under Elizabeth I until his death in 1585, to paint a gallery with representations of the costumes of different peoples. This is plausible: Clinton had been knighted by the father of d'Heere's patron, Edward Seymour I, after playing a part in the capture of Edinburgh in 1544, and so the connection is there. The question is: where was the gallery in which the figures were painted? Was it part of some long since demolished house, or was this a metaphorical 'gallery' of the same kind as the 'theatre' in Ortelius's *Theatrum Orbis Terrarium* and d'Heere's own *Theatre de tous les peuples et nations de la terre avec leurs habits*: a place for metaphorical gatherings not in an actual building or on a stage, but on paper? Tine Luk Meganck reports that the armorial used as a bookplate at the front of d'Heere's *Theatre* has been pasted over by a different one, but that the motto of the Order of the Garter, to which Clinton belonged, can still be seen on the one underneath. If the armorial was indeed Clinton's, presumably the book originally belonged to him, and in that case, it may even be the 'gallery' of costume illustrations that he commissioned. If so, there is no lost series of murals to be found.²⁴⁵

One painting which does survive but whose attribution is disputed is *The Tudor Succession* (ill. 27). This depicts Henry VIII and his three children, all of whom in turn ruled England. Henry is centre-stage, sitting on his throne with the royal coat of arms above him. One hand is on his hip, in a pose similar to that in the famous Holbein portrait, while with the other hand he passes the sword of justice to a kneeling Edward VI. To his right (our left) and further back stands Mary I with her husband Philip II of Spain, and behind them is Mars, the god of war, holding a shield and lance. Finally, on Henry's left (but our right) and on a larger scale than Henry's other children – and in very much the most prominent position – stands Elizabeth I. Close behind her is Peace, standing on the now-discarded shield and lance of Mars, and immediately behind her is Plenty, carrying a cornucopia that overflows with fruit. On the four sides of the frame is painted:

> A face of muche nobillitye loe in a little roome. Fowr states with theyr conditions heare shadowed [represented] in a showe. A Father more then valiant. A rare and virtuous Soon. A zealus Daughter, in her kynd, what els the world doth knowe. And last of all a Vyrgin Queen to Englands joy we see, successyvely to hold the righte and vertues of the three.

The message is clear: Elizabeth combines in her person the good qualities of her father and siblings and is legitimately descended from Henry. After Mary's alliance with Spain has brought about war and England's loss of Calais to the French, Elizabeth has brought peace and plenty. A new treaty had just been agreed with France in April 1572, and according to a couplet painted onto the picture, the painting is a gift from the Queen to her ambassador in Paris, Sir Francis Walsingham: 'The queen to Walsingham this tablet sente, marke of her peoples and her owne contente.'

Since Walsingham started his political career as a protégé of Elizabeth's adviser, Burghley, and since we can assume from d'Heere's sonnet, 'A Milord Bourghley', that Burghley knew him, it is quite possible that the latter commissioned him to paint this picture. Walsingham's connection to d'Heere is in any case referred to in a letter dated July 1576 from William of Orange (*Proceedings of the Huguenot Society*, 4, 1891–3, 39).[246]

Frederica van Dam disagrees with the attribution to d'Heere, however, writing that 'the remarkably small proportions of the depicted persons in relation to the space' and 'the lack of [the] dynamism that can be found in D'Heere's other works as well as his specific way of displaying the anatomy of human figures' make her reject the attribution. On the other hand, Roy Strong argues that the grouping of the figures is very similar to that in d'Heere's earlier picture of *Solomon and the Queen of Sheba* (see p. 23) and his later design of the *Pageant Stage for the Entry of the Duke of Anjou, 1582*.[247] It may be that van Dam's objections can be countered by pointing out that this is not a normal group portrait. It seems clear that Catholic Mary and her Spanish husband need to be set well back, whereas Elizabeth needs to be larger and more prominently placed. Certainly, the figures lack dynamism, but painting the dead father and siblings of a reigning monarch may be assumed to be somewhat inhibiting. Each figure is painted in the clothes of the period when they were alive and reigning, and the painting of differing periods and styles of costume was a d'Heere speciality. The only face to have any expression is that of Mary, who looks distinctly sour. An attribution based solely on taste cannot be certain, but d'Heere's gratitude for the Protestant refuge that he had found from Catholic persecution means that the subject is one that he would almost certainly have accepted if he had been approached to paint it.

Joris Hoefnagel

In 1568, Joris Hoefnagel also chose to work in the safety of London after the arrival of the Duke of Alba, although there is no conclusive evidence that he was Protestant, and he would return to Antwerp the following year.[248] Hoefnagel was the son of rich parents: his father was an Antwerp merchant who dealt in diamonds and luxury goods, and his mother the daughter of a master of the Antwerp mint. Hoefnagel's education was presumably intended to give him knowledge of the wider world in which the family business operated, and he spent time in France between 1560 and 1562 at the universities of Bourges and Orléans. Having received such an education, Hoefnagel was yet another learned merchant like Radermacher and van Meteren, both of whom he met in London. According to van Mander, he was always very studious, working late at night and frequently getting up at four in the morning to write poetry. He was such a good Latinist that he could translate at sight, reading out a Latin text in Flemish. In addition to his linguistic abilities, he was obsessed with art from an early age. His parents evidently regarded this as a distraction from more useful studies, but Hoefnagel seized every opportunity to draw, and if he had no paper, he would draw in the dust on the floor with a finger. One day, an important visitor, observing his aptitude, persuaded his parents to let him draw. This all sounds somewhat hagiographical, but nevertheless van Mander tells us that while Hoefnagel was out in Spain as an agent for the family business from 1563 to 1567, he was gifted some watercolours and began to paint his first panoramic city views. Then, when he returned to Antwerp, he received some advice from Hans Bol (1534–93), an artist known both for his landscapes and as a miniaturist, two areas in which Hoefnagel came to excel.

During his stay in England, he continued his practice of drawing panoramic pictures of places that he visited and of the life that he observed around him. Some of these drawings were later engraved, and were to form a key part of a series of volumes of pictures and descriptions of cities across the world, *Civitates Orbis Terrarum* ('Cities of the Countries of the World'), edited by Georg Braun and Frans Hogenberg and published between 1572 and 1618 (in the end, there were about eighty prints made from Hoefnagel's works across the six volumes in the series[249]). These were envisaged as a companion to Ortelius's atlas, the *Theatrum Orbis Terrarum*, although Ortelius resisted their being published together. One of these drawings (**ill. 28**) gives us an idea of the appearance of Henry VIII's great, but now demolished, palace at Nonsuch, and shows a variety of costumes and activities in the foreground. A print of Seville (**ill. 29**) also shows a wide range of activities in the foreground, including a cuckold wearing an enormous pair of horns while being paraded with his unfaithful wife and mocked. Like d'Heere's costume paintings, these prints can be seen as a contribution to the knowledge of the world so eagerly desired in early modern civilisation.

While he was in England, Hoefnagel made a manuscript book of poems and drawings for Radermacher, which reveals much about their creator and his artistic principles. The roots of his later detailed miniatures, which are also often accompanied by text, can be seen in this work; it consists of twenty-four drawings, each with its accompanying poem written in Dutch, French or Spanish. The opening sonnet is addressed to Radermacher and starts like this: 'The spirit was troubled, restrained by the body, / Distrusting and anxious from great apprehension, / God has roused the spirit quickly out of its misery; / No suffering is so great that time cannot reduce.'[250] Ample cause for the depression that he describes can be found in the state of the Low Countries after Alba's violent suppression of religious and political dissent, and he goes on to thank Radermacher for acting as God's agent in rousing him from inertia to new creativity.

Each page has an image drawn in red chalk with a title and a poem alongside commenting on the image, as in an emblem book. The pictures themselves are set in the streets of Antwerp or the surrounding countryside. The opening picture shows a woman locked in the stocks and is labelled *Patientia* (**ill. 30**). Arms folded, the figure of Patience looks up to heaven as Hope instructs her to, but her expression is more one of resentment than pious resignation. Overhead, a tree branch looms heavily over her in a way that foreshadows one of William Blake's drawings ('The Poison Tree') and with a similar emotional impact.[251] Hoefnagel's accompanying sonnet finishes: 'Therefore take note of me / And place your hope and consolation in the Lord; / Blessed is the person who builds on him alone.'

This representation of patience calling upon the 'consolation' of God in the face of adversity has led some to see a link with the Christianised neo-stoicism of Lipsius's *De Constantia* (although *De Constantia* was not published until some years later, in 1584; see p. 180–1). In any case, the picture here of Patience scowling in the stocks prevents any glib interpretation and suggests that any patience will be hard-won. The figure is clearly allegorical, but the pictures that follow are evidently rooted in the uncomfortable realities of a land in turmoil. Both pictures and verses reflect the hardships of life in the Low Countries after their subjugation by Alba's Spanish forces and the actions of his so-called 'Council of Blood'. One picture shows an evicted family with their sparse belongings beside them after they have been thrown out on the street. As one merchant writing to another (Radermacher), Hoefnagel also speaks of the difficulties of trade under the new regime, which had just initiated a trade war with England that had led to the seizure of English merchants' goods in the Low Countries and vice versa (see pp. 81–6):

We merchants are in a bad way.
We bring princes and countries to prosperity.
Our trade brings prosperity everywhere.
Now they come and confiscate our goods,
Even ransom our persons.
Through war, controversy, or such quarrels
Have patience; the Lord will reward us one day.
God gives, God takes, it is all the Lord's will.

What Hoefnagel does not do, however, is engage in religious polemics, and in this, as in his neo-stoical acceptance of what happens, he is not far removed from Familist attitudes. His writing of his poems in Dutch, French and Spanish is a reminder not only of the international range of Antwerp's merchants but of the cosmopolitan nature of its civilisation (he also writes a separate dedication to Radermacher in Latin). His view that trade is a general good ('Our trade brings prosperity everywhere') is one with which Niclaes, the founder of the Family of Love and a merchant himself, would surely have agreed. He would have seen it as a powerful argument for avoiding the suffering and conflict over what he would have regarded as the unimportant external trappings of religion. At the end of the introductory sonnet, Hoefnagel takes comfort in Radermacher's friendship:

> With you as his [God's] instrument who came to visit me,
> To offer a friendly invitation to the noble and pure art
> That God gave me, I sprang as if from the dead,
> With the spirit full of fantasy, and set it to work.
> ...
> Now then, my work finished, albeit rough and of little impact,
> Goes to Radermacher. He will not scorn you
> Because he thinks as a friend; show him my open heart.

Radermacher is seen as an agent of God's will, reconciling Hoefnagel to exile and teaching him patience, but also encouraging him to take up the 'noble and pure art' that is displayed in his artistic gift. Appropriately enough, the final illustration shows friends sharing a celebratory meal.

Although it is Radermacher who encourages him to turn to the 'noble and pure art', the art itself is seen as nature's – and, by implication, God's – gift, and this requires faithfulness to what he is painting to reveal its truth. Like d'Heere, Hoefnagel must be a *goed Contrefaicter*, one who accepts *natura* as his *magistra* (mistress and teacher). In another tribute to friendship, inscribed in Ortelius's *album amicorum*, the link is clearly made when Hoefnagel writes that:

> Pour suivre Dieu et la nature
> Et pour monstrer l'affection pure
> (N'ayant aultre), j'emplois aussi
> L'art dont nature m'at enrichi,
> Nature seulle, seulle nourrice
> Des bons esprics, abhorrants vice.
> ('To follow God and nature and to show my pure affection (I have no other),
> I employ the talent with which nature, the only nurse of good souls who
> abhor vice, has enriched me.')[252]

The opening sonnet of *Patientia* points to another crucial element in the creative process. Roused from depression, Hoefnagel later finds that his 'gheest vol fantasijen, en ghink hem imploijeren' ('spirit is full of fantasy and [he] sets it to work'). The key word here is *fantasijen*, which is perhaps better translated as 'imagination' rather than 'fantasies'.[253] In other words, Hoefnagel is not engaging in the airy dreaming of fantasy but in the creative power that is better described as imagination, which is the ability to make something of what nature offers. John Keats makes the same point many years when he writes in 'Ode to a Nightingale' that 'the Fancy cannot cheat / As well as she is famed to do', and in 'The Fall of Hyperion' that 'The poet and the dreamer are distinct, / Diverse, sheer opposite antipodes.[254] In *Patientia*, Hoefnagel is not a 'dreamer' but a 'poet' who confronts the harsh conditions of his time. In the Latin prose dedication to Radermacher, Hoefnagel describes the poems that follow as 'hos [...] ingenii sui ludos' ('these contrivances of his wit'). It is the interaction of his *ingenium* (mind) with the truthfulness of what he copies from nature that creates his art: the very title of *Patientia*, for example, is shown entwined with realistic foliage suggestive of the healing herb *rumex patientia* or patience dock (*patientie* in Dutch). So, by exercising his *ingenium*, he uses a copy of nature to convey the assurance that patience will bring healing.[255]

A print of Hoefnagel has been pasted in the previous page of Ortelius's *album amicorum* before the short poem quoted above. At the top of the print is his personal device of a nail on an anvil being struck by a hammer.[256] Written below it is his motto, *Dum extendar*, which may be translated as 'Until I am forged'. This is a play on his name: *nagel* literally means 'nail' and it is used to fix a horseshoe on a horse's *hoef*. But this is far more than just a play on words and images. Just as d'Heere may well have felt that the anagram on his name (*Schade U leer* – misfortune teaches you) was particularly relevant after his exile in London, so Hoefnagel, who also chose to retreat to London, may well have thought that he was being 'forged' by the unhappy experience of exile, just as the lump of iron is hammered out into the extended (and useful) shape of a nail (although he does not actually use the device until a year or two later, when he leaves Antwerp in 1577 after the losses and ravages of the Spanish Fury). Both mottoes reveal an openness to learning by harsh experience that is appropriate to their personal difficulties and in accordance with the Christian stoicism that was to be advocated by Lipsius. It is also very much in accordance with the advancement of learning so valued by the group amongst whom they are depicted in the *Paneel*, which is itself, of course, a picture of the Jews also responding as best they may to the hardships of exile.

PART 2

A CIVILISATION SCATTERED: AFTER THE TIME OF THE PAINTING

CHAPTER 9

Interlude:

Some background history

I wish now to consider what happened to the people that I have discussed and what happened to the civilisation that they had created in Antwerp. First, however, an initial puzzle to be solved is why they all appear in the same group portrait despite their very different religious affiliations. Montano, after all, was a chaplain to His Most Catholic Majesty Philip II of Spain, while we can be reasonably sure that at one point Hooftman was Lutheran (see p. 42), and we definitely know that Radermacher was an elder of no fewer than four Calvinist churches in turn, as he was forced to move from place to place.

There are at least two plausible explanations. The first, Familism, has already been mentioned. Many of these characters have connections with Christophe Plantin, who published books by Dodoens and Heyns, cooperated closely with Montano on the *Biblia Regia*, and sold Hebrew Bibles to Hooftman for export to North Africa. We can also be fairly certain that Plantin (see Chapter 6, pp. 96–7) was a member of the Family of Love. As such, a possible yet contentious explanation is that all these people, despite their different outward religious affiliations, were actually secret Familists like Plantin himself. This theory is impossible either to prove or disprove, as we have seen, because of their strict secrecy. It is only because Plantin is mentioned by name in a book about the Family – albeit as an untrustworthy person who had then joined a splinter group – that we can be confident about even his membership.

A second explanation is that what unites them is simply personal friendship. Radermacher might well be the common link; he is after all right at the centre of the painting. It was he who on behalf of Hooftman, and at the suggestion of Ortelius, had first approached de Vos to paint some of the earlier *portraits historiés* that Hooftman commissioned. As Hooftman's trusted apprentice in Antwerp and then as his agent in London, he will have known all of the Hooftman and Panhuys families and their business associates. And as an active and important member of the Dutch stranger church in London, he will also have had the opportunity to meet anyone from the Low Countries who came to England either on business or to escape persecution, not to mention all those who lived there for longer periods of time, including Emanuel van Meteren, Lucas d'Heere and Joris Hoefnagel.

The way that I propose to tackle this conundrum is to consider the paths taken by the characters in the *Panhuys Paneel* from the time that it was painted, and also to look at the careers of some of their children, which will give us a pointer to their parents' beliefs and whether it is at all plausible to suggest that they might have been Familists. First, however, it will be helpful to provide a context by summarising (and inevitably simplifying) some of the key historical events that they all lived through from just before the time that the *Paneel* was painted in 1574.

In 1573, William the Silent had been forced to recognise that the Calvinist Sea Beggars were the only effective fighting force at his disposal if he was to resist Philip II successfully and defend the privileges and liberties of the Low Countries. Since they were Calvinists, he too became a Calvinist, although they did not share his wish to unite the Low Countries by allowing freedom of worship. (Indeed, the intolerance of the Calvinists was ultimately to prove as divisive as the determination of Philip to persecute Protestants.)

By the time that the *Paneel* was painted in 1574, Requesens, Philip's Governor-General after Alba, had already been obliged to force the city of Antwerp to raise funds to pay his unpaid and rebellious troops after the king's finances had been drained defending against Turkish attacks in the Mediterranean. After agreeing terms with his creditors, Philip obtained the necessary money to pay his troops, and the Spanish army swung into action again, besieging Leiden. Following desperate resistance, the hard decision was taken to breach the dykes and, finding themselves flooded out, the Spanish army withdrew. Following this, Philip ran out of money again (it is estimated that his entire income for any year was consumed by payments of interest and repayments of capital[257]), and he postponed repayment of his debts in September 1575, which not only destroyed his credit but also left his army, many of whom were German and Italian mercenaries, unpaid and mutinous. In March 1576, Requesens died, and the following November, the unpaid Spanish army, owed two years' back pay[258] and undoubtedly resenting the wealth that they could see all around them in one of Europe's most prosperous cities, turned on the people of Antwerp and treated the city as if they had just taken it by storm, burning much of it down and using rape, torture and murder to seize as many valuables as they could lay their hands on. Estimates vary, but about 7,000 men, women and children were killed and approximately a third of the city was destroyed, including the new town hall; it is justifiably described as the 'Spanish Fury'.[259] In response to this and similar outrages, the seventeen provinces of the Spanish Low Countries, regardless of whether they were predominantly Catholic or Protestant, joined together to ratify the Pacification of Ghent, which aimed to raise troops to expel the rebel Spanish soldiers and to reassert the traditional rights and privileges that Philip II had overridden. All this occurred in the interregnum between the death of Requesens and the arrival of his replacement, Philip's illegitimate half-brother, Don Juan (best known to English readers through G.K. Chesterton's poem 'Lepanto' as Don John of Austria, the victor of Lepanto). Don Juan arrived too late to resolve the situation, and he provided the treaty with royal assent in February 1577, following its conclusion at the Union of Brussels.

Despite this alliance, the fault-lines between the predominantly conservative, Catholic and French-speaking southern provinces and the more radical, Protestant, Dutch-speaking northern ones persisted. William the Silent's attempts to gain acceptance of *Religionsvrede* (freedom of worship) failed both in Calvinist strongholds such as Ghent and in the staunchly Catholic south (Antwerp was one of the few cities to accept the principle). By 1579, the leaders of the southern provinces had decided that being dominated by intolerant Calvinists who refused freedom of worship to Lutherans, Anabaptists and Catholics was intolerable. Their leaders also regarded the social radicalism of the Calvinists as a worse threat than the erosion of their privileges by Philip, and so they combined in the Union of Arras, which was soon followed by a peace treaty with Philip. In response, the seven northern provinces united in the Treaty of Utrecht to form the United Provinces, and the war between the rebel forces under William of Orange and the Spanish continued. Given this, it is clear that the *Paneel* was painted in a brief period of calm between the raising of funds for Requesens and the Spanish Fury, which was followed by the continued resistance of the north, including some more southerly cities that are now in Belgium, such as Brussels, Antwerp and Ghent, the home of Lucas d'Heere.

In 1578, Don Juan died and Philip shrewdly appointed Alessandro Farnese, the Duke of Parma, as the next Governor-General. He was the illegitimate son of Margaret of Parma, who had been Governor of the Netherlands until replaced by Alba, and so he already had some understanding of the people with whom he was dealing. He was, in any case, already in command of the Spanish forces in the Netherlands. Farnese also made it clear that there would be no repetition of the harsh treatment handed out by Alba as long as towns returned to their allegiance, and he signed the Treaty of Arras with the French-speaking Walloon provinces in 1579. Thereafter, he began to make rapid progress in consolidating Spanish control of the south and driving back William's forces. His success was such that Lipsius was to describe him as 'conditor Belgii' ('the founder of Belgium').[260] In 1581, William attempted to gain support from France to reunite the provinces by finding an alternative figurehead to himself in the Duke of Anjou, brother of the French king. This plan was hampered by Calvinist suspicions of a Catholic ruler, but failed completely because Anjou resented being what was in effect a constitutional monarch.[261] In 1583, Anjou tried to seize power by treacherously making use of his 'Joyous Entry', the traditional welcome and acknowledgement of a new overlord, to introduce his troops into Antwerp and take control of the city. His trick was seen through, and his attempted coup was bloodily repulsed, after which he returned to France and died soon afterwards. This was a severe setback to William's efforts to unite the Low Countries against the Spanish. Then, in 1584, William was assassinated just as Alessandro Farnese was starting to achieve serious military success. In August of that year, Farnese captured Ghent, and in March 1585, Brussels surrendered to him. Finally, in August of that year, after a siege of more than a year, Antwerp surrendered.

Farnese had favoured a surrender from Antwerp as many lives would have been lost on both sides and much damage done if his army had stormed the city's strong walls (soldiers who storm a city are notoriously hard to control once inside). Moreover, there would have been irreparable damage to the city's trading wealth, which he wished to possess rather than destroy. He achieved his aims by blockading the Scheldt and starving the city into surrender; he was then able to negotiate the handover of the city relatively intact by allowing all Protestants four years in which to settle their affairs and leave for the north or to return to the Roman Catholic Church. Although Farnese obtained his immediate objective, the Sea Beggars based in the ports on the north side of the Scheldt estuary then blockaded the city in their turn, while approximately half the population who did leave took their wealth with them.[262] The decline of Antwerp should not be exaggerated: it became a centre for luxury goods and still had artistic glories ahead, not least the paintings of Rubens and such beauties of sound and sight as are to be found in Ruckers harpsichords.[263] The rebels would lift the blockade of the Scheldt in 1587, preferring to charge a toll, which put up merchants' costs but did allow trade to resume. Despite this gesture, Antwerp was soon to be replaced as a great trading centre by Amsterdam. Quite apart from the political barriers to trade, economic success is hard to achieve without freedom of thought and speech as well as freedom of movement.

After the fall of Antwerp and the assassination of William the Silent, the northern rebels turned to Elizabeth I for help. She declined the offer of sovereignty but agreed to send an army of 6,000 under the command of the Earl of Leicester on condition that he was appointed Governor-General. Leicester, however, made the mistake of siding with the more extreme wing of the Calvinist rebels, who demanded that all trade with Spain should cease. This trade had continued throughout the earlier struggles because both sides needed Dutch ships to transport their goods. The ban, if it had been implemented, would have damaged the income of the northern provinces and ironically reduced their ability to resist the Spanish. It was, in fact, fiercely resisted by the States General, the army and Prince Maurice of Nassau, William the Silent's son. Defeated by this situation, Leicester returned to England in 1586, and after one more attempt to take control, finally resigned as Governor-General in 1588.

Farnese failed to take advantage of this period of discord because Philip II had given him orders to keep his army further south, ready for embarkation to invade England once the Armada had swept the Channel clear – a project that ended in failure. Then, in 1590, he was ordered to invade France to support the Catholic League in the civil war against the Huguenot Henri of Navarre. He had just become Henri IV of France after the assassination of Henri III the year before by a fanatical Dominican friar who had been infuriated by Henri's attempt to escape domination by the Catholic League by assassinating its leaders, the Duke and the Cardinal of Guise.[264] In the meantime, Maurice had trained the Dutch army as a disciplined fighting force that had begun to recapture the cities that had fallen to Farnese, getting as far south as Ostend. Philip then appointed his nephew, Archduke Albert of Austria, as joint sovereign of the Netherlands with his new wife, Philip's daughter, the Infanta Isabella. They were nominally independent and managed to achieve a degree of popularity. The command of the Spanish army was taken over by the Genoese general Ambrogio Spinola, a skilled tactician who recaptured Ostend in 1604. From this point on, the two sides more or less fought each other to a standstill, until a twelve-year truce was agreed in 1609. Although the war resumed at the end of the truce, little further change occurred. Nevertheless, the truce itself was important, since the Spanish decision to enter negotiations was a de facto acknowledgement that the United Provinces had become a separate country.

These military conflicts between north and south and the doctrinal divisions between Catholic and Protestant were to determine the fate of the civilisation that had flourished in Antwerp.

CHAPTER 10

The merchants from the time of the Paneel

The surrender of Antwerp was to prove much more of a turning point in the lives of most of those depicted in the *Paneel* than the Spanish Fury. Both Hooftman (who had died by the time Antwerp surrendered) and Panhuys doubtless suffered earlier losses from the Spanish Fury, as well as having had to raise money for Requesens to pay his troops two years earlier. It is not clear whether they bought off the rampaging Spanish soldiers during the Fury, or how else they managed to protect their belongings, but just as they overcame the earlier damage to trading confidence caused by the *Beeldenstorm* (see p. 49), so they appear to have emerged relatively unscathed by the events of 1575. The evidence for this is not only the alleged ten tons of gold that Hooftman left at his death[265] and the very substantial dowry of £10,000 paid later for the marriage of his daughter, Anna, to Orazio Palavicino,[266] but also the *memorieboek* of his partner, Panhuys, which continues to record the latter's financial affairs and acquisition of property, alongside the birth of his children.

Gillis Hooftman
Hooftman's earlier success seems to have been based on the timber trade in the Baltic, although he also traded as far afield as North Africa. After the Spanish Fury, he may well have been the first merchant from the Low Countries to bypass the Baltic by starting to trade with Russia via the White Sea. This trade route, landing goods at the mouth of the Dvina River on the coast (near where Archangel was to be built shortly after Hooftman's death), became important at this time because of the struggles to dominate the Baltic and its ice-free

ports. To exploit this alternative route, he set up a trading company with the Van de Walle brothers in 1577, just a couple of years after the painting of the *Paneel*. At this time, he will no doubt have had recourse to his bespoke book of maps prepared by Ortelius, particularly the one showing the White Sea (**ill. 9**). He was preceded in this initiative by the English, who were encouraged to trade here by Ivan the Terrible after he had lost his struggle with Poland-Lithuania and Sweden to gain an ice-free Baltic port. The Muscovy Company based in London was in fact the first to use this route, and indeed Ortelius's map was derived from one made by a member of that company, Anthony Jenkinson. Despite this early incursion, we know that by 1600 the Dutch ships at Archangel outnumbered those of the English.[267]

This northern trade may have evaded political dangers, but the weather made it hazardous, and it was a voyage only to be undertaken in the summer months. Despite this danger, it was a lucrative route. In exchange for textiles, salt, wine and precious metals, timber would be imported with rope, saltpetre and fish.[268] A further sign that Hooftman continued to be at the forefront of Antwerp's commercial life is that in 1577, one of his captains was the first to bring goods back from Spain after the Pacification of Ghent.

That his ventures were profitable can be seen from Hooftman's decision to buy the Kasteel Pulhof in 1578, a moated house just to the east of Antwerp (despite its name, it was not so much a 'castle' as a moated manor house). Two years later, he bought the lordships of Cleydael and Aartselaar and also the 'refuge house' of the Abbey of Afflighem.[269] This 'refuge house' would have been where the abbot stayed when he visited Antwerp (Afflighem is roughly halfway between Antwerp and Brussels), and its sale may well have been prompted by the monastery's need to raise money for rebuilding after its buildings were destroyed that year by Protestant soldiers. The abbey's finances were in any case under serious pressure when Philip's ecclesiastical re-organisation assigned 90,000 florins of the abbot's income to pay for the archbishopric of Mechelen.[270] These purchases suggest that Hooftman was preparing for a less frenetic old age, no longer 'living over the shop' in the Pollenaken, his house in Steenstraat alongside the bustle of the river wharfs, but in a quiet and secure moated house outside Antwerp, while nevertheless acquiring a house in the city for when he needed to visit on business.

If that was indeed his motive, then he had little time to enjoy his proposed leisure, since he died in 1581, the year after these purchases. What is clear is that despite the losses that he almost certainly experienced at the time of the Spanish Fury, he continued to prosper, becoming very wealthy under both Calvinist and Catholic regimes. Regardless of his religious beliefs, he chose to conform, taking an oath of loyalty to Philip, observing fast days, going to confession and attending Mass.[271] It is not clear whether he was following the teaching of the Family of Love that one should not change one's outward religious affiliation but concentrate on the inner spiritual life, or simply following Luther's teaching about the importance of being loyal to the state (which required outward religious conformity), or just focusing on self-preservation. This last possibility, however, hardly fits with the risk that he had taken earlier in sending supplies to Vlissingen when it was being besieged by the Spanish (see p. 44). Yet nor does giving help to those opposing the state's authority sound very Lutheran.

Peeter Panhuys

The political and religious positioning of Peeter Panhuys is more apparent in a later crisis: the siege of Antwerp in 1584–5. Like Hooftman, Panhuys was registered as a citizen of Antwerp soon after his arrival, and later served the city as both alderman and treasurer. Almost the only things that he records in his *memorieboek* apart from family births and deaths are some property transactions and his election to various positions on the Antwerp council, regardless of whether the authorities were Catholic or Protestant. In 1573, he had become one of the city almoners with responsibility for collecting and distributing alms for the poor, a prestigious role that was normally given to wealthy citizens (Panhuys twice records the considerable sums of money distributed). Later, in 1578, he was appointed to take on further financial responsibilities as *rentmeester* (steward), and finally, in 1581, he was elected as an alderman and appointed *oppertresorier* (senior treasurer to the city).

This rise in social status within the city was evidently matched by an increase in his wealth, as he started to record various property acquisitions. Yet his life was not without pains. In 1578, he records that his wife gave birth to twin boys: the first was born at half past twelve in the afternoon and the second not until half past six. Unsurprisingly, the second had to be baptised straight away by the midwife and died almost immediately; the surviving boy died seven months later. He must have felt bitter, too, when he remembered his earlier satisfaction in 1579 at having bought the Solhof manor house and its estate at Aartselaar, a village just to the south of Antwerp (now close to the airport), when two years later it became the place where his great-niece, Tanneken van Limborgh, was shot through the head by some soldiers. All the entries in the *memorieboek* are brief, and Panhuys gives no indication as to why the soldiers were there or if anything had provoked what appears to be random savagery. Since Spain was notoriously bad at paying its troops, they were often obliged to forage, and on occasion, as in the Spanish Fury, they would ransack complete cities. The Fury was in the past, however, and at the time of her death, the predominantly Catholic southern states had agreed in the Union of Arras to disengage from the revolt of the northern states and accept again the sovereignty of Philip II. Nevertheless, although Farnese did not treat the Netherlanders with the same violent contempt that Alba had shown them, the unruliness of unpaid Spanish troops did not suddenly disappear. Moreover, the war had not officially ended, since Farnese was gradually reconquering those cities in the south that resisted Philip's authority.

Panhuys appears to have been willing to compromise with the Catholic authorities, following the example of William the Silent while he was in Antwerp, by having his children baptised by the Catholic parish priest up until 1578, as recorded in his *memorieboek* (see p. 43). Nevertheless, his later rise in the city hierarchy to become an alderman and the city's senior treasurer show that he accepted the Calvinist domination of Antwerp.[272] He was obviously trusted by the city council, since when the city was being besieged, he was chosen as an envoy to the northern states to ask for an urgent relief force. After the surrender of Antwerp was negotiated in 1585, he and his wife left the city, as did many other Protestants. However, shortly after their arrival in Amsterdam, his wife Margaret died, followed three days later by Panhuys himself, evidently exhausted and dispirited by the lengthy siege, the long journey, and the loss of his wife and of so much that he had built up. The terms of the surrender gave those who would not conform to Catholicism four years in which to take their property with them and leave the city. One thing that Panhuys must have taken with him was the *Paneel*, since it was one of his descendants who would bequeath it to the Mauritshuis museum at The Hague in the nineteenth century.

Johan Radermacher

The third member of the Hooftman/Panhuys firm to appear on the *Paneel* is Johan Radermacher.[273] Coming from Aachen, he probably began life as a Lutheran, but then veered towards Calvinism while he was in Antwerp. His Calvinist convictions may well have strengthened while he was in London, where he was based as Hooftman's agent until 1580, in which year he returned to Antwerp, perhaps to help the ageing Hooftman. If there had been any doubt about his convictions, he would never have been elected an elder of the Dutch stranger church in London, which was firmly Calvinist.

The Church of England at this point was predominantly Calvinist in its theology, and when Cranmer originally persuaded Edward VI's council to allow the Netherlandish refugees to have their own independent 'stranger' church, it was partly to provide a good example of how a Reformed church should set about its business. However, when it was re-established at the start of Elizabeth I's reign (which had followed Mary's persecution), it was given a more limited freedom, being nominally under the jurisdiction of the Bishop of London. At the time that Radermacher left London, that was John Aylmer, who had been tutor to Lady Jane Grey, the Protestant heir selected to replace the Catholic Mary by the dying Edward VI's will. She was soon overthrown, and Aylmer subsequently showed some bravery in arguing the case against the Catholic doctrine of transubstantiation at the first gathering of Convocation after Mary's accession, before going into exile. After his return, he was made Bishop of London in 1577. He soon made himself unpopular both for the action he took against Catholics and for trying to control the Protestants' tendency to ignore the discipline of the established Church; as such, he probably had little time to worry about the Dutch and Italian stranger churches. Someone whom Aylmer would have known in London, however, was Michelangelo Florio, an Italian Protestant who fled to London and who had also taught Lady Jane Grey (as her Italian tutor). Florio was the author of a biography of Lady Jane, the *Historia de la vita e de la morte de l'illustriss. signora Giovanna Graia, gia regina eletta a publicata d'Inghilterra* ('The History of the Life and Death of the Most Illustrious Lady Jane Grey, formerly chosen and proclaimed Queen of England'), which was to be published by Radermacher in Middelburg in 1607.[274] In his preface, Radermacher states that 'it has been considered worthy to be published by people well versed in theology', by which he presumably means those theologians who shared Florio's and his own Protestant faith. He adds that thanks to God it has been kept 'intact for a period of fifty years against the fire of the Antichrist and preserved against every corruption that could easily have consumed and destroyed it.'[275] There could hardly be a stronger indication of Radermacher's religious commitment than his publication of this account of the life and death of someone who was considered by Protestants to be a martyr for her faith.[276]

His sympathy for the Dutch revolt is also made clear when he agrees to assist Marnix van St Aldegonde, a convinced Calvinist and William the Silent's envoy, in his mission to England to acquire weapons and financial support for the rebellion. The failure of this mission was clearly not attributed to Radermacher, who evidently enjoyed the confidence of both sides when he was entrusted with the key to a box of gemstones that was sent to Elizabeth as collateral for the States General's considerable debts to her. Radermacher was to show the contents to Elizabeth and, if she so wished, to hand them over to her in exchange for a receipt.[277]

After his return to Antwerp in 1580, he became involved in both the church, where he was again appointed an elder,[278] and the administration of the city. He thus found himself working again with Marnix when the latter was appointed by William as mayor of the city in November 1583, shortly before Farnese's siege began. Later, both men were involved in negotiating the surrender of the city after a successful blockade of over a year had brought it close to starvation, and both signed the final agreement that gave Protestants four years in which to settle their affairs and leave or to be reconciled with the Catholic Church. A report survives in Radermacher's hand of how the delegation first went out to meet Farnese on 24 July 1585. It describes how they were greeted with refreshments ('een bancket van confituyren ende fruyt') – a courtesy in stark contrast to the unyielding cruelty of Alba but also a shrewd reminder of the comforts that they would continue to lack if the starving city refused to surrender. After returning to Antwerp for consultations, they came back to Farnese on 12 August, but Radermacher's account breaks off after reporting what the delegation had to say the next day.[279]

After the surrender of Antwerp, Radermacher returned to his hometown of Aachen, where he again served on the council and became an elder of the local Calvinist church. Then, in 1599, when the Catholic party gained control, he had to move once more, this time to Middelburg, where his strong sense of duty meant that he was again elected an elder. In this latter part of his life, he clearly maintained his literary and theological interests, and it was there that he published Florio's life of Lady Jane Grey.

His knowledge, hard work and obvious decency evoked this touching tribute from his daughter, Anna, after his death:

Radermacher was recognized by all his contemporaries as a wise, sensible, learned and pious man. He was at home in every branch of knowledge. He had no pretensions, but was rather modest. He was loved by simple people as well as by the noble, for he knew everything. He could live among all kinds of people, whatever their intellectual or spiritual condition, with the result that everyone liked to associate with him. He was sober in food and drink, because he was not physically strong. Nevertheless, he reached the blessed age of 79. He retained all of his faculties of memory, understanding, hearing, sight, smell and taste up to the end of his life, which is amazing. God also saved him from all the typical ailments of old age. Not one of his children was harmed physically or mentally during his lifetime. That is why we can surely say that our parents were amongst the 'blessed of the Lord'.[280]

Emanuel van Meteren

The most obvious source for van Meteren's life after the time that the *Paneel* was painted is his own *Comentarius* (see Chapter 5). Yet although he records family births and deaths alongside trade difficulties, and makes reference to key political and military events, the *Comentarius* reveals relatively little about van Meteren's own personal character and feelings. The reform of the calendar from 1583 leads him to note that the birth of a daughter in 1582/3 could be recorded either as 30 December 1582 (old style) or 9 January 1583 (new style). He also records the birth of his first grandchild and some medical ailments, but he notes little else about his family that year.

Similarly, he records little more than the bare bones of his international business problems: the need to get safe conducts from William the Silent; fines imposed on Netherlandish ship-owners when William refused to release English ships used for trade with the Spanish; the gradual shift of trade to Hamburg; and finally, the fact that in 1585, after the fall of Antwerp, all trade there comes to an end. On a more personal note, he records that he was chosen as consul to represent the Netherlandish merchants based in London in 1583. There is no mention, however, of his own role as an intermediary that year when Orazio Palavicino, the Genoese merchant, financier and occasional ambassador for Elizabeth I, was trying to raise a loan of £25,000 for the Earl of Leicester to equip his troops before going out to the Netherlands. According to Stone, this scheme failed once van Meteren let slip how risky the venture was, at which point both London and Netherlandish merchants withdrew.[281]

On the military and political front, we hear of the Spanish Fury, the Pacification of Ghent and the subsequent arrival of Don Juan, and then the latter's death and replacement by Farnese. We learn of Farnese's gradual recovery of lost territory, but again there is only the occasional hint of van Meteren's own feelings, as when he describes the fate of Mechelen, which was, he writes, 'iammerlijk gheplondert' ('pitifully sacked'). We also hear about his father-in-law's grievously heavy financial losses when the Spanish sack Breda. Prior to this, he had mentioned the return of the Catholic south's allegiance to Philip followed by the Act of Abjuration, in which the seven northern provinces formally renounced their allegiance, transferring it to the Duke of Anjou. Next, we hear of the 'French Fury', Anjou's treacherous attempt to capture Antwerp in January 1583, its humiliating failure, and his withdrawal to France.

After this, he records the assassination of William the Silent, the fall of Antwerp and the arrival of the Earl of Leicester with the English expeditionary force in 1586. At this point, unsurprisingly, some key moments of English history are mentioned: the Babington plot to assassinate Elizabeth I in 1586 and replace her with Mary Queen of Scots, her Catholic cousin, along with the execution of the latter in 1587 and the failure of the Armada in 1588. Once more, van Meteren's feelings are clear: the storm that scattered and destroyed much of the Spanish fleet is described as 'een wonder werk Godes' ('a wondrous work of God'). Very occasionally, van Meteren includes events from further afield that influence European power struggles: he mentions Sebastian of Portugal's death in Morocco after a rash military adventure, which opened the way for Philip II to lay claim to Portugal and its overseas empire; the religious civil wars in France, in which Philip intervenes, are also briefly mentioned when van Meteren records how the Guises drive Henri III out of Paris, thereby forcing him into an alliance with the Protestant Henri of Navarre, the future Henri IV. He then switches into what one can only describe as a fast-forward mode as he alludes to the assassination of both Henris in 1589 and 1610, respectively.[282]

Reading the latter part of the *Comentarius* long after the events it describes have happened, it all seems something of a whistle-stop tour, and presumably by the time the last entries were made, van Meteren's mind had already turned to the writing of his history of the struggle for independence, which he planned to be much more detailed. In the entry for 1583, he notes that as well as being chosen as consul for the Netherlandish merchants living in London, he was starting in November of that year to gather material for his history from his cousin Abraham Ortels (Ortelius). At the end of his last entry, he signs his full name, Emanuel van Meteren, and adds his motto, 'God met ons' ('God with us'), which is the meaning of his first name.

The political events mentioned in the *Comentarius* clearly provide little more than a context or timeline against which to set the family events that he records, but as well as collecting material from Ortelius and others, he will have found plenty more information in the archive that he was building up as consul to the Netherlandish merchants in London and in the letters that he received from his wide range of contacts when serving as postmaster for the Netherlandish community there. For example, while he only devotes a single sentence in his *Comentarius* to the arrival of Don Juan in the Netherlands as Philip II's new Governor, a much fuller account can be found in a letter written in French and dated 11 January 1577 that he received from Marnix.[283] Apart from beginning and ending the letter with polite enquiries about van Meteren's health, the whole letter is devoted to the arrival of Don Juan. Marnix is writing from Brussels, where the States General (representing all the provinces of the Netherlands) had been meeting together after the agreement of the Pacification of Ghent (see p. 142), and he reports that although he had gone there to suggest various offers of help from Germany, 'la grande irresolution des Etats a tourné le fruict de ma negotiations [sic] en vain dilays' ('the indecision of the Estates [about whether to compromise with Don Juan] has destroyed any possible benefit that might have arisen from [his] negotiation with frustrating delays'). He goes on to record the arrangements to safeguard Don Juan (a guard of 3,000 men and hostages) but reports that the Estates are divided on this matter too, with some members saying that there should be no negotiations until all Spanish soldiers had left. In the meantime, the theology department of the strongly Catholic Leuven University have confirmed that there is nothing prejudicial to Catholicism in the Pacification of Ghent, and the Council of State have said that there is nothing in it prejudicial to the king's authority. In response, Don Juan states 'qu'il chemine de droit pied' ('that he will act honestly'). To this, Marnix says with weary scepticism, 'les povres gens se laissent abuser de semblable mines' ('the poor people let themselves be hoaxed by such outward shows or pretences'). As a committed Calvinist who clearly does not trust Don Juan at all, it is probably with a certain malicious pleasure that he adds that his foe has confined his mother to a nunnery and that she now says that he is not the illegitimate son of Charles V, but of a baker. He notes that the time and circumstances seem to fit this claim and that quite a few people believe it. Even if Marnix himself believes the story to be fake, he seems to be quite happy to pass on a rumour that discredits an opponent. Another rumour that he mentions is the belief in some Spanish quarters that Elizabeth I might make English ships available to aid the withdrawal of the Spanish troops. Marnix is not sure whether she would do anything so ill-advised. (She did not; most of the Spanish troops withdrew to Luxembourg which had not signed the Pacification of Ghent.)

With material as richly detailed as this, the sources for van Meteren's history become much clearer. It is noteworthy that when he starts to gather the necessary information, he clearly thinks that he is describing the emergence of a new country, referring to it as the *Vaderlande* (Fatherland), although its precise boundaries were still to be determined by the long-drawn-out war that lay ahead. This major history of the Netherlandish rebellion against Philip, titled *Belgische ofte Nederlantsche historie van onsen tijden* ('A Belgian or Netherlandish History of Our Times'; hereafter referred to as his *History*), was to occupy him for much of the rest of his life. Although it was first written in Dutch, it was, in fact, first published in German. The Universal Short Title Catalogue lists 111 editions published between 1596 and 1647, of

20. *Johan Radermacher* by an unknown artist, 1607.
(Rijksdienst voor het Cultureel Erfgoed, Amersfoort)

21. Portrait of Emanuel van Meteren and his wife
Hester van Corput, attributed to Joris Hoefnagel, from
Comentarius by Emanuel van Meteren, 1576.

Anno 1576.
ætia. 32.

Sÿ was lanck
vÿf voeten 1½ duim
gemeten, enghe[?]e
voeten va̅ 1½ duÿme

22. A double-page spread from the Old Testament part of the *Complutensian Bible*, 1520, showing the Vulgate translation in the centre of each page, but a double column of Greek (with interlinear Latin translation) in the centre of the double-page spread.

(Chained Library, Hereford Cathedral)

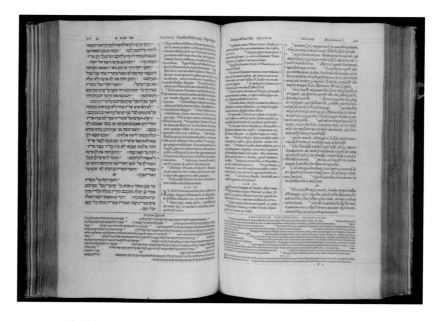

23. A double-page spread from the Old Testament section of Plantin's *Biblia Regia*, first printed 1568. *(Yale University Library)*

BIBLIA SACRA

HEBRAICÈ,
CHALDAICÈ,
GRÆCE,&
Latine

PIETATIS CONCORDIÆ. Iſaiæ,11

PHILIPPI II. REG. CATHOL. PIETATE,
ET STVDIO AD SACROSANCTÆ
ECCLESIÆ VSVM

CHRISTOPH. PLANTINVS EXCVD. ANTVERPIÆ.

24. The opening title page of Plantin's *Biblia Regia*, based on Isaiah 11: 6–7.

25. *Portrait of Maerten de Vos* engraved by Aegidius Sadeler
after a painting by Joseph Heintz the Elder, 1592. De Vos's
motto, *puro astu et labore*, can be seen at the top.

(Rijksmuseum, Amsterdam)

26. Watercolour of Stonehenge by Lucas d'Heere in his *Short Description of England, Scotland and Ireland*, 1573–1575.

(British Library, London)

27. *An Allegory of the Tudor Succession* by Lucas d'Heere, 1572. Henry VIII is shown with all three of his children who reigned after him successively.

(Sudeley Castle, Gloucestershire)

28. *Palace of Nonsuch* by Joris Hoefnagel in *Civitates Orbis Terrarum* (vol. 5),
first printed 1598. Notice the many characters in the foreground. *(Ghent University Library)*

29. *View of Seville* by Joris Hoefnagel in *Civitates Orbis Terrarum* (vol. 5),
first printed 1598. *(Ghent University Library)*

30. *Patience*, the opening illustration in *Patientia* by
Joris Hoefnagel, 1569. *(Bibliothèque Municipale, Rouen)*

Chapter 12

31. *St Thomas* by Maerten de Vos, 1573. This grisaille image is on the left exterior wing of the triptych painted for the Furriers' altar in Our Lady's Church (now the cathedral) and is clearly intended to look like a statue.

(Koninklijk Museum voor Schone Kunsten, Antwerp)

32. Portrait of Antonius Anselmo, his wife Johanna Hooftman
and their children by Maerten de Vos, 1577.

(Musées Royaux des Beaux-Arts, Brussels)

Omnia ego foueo et nutrio, quæ terra creauit Nil sine me vitam ducere namque potest

33. *Air* by Maerten de Vos, engraved by Adriaen Collaert, 1580–84.

(Rijksmuseum, Amsterdam)

34. Folio XX in 'Aier' in the *Four Elements* by Joris Hoefnagel, 1575–89.
(National Gallery of Art, Washington, DC)

35. Folio LIV in 'Ignis' in the *Four Elements* by Joris Hoefnagel, 1575–89.
(National Gallery of Art, Washington, DC)

36. *The Four Philosophers* by Peter Paul Rubens, 1611–12. Lipsius sits beneath a bust of Seneca. On either side of him are his future editor, Joannes Woverius, and the artist's brother, Philip, and on the left is a self-portrait of the artist.

(Pitti Palace, Florence)

Chapter 13

37. *Amicitiae Monumentum (Allegory for Abraham Ortelius)*
by Joris Hoefnagel, 1593.

(Plantin-Moretus Museum, Antwerp)

which seventy-four were in German and only twenty-four in Dutch. Other editions were in Latin or French, and there were some partial translations into English as well. It would be fair to say that van Meteren was writing for an international audience and that his *History* played a major part in shaping European understanding of what had happened in the Netherlands and its widersignificance.[284]

It was not intended as a 'history' as it was first written, however, but more as a series of *memorien* (notes) that could be used by some more 'gheleerden History-schryver' ('scholarly historian') to produce a formal history, written in 'een heerlicke ende aenghename style' ('a grand and agreeable style').[285] He had therefore sent copies of these notes to various friends, such as Ortelianus, his first cousin once removed, and Marnix. He may well have hoped that the latter would turn his raw material into a formal history that could be published. As William the Silent's right-hand man, Marnix was not only very much involved in the events described, but he was also a writer of some distinction, having written a satire on abuses in the Roman Catholic Church, *De roomsche byen-korf* ('The Roman Beehive'), and a metrical version of the Psalms (early versions of a number of his psalm translations can be found in Radermacher's *album*). In fact, it was van Meteren's own plain account that was first published after it had been translated into German: Ortelius had sent it to the printer Frans Hogenberg in Cologne, who had had it translated to provide an accompanying narrative to go with some engravings of the Netherlands Revolt that he was printing. In an age without the protection of copyright, there were soon other German editions published without van Meteren's agreement, and then a Latin translation that incorporated additions by 'papist writers'. In order to defend the integrity of his work, van Meteren quite understandably took up the offer of a Delft printer to publish a version in Dutch for presentation to the States General, and so a revised edition in Dutch that took the story up to the death of Philip II in 1598 was then printed in 1599.[286]

Arguably, the *History* helped to establish not only a new sense of national identity but also the language that was an integral part of that identity. The desire to establish Dutch as an independent language and not simply a dialect of German presumably lay behind Radermacher's incomplete grammar and the vernacular poetry written by the likes of Lucas d'Heere and Joris Hoefnagel. Ironically, the very plainness of style that van Meteren was ashamed of may well have helped it spread. Marnix had made clear his reservations about the style in another letter to van Meteren, in which he wrote that he had heard that the latter was thinking of having it translated into Latin; he recommended that he choose someone who can improve his style in the process since in the original Dutch it is 'een weynich slap' ('a little feeble').[287] Nevertheless, the majority of editions were in neither Latin nor Dutch, but German.

Although a national history, especially one which describes the emergence of a new state, can be seen as a patriotic endeavour, historians across Europe were not led by patriotism to ignore what 'old-fashioned' historians might call 'facts'. The concept of a subjective 'truth' had not yet been exploited to spread confusion. It is true that Marnix reports the rumours about Don Juan's parentage (see above), but he does not actually claim that they are true. Although the *History* was clearly seen by Catholics as presenting a Protestant account of what had happened, and by the Spanish as representing the arguments of rebels, the Dutch States General was nevertheless unhappy with some of the things that van Meteren wrote, as were various synods of the Reformed Church.[288] The reason for this was not only that van Meteren had had access to sources that the government would clearly have preferred to remain confidential, but also that his intentions were eirenic, and he does not regard any party as being beyond criticism, as can be seen in these excerpts from the preface to the first Dutch edition. He observes that: 'A History of this kind could give the inhabitants of the Netherlands and other nations an insight into the actual course of events of these wars and provide them with a mirror showing God's just verdicts and providential grace....'[289]

This understanding of history as revealing the unfolding of God's providential purposes sounds distinctly Reformed, although not as obviously partisan as when, in a letter to Ortelius, he specifically attributes quarrels amongst Catholics (such as that which led to the expulsion of the Jesuits from France) to 'Godes voorsightigheyt' ('God's providence').[290] He is more even-handed in his *History* than this might suggest, as he criticises almost all parties to the conflict. The value of his account, he writes in his preface, is firstly that:

Roman Catholics might realise the brutal crime of which they are guilty by trying to enforce the Catholic religion everywhere in the Netherlands by means of rigorous edicts [the 'placards']; through these measures they have tried to violate the innate consciences of the free Netherlander using inquisitorial methods of investigation. In this way they have given the Prince an opportunity to bring in the Spaniards under the pretext of maintaining the Romish religion and with their help to suppress the freedom of the Netherlands, to usurp the riches and to establish an absolute rule of Spanish origin, thus acting very much against the interests of the Catholic religion; for in this way these Catholics drove the cautious 'Political' Magistrates (who were opposed to Spain) into a corner and forced them to look to the Reformed Church for assistance and to ally themselves with it.

The placards referred to above were the edicts that the state used as punitive measures in support of Catholic attempts to suppress religious beliefs that the Church authorities deemed heretical. Not only were Spanish attempts 'to violate the innate consciences of the free Netherlander' a 'brutal crime', they were also counter-productive, since they drove the 'political' members of the ruling class to turn to the Reformed Church for support, as William the Silent himself had been forced to do. Van Meteren's use of the term 'political' here echoes the French term *politiques*, which was used in their religious wars to describe those who thought that rather than supporting the Catholic League in their rebellion against Henri III (who was himself a Catholic), compromise and tolerance were the only way forward if France was not to be completely devastated.

The religious neutrality of the *politiques* who fail to recognise God's providential working through history also comes in for criticism, however. For van Meteren, they must not be lukewarm, but should 'recognise in the outcome of the various events the wise and righteous judgements of God, and moreover find that He does not give his commandments in vain but that He wants to be served and honoured in this world with body and soul.'

He also criticises excessively zealous reformers: 'those who adhere to the Reformed Religion might learn from this history the damaging effects of their over-impetuous and immoderate religious fervour, that has led more than once to great confusion in the various provinces.' His thinking here may well be in regards to the aggressiveness of the Reformed regime in Ghent, whose persecution of Catholics helped to swing the support of the predominantly Catholic southern provinces behind Philip II. These criticisms were excised from subsequent editions, however. After his death, subsequent editions not only removed criticisms of the Reformed Church but also material about contemporary events in other countries. With these redactions, the work of someone who was international in outlook and who travelled regularly from London to the European mainland was turned from a European history into a much narrower, nationalistic one.

Van Meteren's lack of experience with the realities of publishing is revealed, incidentally, not only in his hoping that a more experienced writer would use his notes to produce a more polished history but also in his evidently naïve enquiry to his cousin, Ortelius, about the chances of being paid for his work. Ortelius replies that he hardly knows what to say, but, as many writers have since discovered, authors don't usually make money from their books. The best that can usually be hoped for is that the printer may give you a few copies. Ortelius even adds that some authors actually pay the printer to get their book published.[291]

Abraham Ortelius

Ortelius himself was also a merchant, and although he does not appear in the *Paneel*, he had links with everyone in it. Moreover, his commitment to maintaining friendships with all his contacts both by correspondence and in his travels across Europe could be seen as typifying the spirit behind the *Paneel*. In 1575, he had made a journey across the southern part of the Spanish Netherlands and on to Lorraine and Trier with Johan Vivien (Vivianus) and two other friends: Hans van Schille, author of the first book on military architecture to be printed in the Netherlands, and Hieronymus Scholiers, a scholar who was skilled in reading and transcribing manuscript texts. Plantin would later publish an account of this journey that Ortelius and Vivianus wrote together.

Vivianus was another skilled writer who wrote paraphrases in Latin verse of the Old Testament Books of Proverbs and Songs (many of his translations can be found copied into Radermacher's *album*). Vivianus was also a noted collector of coins, which provided valuable evidence for humanists piecing together early history.[292] There are many links between him and other members of the group of merchant scholars around Hooftman, Panhuys and Radermacher. During the Calvinist rule of Antwerp, he was an almoner of the city and must therefore have worked with van Meteren. After the fall of Antwerp, he withdrew to Aachen, where he became very friendly with Radermacher and was godfather to two of his daughters, Hester (1586) and Johanna (1590). Furthermore, two of his own daughters married two of the sons of Panhuys, Catharina and Margaretha, who married Bartholomaeus and Gillis, respectively (the two youngest Panhuys children shown on the *Paneel*). In addition, Margaretha, the elder sister of Bartholomaeus and Gillis (standing just behind her kneeling elder sister on the *Paneel*) married Nicolaas Malapert, who was the brother of Vivianus's own wife.

After the Spanish Fury in November 1576, Ortelius unsurprisingly decided to move abroad, travelling to England and Ireland. He had many friends and scholarly contacts there, such as Hoefnagel and d'Heere, not to mention his cousins, Emanuel van Meteren and Daniel Rogers, and his nephew,

Ortelianus. He was particularly eager to learn what Martin Frobisher had learnt on his return from a search for the much-hoped-for Northwest Passage to the Pacific.[293] Crucially, it was on this visit that Ortelius met and encouraged William Camden, who had just started the research for his great account of the topography and antiquities of Great Britain and Ireland, *Britannia*. Camden's research included not only travelling to the places he was describing but also researching written sources, both printed and manuscript. He continued to work on *Britannia* after its first publication in 1586, and the last edition to be published in his lifetime (the folio edition of 1607) contained maps by Christopher Saxton and John Norden, as well as engravings of medals and historical sites. It is a work worthy of being compared with Ortelius's own. Camden acknowledged the inspiration given by Ortelius, that 'great Restorer of old Geography'[294], and, like Ortelius himself, his careful investigation of primary historical resources provided a valuable basis for further research. The fruit of Ortelius's own continuing research can be seen first in his *Synonymia Cartographica* (1578), which was praised by Lipsius[295] and which is a kind of concordance providing both the original and the modern names of places important in secular and biblical history. Naturally progressing from this is Ortelius's *Parergon* (Supplement), which contains historical maps that he had designed himself and which, from 1579, he adds to the modern maps of his own *Theatrum*. One map, dating from 1579, illustrates the missionary journeys of St Paul. Since it was Ortelius who provided advice to de Vos when he was painting his five pictures of St Paul's life for Hooftman while Radermacher was away in London, it seems quite likely that this experience triggered his interest and perhaps influenced him.[296] The 'theatre' of the world that he had set out in his great atlas has now become, as it were, the stage set on which its history was played out.

Ortelius was perhaps more an antiquarian than a cartographer, but in the latter capacity he did put forward one notable idea. Having noticed how the coastlines of the Americas and of Africa and Europe complemented each other, he was the first person to propose the theory that we now know as continental drift (although he clearly had no thought of plate tectonics). His insight was not finally confirmed, however, until the twentieth century.

After Antwerp was starved into surrendering to Farnese's Catholic forces in 1585, all members of the city's civic guard, including Ortelius, were vetted for religious orthodoxy (i.e. loyalty to the Catholic Church), and those who were considered suspect were required to surrender their arms. Ortelius, with his Protestant family background and friendship with such prominent Protestants as Peeter Heyns, was among their number. Although the decision was subsequently reversed and his arms restored to him, not all suspicions were allayed, and the following year, the privy council asked the city council whether Ortelius was a Lutheran. In reply, they confirmed that his weapons had been confiscated because of a misunderstanding and that he was a good Catholic. Although they were certainly right in saying that he was not a Lutheran, it becomes clear from later correspondence with his nephew Ortelianus that he was by no means committed to the Catholic Church (or very probably, to any other denomination).[297]

Ortelius regarded Ortelianus as his protégé, and attempted to guide his reading and intellectual development when he was a young man. Despite this, it was not until Ortelianus was thirty that his uncle wrote to him in 1592 suggesting some theological reading. Ortelianus had evidently been reading works by a fourteenth-century German Dominican priest and mystic named Johannes Tauler, as well as works by Nicolaus van Esch (Eschius), a sixteenth-century Dutch priest, and had written to Ortelius that he had found them tainted by superstition. As an alternative, Ortelius suggested that he might try *Paradoxes* by Sebastian Franck. Franck had originally been a Catholic priest but had subsequently preached the Reformation at Nuremberg as a Lutheran, before moving to Strasbourg and becoming an Anabaptist. After all this, he complained that the Anabaptists, like every other Christian body, were too dogmatic. He argued that every denomination was at fault and that the only doctrine a Christian needed to know was contained in the Ten Commandments and Apostles Creed; he claimed even the Bible itself contained inconsistencies that could only be resolved within the inner spiritual life. To recommend the writings of someone whom every denomination of the time regarded as a heretic was so risky that that Ortelius writes under the pseudonym Bartholus Aramejus (an anagram of Abraham Ortelius) and refers to Sebastian Franck's writings simply as 'Paradoxa S. F.'[298] To recommend such a writer tells us a good deal about the older Ortelius's lack of commitment to any particular church as an institution with its own specific doctrines. It suggests that little has occurred to change his mind since he wrote disparagingly of the 'Catholic evil, Geuzen fever and Huguenot dysentery' (see p. 68). Detachment of this kind is not inconsistent with being a member of the Family of Love, but equally one senses a certain reluctance to commit to any organisation. It sounds more as though he is thinking 'a plague on all your houses'. Certainly, in the absence of hard evidence such as exists in the case of Plantin, it is impossible to argue confidently that he was a Familist.[299]

Daniel Rogers

It is hard to avoid the feeling that in the case of Ortelius's and van Meteren's first cousin once removed, Daniel Rogers, a significant academic and poetic talent was left unfulfilled. A few poems by Rogers survive, published in a slim volume by Plantin and in various *alba amicorum*, but he never completed his history of the ancient Britons (although he did provide some material for Camden's *Britannia*). Instead, from the 1570s, he was caught up in the diplomatic efforts demanded by the threat of Catholic Spain. He spent much time in the service of Elizabeth I, travelling abroad to liaise with both William the Silent and the Protestant German princes, and on one occasion arranging a loan of £20,000 for the Dutch States General; he also travelled with Sir Philip Sidney on his mission to woo the support of the German princes. On one occasion, his mission was to persuade William the Silent and John Casimir, the Count Palatine, to form an alliance against Pope Gregory XIII. Later, on a mission to Emperor Rudolf II in 1580, he was captured and held to ransom. The English court did little to help his release, although finally, after his friends made a considerable fuss, he was released in 1584 for a ransom of £200. To repay this, he was authorised to raise a levy on the English clergy, something which one imagines was much more easily said than done. Elizabeth also offered him the treasureship of St Paul's Cathedral, but since he was not ordained, he was unable to accept this. Later, he received some recompense when he was appointed as clerk of the Privy Council, and he also became the MP for Newport in Cornwall. As Palavicino was later to learn (see p. 170), being an ambassador for Elizabeth was not a rewarding task.[300]

CHAPTER 11

The next generation

The Panhuys family

After the death of Peeter Panhuys, his oldest surviving son, Bartholomaeus, took over his *memorieboek* and continued this family record of births and deaths.[301] He begins by adding a note to his father's entry for 1582 which records the birth of his youngest sibling, the third Peeter (the first two both having died during childhood). Next, he records the surrender of Antwerp in 1585 after a thirteen-month siege and the subsequent death of his mother on 10 November that year, followed by his father's death three days later. Apart from his description of his mother as being of 'zaligher memorie' ('blessed memory') and expressing the hope that God will give them both 'een vrolijke verrysenisse' ('a joyful resurrection'), he expresses no emotion. Nevertheless, it is easy, not to mention painful, to imagine the disorientation and distress felt by the Panhuys children when, having been obliged to abandon their home in Antwerp and move to Amsterdam, their parents died within days of their arrival and within a few days of each other. Their seven surviving children's subsequent reactions and careers tell us a good deal about the impact of Philip's determined persecution of Protestants and the breaking up of the tolerant civilisation that was centred on Antwerp, but also tell us something about the upbringing the children had. Their subsequent lives place them firmly in the Protestant camp, and there is no hint at all of any Familist upbringing. I consider them briefly in the paragraphs below.

After their exile from the cosmopolitanism of Antwerp, there seems to be an initial and very understandable withdrawal to the safely familiar, since Anna, the oldest surviving child (born 1565), marries Willem van Schuyl in April 1586 within five months of her parents' death. Schuyl, like her father, came from Walhorn. He was presumably a man of some substance, but probably more important to Anna would have been that he came from a family that her parents had known and which could be trusted to provide stability. He had worked as the royal agent in the county of Daelhem and Fauquemont, which was a small territory that had come under the sway of the Duchy of Brabant in the Middle Ages. Philip II's inheritance of the Duchy from his father had been uncontentious, and I doubt that Schuyl's employment as his agent proves anything conclusive about either his religious or political sympathies, any more than working as a civil servant today implies support for the party in power at the time. (Anna is the kneeling girl at the front right of the *Paneel*, looking confidently out of the picture.)

The next Panhuys child was the first Peeter (born 1566), who looks out from the *Paneel* a good deal more apprehensively, with his father's hand resting reassuringly on his shoulder. He, however, had died in December 1576 in Mons, where he had presumably been sent for safety shortly after the Spanish Fury had devastated Antwerp, perhaps with some of the Malapert family.[302]

Margaretha (just behind Anna; born 1568) married Nicolaas Malapert, whose sister Catharina had married Vivianus, the friend of Ortelius who had journeyed with him across the southern Low Countries and had co-authored the book about their travels that Plantin had published (see p. 158). The Malaperts were a merchant family from Mons who had settled in Antwerp and would have been well known to the Panhuys family. Like them, they were probably Protestant: in a secret report by Jerónimo de Curiel, an agent of Philip II in Antwerp, they are described as Calvinists (*de la seta calbenista*), along with Gillis Hooftman and Peeter Panhuys (see p. 40). As a Protestant, Nicolaas had left Antwerp after its fall and moved to Bremen.[303]

In 1601, Bartholomeus (standing between his mother's knees; born 1570) married Catharina Vivien, the daughter of Catharina Malapert and Vivianus (whose own father had also married a Malapert, Barbara). Bartholomaeus gives an account of his university studies from which it is clear that the enforced withdrawal from Antwerp did not mean a withdrawal from wider European connections. In studying the law, he attended not only the university at Leiden, where he had been enrolled by his father, but also Heidelberg, Padua, Siena and Basel, where he obtained his law degree. Finally, he was made a doctor of law at Orléans in France. (One university noticeably absent from this long list is the nearby and strongly Catholic university at Leuven.) After this, he practises law at Spiers in Germany and later represents the state of Holland in France in a case dealing with compensation for a ship that had been seized near La Rochelle. Having learnt at first-hand about German and French legal practice, he then goes to The Hague to learn Dutch practice.

Gillis (on his mother's lap; born 1574) also marries within the close social and family group, marrying his sister-in-law, Maria Vivien (a daughter of Vivianus and sister of Bartholomaeus's wife, Catharina), in 1602.

Johan (born in 1575 and so not on the *Paneel*) first marries Geertruit Montens, the daughter of Godevaert Montens, who was treasurer and general steward to Prince Maurice, whom he succeeds in both these posts after his father-in-law's death. When he marries again, it is more within the family's social group. His new wife is Elizabeth van der Meulen, a daughter of Suzanna Malapert, and a sister of Catherina and Nicolaas.

In 1601, Barbara (born in 1579, thus after the *Paneel* was painted) marries Jan Hesse, whose mother was a Margaretha van Nispen and appears to have been a cousin of Gillis Hooftman's third wife.

Peeter, the youngest of the siblings (born 1582), marries Maria Godin in 1606. She, as far as I can establish, was a first cousin of her brothers' mothers-in-law, Catherina and Susanna Malapert, and also of her brother-in-law, Nicolaas Malapert.

Finally, after the death of her first husband, Barbara marries Caspar van Vosbergen. Together with his brother-in-law, Bartholomeus, he was a guardian of Johan Panhuys's children after the latter's death.

My purpose in testing the reader's perseverance with this convoluted recital of family history – it was not only the Habsburgs who intermarried – is to draw attention to a certain narrowing of cultural horizons. Exiled Protestant families, having lost their immediate social roots, naturally looked amongst their own kind for partners. The opportunity for wider relationships enjoyed by the previous generation when they moved to Antwerp had disappeared. The careers of two of the sons of Peeter Panhuys also confirm the hardening of a confessional divide across the Low Countries. As mentioned above, Johan succeeded his father-in-law as treasurer and general steward to Prince Maurice, and after his early death, he was succeeded in turn by his brother Bartholomaeus. In addition, Barbara's second husband, Caspar von Vosbergen, was a friend and confidant of the Prince, although he held no official post. In other words, the family are very much supporters of Prince Maurice, the eldest son of William the Silent by his second marriage (Maurice's elder half-brother would be held as a hostage by the Spanish until he died). Maurice was not only a pioneering military strategist who succeeded in driving the Spanish out of the north and east of the Low Countries, but he also became theologically uncompromising in his support for the Gomarists (strict Calvinists) as opposed to the Arminians (who wished to soften the doctrine of predestination by allowing more scope for the influence of free will). This may have partly been political opportunism on his part to gain allies when he turned against Johan van Oldenbarnevelt, who supported the Arminians and who had negotiated the Twelve Years' Truce with Spain against the wishes of Maurice, and whom the latter had subsequently executed. Whatever his motives for supporting the Gomarists, there is no doubt at all that Maurice did not share the Familists' tolerant lack of concern for outward doctrines and observances, and it seems highly unlikely that the next generation of the Panhuys family would have done so either, since they were so closely involved in the Prince's inner circle.

Orazio Palavicino, Hooftman's son-in-law

Orazio Palavicino (c. 1540–1600), who was to marry Hooftman's daughter Anna (kneeling left foreground with her mother's hand stretched out to touch her), would certainly have known both Gillis Hooftman (a fellow creditor of Elizabeth I) and Peeter Panhuys. His activities before he married Anna quite late in life throw some light on English interventions in the Eighty Years' War, as well as revealing the international nature of Antwerp life. Anna Hooftman's marriage to him confirms once again how the next generation's marriage choices mark a clear move to one side of the religious divide. These facts justify, I hope, my decision to introduce this stranger into our group, whose varied and active life cannot be dealt with quickly!

Palavicino came from a noble Genoese family who made a great deal of money as lessors of the monopolistic mining rights of the papal alum mines at Tolfa. Alum was used as a dye-fixer for textiles and was essential for the production of woollen cloth, a key part of both the English and Netherlandish economies, and therefore commercially extremely valuable (see p. 31). Palavicino's father and uncle controlled the importation of the ore from 1541, and he and his two brothers were strategically established as agents of the family business in London, Rome and Antwerp, from where they oversaw the family business.[304] When their father died in 1581, he left them an enormous fortune, estimated at 400,000 scudi.[305]

Orazio was the family's agent in Antwerp.[306] Before their monopoly expired in 1578, the family sought to undermine the new grantees by buying up alum stocks in advance and negotiating monopoly agreements with the major consumers in England and the Low Countries. The plan backfired in England both because of Burghley's enlightened anxieties about the consumer (he was Elizabeth I's Lord High Treasurer at this time) and because of attempts by the customs official Thomas Smythe to manipulate the same markets to his own advantage. In the Low Countries, however, the Palavicino family were able to negotiate a six-year monopoly of alum imports, in return for which they loaned stocks of alum allegedly worth about £30,000 to the States General, who could then sell it to the cloth industry to raise money to support the war effort. This loan was underwritten by Elizabeth I and the City of London, which meant that Palavicino's personal financial interests were now aligned with English policy. Although the loan never was repaid, the interest payments were extremely lucrative, and by 1593 (when Elizabeth stopped them[307]), Palavicino had received £45,479 11s. 11d., a sum far greater than the estimated (and disputed) value of the alum. Claims for outstanding interest were still being made by his son, Toby, as late as the 1620s. During the early 1580s, Palavicino moved to Paris, where he ran the family's business and where his international trading contacts made him a very useful source of intelligence to the English government. He was also used to transmit funds by bills of exchange to support the Duke of Anjou's campaigns against the Spanish in the Low Countries.[308] (This English support may have been motivated not only because Anjou was fighting the Spanish, but also by the need to compensate for the affront that he and the French royal family had suffered when Elizabeth decided not to marry him. These motives were probably considered to have justified the expense despite Anjou's spectacular military incompetence and political untrustworthiness.)

Like Hooftman, Palavicino had very diverse business interests, including banking. In 1591, he secured a portion of Sir Edward Stafford's licence for the export of undressed cloths, which were sold to Merchant Adventurers; less creditably, he is reputed to have speculated in corn in times of dearth. His main source of income, however, was lending money on a large scale, which brought with it political implications. In 1585, after his failure two years previously, he successfully negotiated a loan from city merchants for the strongly Protestant Earl of Leicester as the latter prepared to lead the English military support for the Dutch revolt against Philip II after the fall of Antwerp. Then, in 1592, he acted as agent for a consortium of Dutch merchants for the purchase of the large quantity of pepper from a captured Spanish carrack, the *Madre de Dios*, that Elizabeth had unjustly claimed for her share as a partner in the jointly funded expedition that had captured it (despite the fact that her investment had been proportionately smaller). Palavicino suggested that part of the payment would be the repayment of his loan for the alum offered to the States General to finance their war against the Spanish. From this, we can clearly see he was working for his own interests and not simply those of the Dutch merchants. Fortunately for Palavicino, he was finally outbid by some London merchants, who appear to have received a very poor bargain. He did, however, buy £24,000 worth of other goods from the captured ship; the arrangements were sufficiently suspect that protracted litigation followed, the aftershocks of which were still being fended off with masterly delaying tactics in 1610 by Sir Oliver Cromwell, uncle of the Lord Protector of the same name and Anna Hooftman's second husband, ten years after Palavicino's death and nearly twenty years after the original capture of the *Madre de Dios*.[309]

When he was first in London, Palavicino was probably the young Italian who was detained at the Portuguese ambassador's house for attending Mass.[310] One of his brothers, Camillo, was a Jesuit priest,[311] but Palavicino's allegiance to the Catholic church was strained by the Pope's arrest and torture of another brother, Fabritio, through the Inquisition. This had occurred not for reasons of heresy but because of the part the family had played in raising financial support for the States General's rebellion against Philip. This exploitation of the papal monopoly that they had been granted, followed by their efforts to undermine it for those who succeeded them, was as good as heresy in the Pope's eyes, who doubtless considered his financial prosperity coincided with whatever was 'most advantageous to the service of God and the weakening of the enemies of his Holy Name?'[312] By 1583, the English authorities noted that Palavicino was 'of no church' (that is, not attending any church) and in 1584, Horatio was condemned by the Inquisition *in absentia* and his goods in Genoa seized. Now perforce Protestant, Palavicino chose to use the language of the Puritan 'godly' in his correspondence with Walsingham, the more Protestant of Elizabeth's two principal councillors, describing the Pope as the Antichrist, but writes less intemperately when communicating with Burghley. Despite his tailoring his language to his audience, he seems to have been sincere, at least in his commitment to opposing Catholic Philip II, but it would be very difficult to argue that he was driven solely by theological commitment as opposed to commercial self-interest and family loyalty.

When it came to marriage, however, he certainly looked for a Protestant wife, while not neglecting financial and social issues. He had first approached François de la Noue, the leader of the Huguenots at La Rochelle (another key trading port), who was a distinguished soldier and very much a Huguenot hero (a poem celebrating his bravery when he lost his left arm at the siege of Fontenay in 1570 can be found in Radermacher's *album*). In 1572, de la Noue led a force of Huguenots and Dutch exiles across the French border to capture the town of Valenciennes. From there, he had led a daring raid on Brussels in an unsuccessful attempt to capture Alba.[313] The tide of war was to turn after the St Bartholomew's Day massacres later that year, which abruptly halted French Huguenot support for the Dutch rebels. Subsequently, de la Noue was to campaign against Farnese in the Low Countries. Such a man was not afraid of speaking his mind, but he suggests with relatively tactful irony that his daughter (whom Palavicino had never seen) might disgust him by her lack of a courtly upbringing, without hinting that faced by an older man, it might be his young daughter who was 'dégoutée':

> 'Elle est laide et le Sr Palavicino est beau gentilhomme. Elle est pauvre et il est riche. Elle n'a esté nourrye es cours, et il est gentil courtizan. Toutefoys j'estime qu'elle a de la piété. Et qui sçait, s'il l'avoit vue, s'il en seroyt dégouté.'
> ('She is ugly and Signor Palavicino is a handsome gentleman. She is poor and he is rich. She was not brought up in a court and he is a noble courtier. I have always thought her to be pious. And who knows, if he were to see her, might he not be disgusted?')

This unusually liberal sixteenth-century father concludes that a daughter should at least be allowed to meet a potential husband before being expected to marry him: 'J'ay tousjours estimé qu'en tells affaires ung peu de conversation estoit bien requise' ('I have always thought that in such matters a little social converse was a necessary preliminary').[314]

Apart from the desire to have legitimate heirs to whom he could leave his considerable wealth, Palavicino's motives were unclear. Was it merely to ease the discomfort of his arthritis (Stone points out that sexual intercourse was thought to be a means of keeping the affliction at bay)?[315] Or was it to demonstrate to Burghley and Walsingham that he was committed to the Protestant cause beyond all doubt? Or perhaps he was thinking of playing a more active role in the Wars of Religion? After all, de la Noue, his proposed father-in-law, had proved a brave and resourceful general.

Whatever the case, when Palavicino next made marriage proposals it was to another Protestant family, albeit a merchant one, rather than of the minor nobility. Unfortunately, we lack information about how he approached Antonio Anselmo, Gillis's son-in-law and Anna Hooftman's guardian, or whether there was 'ung peu de conversation' first. If so, it must have been hard going for a girl of about sixteen to be with a man easily old enough to be her father, who was suffering not only from arthritis but also gout and gall stones, a painful combination that almost crippled him.[316] It seems certain, however, that the arrangements were financially advantageous for Palavicino (Anna's dowry was estimated by one contemporary as worth £10,000, an enormous sum at the time), as well as religiously appropriate, if socially somewhat *infra dig*, as Burghley rather unkindly indicated by his incredulous tone in a letter to Palavicino enquiring what is happening: 'I ... will make an ende of this my letter with a matter of sum mirthe, whiche is to knowe of yowe truly whether yow be married or Contracted to a Ritche Yonkers daughter of sum of the Fowkers [Fuggers] or such like, for soe I heare that Monsieur Tiligni hath reported heare since his comminge hither.'[317]

Whatever Palavicino's motives, he certainly adhered thereafter to the Church of England, arranging for the baptism of all three of his children at the church in Babraham near Cambridge, where his house was. He was granted letters of denization (naturalisation) in November 1585 and was knighted by Elizabeth I in November 1587. In 1588, inspired by 'l'ardore dell'animo mio' ('the ardour of my spirit'), he volunteered for service against the Armada and also wrote a propagandist pamphlet on the campaign. His biographers suggest – perhaps a little unkindly – that it was probably his talent for self-promotion which accounts for his otherwise inexplicable appearance among the naval commanders commemorated in the Armada Tapestries presented to the Lord Admiral by the Dutch government (who may also have wished to flatter the person to whom they owed such a substantial debt, and who was not backward in demanding payment).[318] His close relations with Elizabeth are clear from the fact that he was among the sixteen knights to receive New Year's gifts of gilt plate from the monarch in 1589, and the exchange of presents continued throughout the 1590s.

Palavicino's commitment to his newly adopted country, his wide contacts in the commercial world (frequently used by the English for the transfer of large sums of money by the use of bills of exchange, and for obtaining intelligence of developments abroad), and his descent from an aristocratic Genoese family were sufficient to commend him to Elizabeth as an ambassador. He felt that the Spanish threat should be dealt with in France rather than in the Low Countries, and it was he who was chosen for a confidential visit to Henri III of France in August 1585, when it looked as though Henri was about to throw in his lot with the Spanish-backed Catholic League led by Duc de Guise in order to crush the Huguenots, and it was feared that Philip II's plans to dominate Europe were coming to fulfilment. Under the cover of appealing for a repayment from Henri of the moneys loaned to his brother Anjou, who had recently died, Palavicino was to warn Henri of the dangers of a Guise alliance and the personal ambitions of the Guise family. If he were to reject the Catholic League, Elizabeth would offer Henri such help as he might need: 'she offers herself and her forces with hearty goodwill to give him that assistance in all those actions that he may reasonably demand of her'.[319] Perhaps unsurprisingly, this distinctly vague offer did not persuade

Henri, and Palavicino's mission was in vain, but it was a mark of Elizabeth's confidence in him that he was chosen to make it.[320]

From March 1586 until April 1587, he was employed on an embassy to the German princes to persuade them to levy troops to assist the Huguenot Henri of Navarre and to free Henri III from the domination of the Guises and the Catholic League, who were supported by Spain.[321] Palavicino's mission was not an easy one: Elizabeth expected the Germans to pay for an army of 23,000 men in France for an indefinite period for a mere 50,000 écus (then worth £15,468 15s. 0d.); clearly, she underestimated the reluctance of Lutheran Brandenburg and Saxony to get involved, and she was banking on the Calvinist John Casimir of the Palatinate, whose reliability was in doubt, to act as her agent. In June 1586, Elizabeth agreed to supply an extra 50,000 écus, enabling Palavicino to negotiate the Treaty of Friedelsheim in January 1587, by which Casimir agreed to support an army of 9,000 in France for three months. Elizabeth undermined this, however, by her subsequent claim that she had only meant the extra 50,000 écus to be paid if the Germans contributed their share.

Palavicino was convinced of the need for a negotiated peace. He put out feelers to Philip II through his brother Fabritio and the Genoese authorities in 1586 and also, mischievously hoping to exploit the tensions between Philip and his general, wrote to Parma to encourage him to take on the sovereignty of the Netherlands in 1588 (see p. 142). Palavicino also recognised the need to negotiate from strength and therefore pressed the queen on the need for intervention in France in 1587/8. Nevertheless, Elizabeth rejected his counsel until the dire position of Henri of Navarre after the assassination of Henri III necessitated a rethink. In March 1590, Palavicino was sent to negotiate joint action by the German princes in France, but his efforts were undermined by Elizabeth's diversion of her interests elsewhere. His diplomatic efforts on a further embassy to Germany beginning in December 1590 bore fruit in the Union of Torgau[322] (February 1591), by which Elizabeth was pledged to pay £15,000 to support the princes' campaign in France. Unfortunately, Elizabeth claimed that Palavicino had exceeded his instructions by granting £5,000 more than she had intended, even though his instructions had left him with discretion to agree to that amount if necessary. Although Robert Cecil turned to him for help in constructing his spy network in 1596, Elizabeth's fury over the German embassy of 1590–91 ended his diplomatic career.

The other use that Palavicino made of his international contacts for the Protestant cause was in transferring money and passing on intelligence, which, given the unreliability of the average spy of the period, was an important and relatively reliable source of information. Palavicino's brother in Genoa was able to send information from Italy, and his own business contacts in Paris provided Walsingham with a means to pay the spy Nicholas Berden and to receive information back from him. At first, Palavicino did no more than this, but in due course he came to act as a spymaster as well.[323]

One of Palavicino's tasks was to keep an eye on the English ambassador in Paris, Sir Edward Stafford, who had become addicted to gambling. For this role, Palavicino was acting more for Burghley than for Walsingham, since Stafford was Burghley's nominee. Indeed, one of Walsingham's spies had told him that Palavicino was concealing the truth about Stafford, but in fact Palavicino was giving a blunt enough assessment, but to Burghley instead: 'I fear that he [Stafford] is too impetuous in his judgements, and that from little points he infers maxims and general conclusions, in my opinion false, or at any rate very uncertain in the consequences he draws from them. [...] he fills his mind and his letters with fears and disorder.'[324]

The arrest of van Meteren (see pp. 89–91) was presumably motivated by the fear that he might have been acting as a spy in a similar way to Palavicino. We do not know whether Hooftman ever passed on sensitive information as Palavicino did, but it is clear that on one occasion at least he was trusted with confidential information and used the resources available to him as an international merchant for political purposes when he arranged for supplies to be sent to Vlissingen while it was being besieged by Alba's troops in 1572 (see p. 44).

In Palavicino's case, it might seem to a cynic that his principal successes in helping the Protestant resistance in the Low Countries were limited to making a handsome profit out of the interest paid by Elizabeth in exchange for making his stockpile of alum available to the States General, and to arranging a loan for Leicester at what would undoubtedly have been an advantageous rate of interest before the latter led a not very successful English force to the region. On the other hand, he clearly made a serious commitment to his work as ambassador (being an ambassador was unpaid and was only to be undertaken by a really wealthy man since it could prove remarkably expensive). He did his best to persuade German princes to intervene and urged the desirability of a negotiated peace, although his missions were invariably hamstrung by Elizabeth's unwillingness to make a serious financial commitment to funding any effective intervention. Indeed, it is doubtful whether any diplomat could have made a success of Elizabeth's half-hearted and under-funded policies. Stone sums it up as follows: 'Liable to diatribes from the queen for excessive generosity and slanders poured direct into Walsingham's ear for excessive meanness, to reproaches from Stafford [the English ambassador in Paris] for war-mongering and suspicions of Leicester for peace-making, Palavicino was forced to walk the slenderest of tight-ropes.'[325]

If so far I have painted a less than flattering picture of Palavicino as someone who always had an eye to the main financial chance, his peace proposals, which emerged shortly before the Armada, when he was endeavouring through his Genoese contacts to discover the terms on which Philip II would settle for peace, deserve recognition as being enlightened (but they depended on compromise, which was not Philip's strong point). Under Palavicino's proposals, Elizabeth was to leave the Americas and Indies alone, issuing no more licences for privateering attacks on Spanish treasure ships, offer compensation for Drake's raids, and permit the Low Countries to return to Habsburg sovereignty; in return, Philip would once again allow the provinces their ancient privileges. Both Elizabeth and Philip would withdraw troops from the Netherlands, and Philip would provide security for the repayment of Dutch war debts to England (a singularly optimistic suggestion since the money had been used to fight Spain, but presumably intended to be a way of getting the perennially hard-up Elizabeth onside). Freedom of conscience would be decreed, with some concessions: for example, public worship in the southern states would only be Catholic, but travellers from the south would be allowed to attend Reformed services in the north if they wished. Obedience to the magistrates in civil affairs would be safeguarded. Such a treaty could well have been transformative and, if followed elsewhere, might have saved much blood and suffering. But since Philip was very clear that he wanted no truck with heretics and wanted to regain what he not unreasonably considered to be his rights in the Netherlands, it soon became clear that the scheme was a non-starter, and it was quietly forgotten.[326]

It also seems fair to acknowledge that Palavicino's personal commitment when he served on one of the English ships harrying the Armada was not profit-making and was certainly risky, not least for a man who was nearly fifty (a comparatively advanced age by sixteenth-century standards). Nor was he lacking for ingenuity when fighting for the Reformed cause. After the failure of the Armada and Spanish attempts to blame Parma for the failed invasion, Palavicino decided to see if he could exploit the rumoured friction between Parma and Philip.[327] To test the waters, Palavicino sent a Genoese merchant based in Antwerp to give Parma a letter in which he expressed shock that Parma should be treated so poorly by Philip and said that if Parma were to take on himself the sovereignty of the Low Countries, he would have the support of Elizabeth. Since there were witnesses present when Parma received this letter, he could not afford to be seen to hesitate, or the message would go back to Philip that he was tempted by the thought of treason, and so he leapt to his feet and seized the unfortunate messenger by the throat, threatening to kill him. The witnesses could therefore testify to Parma's indignation. Although Palavicino's intrigue was unsuccessful, it may well have contributed to Philip's suspicions and Parma's intended disgrace, which was forestalled, however, by the latter's death shortly afterwards. As an attempt to win over the most able of the Spanish commanders of the Netherlands up to that time (and one who had proved willing to engage in realistic negotiations to ensure the peaceable surrender of Antwerp), the plan was admirably ingenious but undeniably a very long shot.

Hooftman's engagement in the struggle had also involved financial commitment, but in his case, loss rather than profit, as when he responded to the city's request for financial help to pay off the Spanish soldiers in Antwerp who were demanding their back pay by threat in April 1574 (see p. 44). As well as acting as a member of the committee instructed to find ways of maximising the city's income and cutting expenditure, he was also one of those citizens who made a personal contribution to raise the necessary money, a deed that can only be seen as being done for the public good to ensure peace. Given Hooftman's role in coping with the pressure on the city's finances, and that the Genoese 'nation' was asked to make the largest contribution of all the Italian 'nations', along with the fact that Palavicino was probably the wealthiest Genoese based in Antwerp, it seems most unlikely that they would not have met, even though Palavicino did not marry Hooftman's daughter Anna until 1591, ten years after his death.[328] A question that cannot be answered with confidence is whether they would have agreed on religious matters. Hooftman's provision of relief supplies for Vlissingen suggests that he was definitely Protestant, but it is clear that he was willing to conform outwardly to Catholicism. A similar willingness to compromise can be seen in Palavicino's proposals for a treaty allowing freedom of conscience. I suspect that both saw unhindered trade as being of greater benefit to all than religious intolerance, but this, I admit, is just speculation.

Anna's marriage in 1591 to Palavicino, a Genoese nobleman who was a naturalised Englishman, shows her guardians' willingness to venture much further on her behalf than her Panhuys cousins were willing to go. Once again, though, the marriage was to a Protestant who had worked hard in his diplomatic endeavours to support the Dutch revolt, or at least to negotiate a peace that would offer Calvinists freedom of worship. Whether the young Anna was happy in her marriage to this elderly, gout-ridden merchant, banker, ambassador, spymaster and general wheeler-dealer is a good deal less certain, although she did bear him three children. What is certain is that she married again at the earliest possible opportunity, exactly a year and a day after the death of her first husband. Her second husband was Sir Oliver Cromwell, uncle to the future Lord Protector of the same name, but a Royalist and certainly no Puritan. He was quite different from Palavicino in that he spent money rather than making it, his extravagant entertainment of James I and VI failing, however, to secure him any great post at court. Whether James's decision to knight Anna's younger brother, Gillis, was merely a financial one is not altogether clear, although 'cash for honours' was a common practice at his court.[329] At all events, we see that at least two of Hooftman's younger children become firmly established in Protestant England, just as those of Panhuys had gathered round the Calvinist court of Prince Maurice.

CHAPTER 12

Scattered

Plantin and his authors

It was in 1576, not very long after the *Paneel* was painted, that Plantin moved his business to a site on Antwerp's Vrijdagmarkt (Friday Market), where his property survives today as the remarkable Plantin-Moretus Museum, which preserves not only the buildings but also Plantin's printing presses, fonts and archives. However, it was at the end of that same year that the discontent of the unpaid Spanish troops erupted into the savagery of the Spanish Fury. In a letter to Montano, who was now back in Spain, Plantin's son-in-law, Moretus, describes how the printing works had narrowly escaped being burned down no fewer than three times. Plantin, he explains, had gone to Liège and on to Paris to raise the money to pay back his friend Luis Perez, who lent him 2,867 florins and 8 sous to pay off the Spanish soldiers. Perez was a wealthy Spanish *converso* (converted Jew) based in Antwerp who was probably a member of the Family of Love but outwardly Catholic. He was a merchant and bookseller, and a friend of both Montano and Plantin. That Plantin even recorded the sous indicates, I suspect, how determined he was to repay every last sou of the loan from his close friend that had enabled the survival of his business.[330]

Plantin returned to Antwerp in May 1577, having sold off his Paris business for less than half of what he considered its true value.[331] He then restarted the Antwerp business. In a letter of February 1578, he writes that God had given him patience to face the recent calamities, but he seems also to have been given remarkable energy to revive his business, since he describes how he had moved from using one press to using two, and then three, and then five. This was impressive progress, albeit on a significantly smaller scale than before; moreover, he still had fifteen unused presses even after he had sold two of them to raise some cash.[332] This rapid recovery meant that by the middle of

1579, and despite his financial difficulties, he was able to buy the Friday Market property that was to become both his home and his printing works. (He never, however, fully recovered the losses caused by publishing the *Biblia Regia*.)

One source of income that he found in 1578 was to act as official printer to the States General, who were now the new authorities, since they were acting as the government after the death of Requesens and the Pacification of Ghent. Plantin claimed that he was obliged to print everything that they 'ordered' him to, and, not surprisingly, this included anti-Spanish material. This can hardly be squared with his protestations to Philip II that he wished to print the polyglot Bible nowhere except in a city owing loyalty to the 'our most Catholic King'.[333] Plantin was, however, a Frenchman, and I suspect that his primary loyalty was not to any king (especially one who did not honour his debts) but to his family and business. In 1579, he published another work that would not have pleased the Spanish: a translation into French of an attack by Bartolomé de las Casas on the abuses of Spanish settlers in the New World, *Tyrannies et cruautez des Espagnoles perpetrées ès Indes Orientales*, which was highly critical of the Spanish colonists' violence and enslaving of the native population in their efforts to gain maximum profit from their colonies. These same settlers, of course, contributed to the wealth on which Philip depended (although it did not prevent his occasional bankruptcy). As such, Plantin must have known that it would displease Philip's government and so it was published under the name of his son-in-law, Raphelengius, but it could hardly have been published without his approval.[334]

At about the same time, Plantin began to publish some of the works of Hiël. It had been in 1573 that a group of Familists, including Plantin and his fellow members, had broken away from the increasingly hierarchical leadership of Henrik Niclaes and become followers of Hendrick Jansen Barrefelt, who called himself Hiël (Life of God). Plantin began to publish some of his work in the late 1570s, albeit *sine nota* (that is, without any acknowledgement that he was the publisher).[335]

In 1581, Plantin visited the new university that had been set up at Leiden after the year-long Spanish siege had been repulsed by heroic resistance and the eventual arrival of William the Silent's forces under Admiral Boissot. It was presumably from this time that he began to consider moving there from Antwerp, doubtless encouraged by his friend Lipsius teaching there since 1579. In addition, although it was a Calvinist institution, the university was tolerant of those loyal to other churches, at least initially. In the meantime, Plantin continued to publish an impressive range of books. In 1581, for example, he published the *Kruydtboeck* of Matthias de l'Obel, the father-in-law of Ortelianus. The *Kruydtboeck* was a Flemish translation of a botanical work first published in Latin by Plantin in 1576, *Plantarum seu Stirpium Historia* ('A Study of Plants and Shrubs') to which was added a revised version of an earlier work. This was no mean task: not only does de l'Obel describe and illustrate a vast range of plants, he also includes a history of botany and an account of the medical uses of plants. There are over 2,000 illustrations, some of which Plantin had used previously when publishing the works of Dodoens and Charles de l'Ecluse. De l'Obel's classification of plants by leaf shapes made him one of the first botanists to distinguish between monocotyledons (grass-like plants) and dicotyledons, although as an early twentieth-century historian of herbals writes in a perceptive description that captures the generosity of spirit and love of learning that mark out a great civilisation:

> Between [Dodoens] and his two younger countrymen, de l'Ecluse and de l'Obel, there was so intimate a friendship that they freely imparted their observations to one another, and permitted the use of them, and also of their figures, in one another's books. To attempt to ascertain exactly what degree of merit should be attributed to each of the three would be a task equally difficult and thankless.[336]

By 1583, Plantin had made his decision. He had already sold his Paris business and his house in the city the previous year, and subsequently moved to Leiden, where Lipsius had fled in 1579 after his property had been looted for a second time by Spanish soldiers. In 1584, Plantin became the university's printer, having apparently been promised that he would not be made to publish anything against his conscience. At the end of 1583, he had drawn up a list of all the expenses that he had undertaken for Philip II in publishing the polyglot Bible in a final attempt to get some restitution. An earlier subsidy that he had been given had in effect been withdrawn when it was included as half the payment for a separate order of missals and breviaries that he had supplied. Plantin calculated that Philip owed him just over 45,000 florins, a sum that he was never to receive.[337] Thereafter, his standard excuse when accused of disloyalty in going to Leiden and working for Protestants was that financial need and the States General had forced him to do the work that Catholics and supporters of Spanish rule objected to; he also claimed that he was not opposed to Philip II, but only his bad advisers.

He continued to publish works of major academic importance while he was in Leiden, including *De Thiende* ('The Tenth') by the mathematician Simon Stevin, which was the first book to consider the decimal system, and

De Constantia by Lipsius, who was still teaching in Leiden. This was by far the most widely read of all his works, and Plantin published it in Flemish and French translations as well as in the original Latin.

Plantin seems to have felt quite settled in Leiden. In a letter written to Montano after his return to Antwerp, he praises the tolerance of the Calvinist university, saying that he, Lipsius and others were accepted there 'sine ullo discrimine religionis' ('without any religious discrimination') as long as they acknowledged the authority of the government in secular matters. Dodoens had lived there in contentment for the last two years of his life, teaching at the university.[338] Nevertheless, when Plantin learnt that the siege of Antwerp was over, he returned to the city, made sure that he was reconciled with the Catholic authorities, and passed oversight of the Leiden business and property to his son-in-law, Raphelengius, who succeeded him as university printer in 1586 and became professor of Hebrew shortly afterwards. Raphelengius subsequently published a number of dictionaries of oriental languages and later converted to Calvinism, much to the disappointment and surprise of his family.[339]

In the remaining four years of his life back in Antwerp, Plantin continued to advance the spread of knowledge, publishing at an impressive rate of about forty books a year, including translations of works such as an Italian edition of Guicciardini's *Description of all the Low Countries* and a Spanish edition of Ortelius's *Theatrum Orbis Terrarum*. Nevertheless, it was a struggle for the rest of his life to pay off his debts so that he could leave the business unencumbered to his family. His efforts were made more difficult because, after the siege and the departure of so many Calvinist businessmen – not to mention the blockade of the Scheldt – Antwerp was no longer a thriving financial hub, and matters were made worse still by a poor harvest. The survival of his printing house in Antwerp for many generations until its donation to the city as a museum in the nineteenth century is a testament to his lifelong perseverance and would have delighted him. It has to be admitted, however, that the range of publications after his death became much narrower as philosophy, literature and science were replaced with a stream of prayerbooks and missals – genres that were profitable in Spain and safe in Catholic Antwerp.

Montano

Throughout this time, Plantin kept in touch with his authors and friends by means of a frequent exchange of letters, not least with Montano and Lipsius. Despite Montano's fear of the Spanish Inquisition and the hostility of his theological opponents, he had been obliged to return to Spain in 1576 at the king's command to look after the El Escorial library. Writing to

Ortelius, another close friend, Montano reveals his sadness at leaving the Low Countries and says 'Vix credi potest ... quam arctis charitatis vinculis tibi tuique similibus devinctus sim' ('I can hardly believe how tight the bonds of love are that bind me to you and those like you'[340]).

The ongoing correspondence between Plantin and Montano not only covers academic details of book purchases and publishing, but also reveals their concern for each other's welfare. Plantin tries to reassure Montano about the attempts of Leon de Castro (a reactionary Spanish biblical scholar) to have his works condemned by the Inquisition and begs him not to 'meliores horas ... perdere' ('waste valuable time') defending himself against ignorant people motivated by envy.[341] In another letter of July 1578, he hopes that Montano can draw the king's attention to the turbulent situation in the Low Countries, and expresses the opinion that the only hope for 'Religionis pax' ('religious peace') is the introduction of an 'ad modum in Germania concessum tempore piae memoriae Caroli V' ('similar arrangement to that made in Germany in the time of Charles V of blessed memory').[342] This is a reference to the Peace of Augsburg which allowed Lutheranism and Catholicism to co-exist in the lands of the Holy Roman Empire and which had been agreed during the reign of Philip's father, Charles V. Plantin might seem to have unrealistic expectations of Montano's influence on Philip, but Montano was trusted by Philip, who had sent him in January that year to King Sebastiano of Portugal to discourage him from his planned crusade against the Moors in Africa. Although Montano was unsuccessful in his mission (and Sebastiano's ill-advised expedition led to his death in battle), it is evidence of Philip's high opinion of him.[343] The other thing that Plantin overlooked was that the Peace of Augsburg allowed each ruler to determine religious practice in their own territory, and Philip was the ruler of the Low Countries by legitimate inheritance and had made his decision.

Montano's letters to Plantin range from homely matters to academic ones. In one, he tells Plantin that the books that he had asked for have arrived in good condition but that unfortunately the bulbs and plants have not survived their long journey. He appends to the end of this letter a very long list of plants that he would like to be sent to him. Just before this, he explains that he has asked before and now again asks 'amanter et studiose' ('lovingly and eagerly') for a copy of 'elucidationes in Apocalypsin' ('explanatory notes on the Apocalypse'), by which he seems to mean Hiël's commentary on the Apocalypse or Revelation of St John the Divine. He needs the book to help him write his own commentary on this, the most obscure book of the New Testament.[344] Although Montano cautiously avoids referring to Hiël by name, nine tenths of what he writes on Revelation can be shown to be drawn from Hiël's *elucidationes*, as Maurice Sabbe showed when he made a detailed comparison of the two men's notes.[345]. This presumably explains why he sends money to Hiël via Plantin's friend Luis Perez.[346] He is also grateful to Perez for sending him notes on Ezekiel, which he also uses. Perez was almost certainly a follower of Hiël and seems to have acted as a go-between in passing on the latter's writings. In another letter, Plantin assures Montano that Hiël will not regard any of this as plagiarism, but is 'de voluntate vero' ('truly willing') to have his work used in this way.[347]

In the final years of his life, Montano withdrew to his country house where he wrote his final work in two parts, *Anima* ('The Soul') and *Naturae Historia* ('A Study of Nature'). The first is firmly based on the Bible, tracing the Jews from Genesis and the Fall (the act of disobedience when they eat the fruit of the forbidden tree in Eden that is interpreted as the cause of original sin) through to the time of Jesus and the Resurrection. *Naturae Historia*, meanwhile, offers an inclusive classification of natural phenomena (God's creation), drawing on geology, physics and biology.[348] Although Montano continued to write, he was well aware of the need for caution and the likelihood that new ideas would be obstructed by envy, as he writes in his dedication to Lipsius of his commentaries on thirty-one of the Psalms (*Commentaria in XXXI Davidis Psalmos priores*) which was published posthumously in 1605 in Antwerp by Moretus, Plantin's son-in-law. In this, he writes that good men should not be distracted by detractors' 'ignavo latratu aut maligno obloquio' ('cowardly barking or malicious abuse').[349]

Lipsius

It was in 1577, soon after its opening, that Jan Dousa invited Lipsius to join the new university at Leiden, and it was while he was there that he published his two most influential books, *De Constantia* and *Politica*. The first of these was to prove enormously popular, being translated into a variety of languages and reprinted many times. It was translated into English by Sir John Stradling, a friend of William Camden, and published in 1595 in London as *Two Bookes of Constancie*.

In *De Constantia*, Lipsius gives the Stoic ideas of Seneca a Christian turn. The book takes the form of a dialogue between his friend Langius (a canon of Liège) and Lipsius, who is talking of emigrating to avoid the political turmoil of the Low Countries. Langius is the mouthpiece of Lipsius's ideas and advises the fictional Lipsius to be constant in the face of the war and savagery around him. He does this by arguing that God is not subject to necessity and that, though this unpredictability requires the movement from creation to change and decay, God is in fact at work even through what he describes as 'divinae clades' ('disasters permitted by God'), which serve to chasten and guide humanity. The right use of reason will therefore guide him to escape 'mala publica' ('public evils') not by a change of location, but by a change of mental attitude, whereby the mind is moved 'non ab Opinione, sed à iudicio & recta Ratione' ('not by mere opinion but by right and well-judged reason'; *Constantia* I, 4). This neostoicism, Christianised by the assertion that God's providence prevailed over fate and the disasters brought by necessity, understandably had great appeal in the times of hardship that were being seen across so much of Europe.

It was, however, a later work, also published at Leiden but under the name of Plantin's son-in-law, Raphelengius, that was to cause Lipsius trouble. This was *Politicorum sive civilis doctrinae libri sex qui ad principatum maxime spectant* ('Six Books on Politics or Civil Doctrine', normally referred to as *Politica*). If *De Constantia* was about private life and how to face hardships and injustice with stoic endurance, *Politica* was about public life and how to govern a state. It was dedicated to Prince Maurice, who had been studying at Leiden when his father, William the Silent, was assassinated in 1584. He succeeded his father since his elder half-brother was held hostage by Philip II until his death. The book drew heavily on Lipsius's unrivalled knowledge of classical texts. Of the 2,069 quotations in it, no fewer than 528 are from Tacitus. Its advice for a young ruler sits somewhere between the ruthless *Realpolitik* advocated by Machiavelli in *Il Principe* and the typical 'mirror for princes' books that urged virtue upon rulers. After arguing the need for virtue and prudence in the first of the work's six books and having dealt with the ruler's need to act with justice and clemency, Lipsius then turns to the issue of prudence. Prudence requires an understanding of what must be done and what must be avoided; it also requires making the right decisions based on memory and a knowledge of history. Moral decisions are especially difficult for leaders, and so Lipsius introduces the concept of *prudentia mixta*; that is, there needs to be a prudential qualification of moral values, and a balance between *honestas* (honourable) and *utilitas* (useful) behaviour, because 'Necessity, being a great defender of the weakness of man, breaks every law.'[350] For Lipsius, order and peace are more important than individual liberties (even religious ones), and therefore if anyone dissents from the religion endorsed by the state, they must be driven out. At this point, Lipsius quotes Cicero's *Philippics* – 'Ure, seca' ('burn and cut out') – which would go on to prove costly.

The book was soon put on the Vatican's *Index Librorum Prohibitorum*, but Lipsius had other troubles that were closer to home. It was his assertion that the need for order and peace was more important than religious liberties that horrified some of his colleagues at Leiden. Religion freedom was permissible in private, he argued, but religious dissidents whose open actions led to civil conflict should be suppressed with force. Given that heretics could be burned, his quotation of Cicero at his fiercest was tactless: 'Burn, cut – for the whole body [i.e. the state] is more important than some of its limbs.'[351]

It is unsurprising that such a statement at a time of civil war and religious persecution made tempers flare. However, Lipsius was making a genuine attempt to offer a solution, even if it seems a very illiberal one to modern readers: a strong ruler who would not tolerate dissent was needed to impose order. In support of this position, Lipsius could point to the fact that his friends in Antwerp had been lucky to escape with their lives after the Spanish Fury and that the ultimate cause of this could be attributed to the rebellion (even if the immediate moral responsibility lay with the Spanish soldiers and not the rebels). Similarly, Montano, shocked by the wanton destruction of the library at the monastery of Dunes (see p. 116), initially approved of Alba's fierce suppression of religious and political opponents to restore order. Plantin himself (see p. 179), meanwhile, had favoured the Peace of Augsburg as a model to establish accord; this had required everyone in each state within the Holy Roman Empire to adhere to their own ruler's religion (*cuius regio, eius religio*), but had removed the ability of citizens to exercise their individual conscience. Furthermore, at the time of the debate, Farnese's drive to re-impose Spanish control had been much more successful because he had displayed clemency, just as Lipsius recommended in an earlier part of the *Politica* (for example, Farnese had allowed the Protestant citizens of Antwerp four years to sort out their affairs and leave, although he nevertheless insisted that those who remained must return to Catholicism).

The next year, there was a bitter public debate in Leiden between Lipsius and Dirk Volkertszoon Coornhert, an ardent champion of freedom of conscience. Understandably, Coornhert wanted to know whether Lipsius's ideas meant that the Spanish kings, who were legal rulers of the Low Countries by descent – and Lipsius favoured monarchy – were right to burn Protestants. The university authorities, wanting to keep such a prestigious scholar, persuaded Lipsius to make clear that his provocative quotation from Cicero, 'ure, seca', was intended to be taken metaphorically and not literally. The damage was done, however, and the following year, after eleven years in Leiden, he slipped away and was reconciled with the Catholic Church. He soon took up a teaching post at Leuven

University, a Catholic institution. A revised edition of *Politica* was published in 1591, and in 1596 it was removed from *Index*.[352]

In an attempt to clarify what he had said in *Politica*, he used one of his last works, *Monita et Exempla Politica*, to praise clemency rather than firm punishment, approving the more conciliatory approach of Archduke Albert and Archduchess Isabella of Austria, joint rulers of the Spanish Netherlands from 1598–1621 (after their deaths, sovereignty reverted to the Spanish crown). By this stage in his career, his praise of the 'clementia prncipis' ('clemency of the prince') had also become a praise of the Habsburgs' 'pietas austriaca' ('Austrianpiety').[353]

On his move to Leuven, his Catholic friends clearly expected such a well-regarded scholar to write something in support of the church with which he had become reconciled, and the opportunity to do so arose after he made a pilgrimage to the shrine of Our Lady of Halle. This was a statue of the Virgin, crowned and nursing the infant Jesus. Since devotion to sacred images was regarded as a form of superstition by Protestants and was one of the factors that had led to the *Beeldenstorm* (see p. 49), there could hardly have been a more emphatic statement of his renewed loyalty to the Catholic Church than Lipsius's decision to publish a treatise about the miraculous deeds linked with the shrine, *Diva Virgo Hallensis* (1604). In it, he makes clear his personal belief in the efficacy of praying at shrines. He begins by giving an account of his first visit to the shrine and closes with a description of his second visit, when he made the highly symbolic offering of a silver pen. Naturally, this upset many Protestants, although it does not seem to have harmed his relationships with close friends regardless of their religious affiliations.

His first visit to Halle was in 1601, and the following spring he fell ill. He prayed to the Virgin of Halle for healing, and after he recovered, he fulfilled the vow that he had made by returning to the shrine and making a votive offering of a replica silver pen, which was displayed beside other offerings and was accompanied by a brass plaque inscribed with a Latin poem that Lipsius had written. He makes clear that the pen represents his lifetime's studies devoted to searching for 'Scientiae, Prudentiae, Sapientiae' ('knowledge, prudence and wisdom'). He concludes by praying that in place of any 'famae fugacis in vicem' ('ephemeral fame') that his work has brought him, the Virgin may grant him 'perenne gaudium / Vitamque' ('everlasting joy and life').[354]

Rembert Dodoens

Dodoens had left the Low Countries long before the siege of Antwerp, at around the time that the *Paneel* had been painted. Shortly before that, his house in Mechelen had been ransacked by Spanish soldiers, who were again causing mayhem because they were not being paid. His earliest studies at Leuven University had been in medicine, and he then went on to Vienna where he held the post of court physician for the Holy Roman Emperor, Maximilian II, and his successor, Rudolph II. His decision to move to Vienna was probably influenced both by the desire to avoid future violence at the hands of Spanish soldiery and by the knowledge that Charles de l'Ecluse, a friend and fellow botanist who had translated the first version of his *Cruydeboek* into French, was living there.

Dodoens left Vienna in 1580, spending time in Cologne, where he published two further books. Following this, he went to Antwerp, where he oversaw the publication by Plantin of his last and most inclusive herbal which gathered together much of his earlier work, *Stirpium historiae pemptades sex sive libri XXX* ('Six Sets of Five Books'[355] or 'Thirty Books of the [Natural] History of Plants'), a richly illustrated work, sometimes with as many as three woodblock illustrations per page.[356] This was one of two books plagiarised by John Gerard for his *The Herball or Generall History of Plants* (the other was de l'Obels *Stirpium adversaria nova* [1571]). However, whereas Dodoens prefaces his book with a long list of other scholars cited, Gerard afforded no such courtesy to those whose work he exploited.[357]

In 1582, Dodoens accepted the appointment as professor of medicine at Leiden, whilst Lipsius was still there. According to Plantin, he was happy there, although he appears to have remained Catholic. Plantin refers to this in the same letter in which he describes to Montano how he and Lipsius were allowed to live peacefully under the Calvinist authorities.[358]

Peeter Heyns

While Lipsius had moved away to that part of the Low Countries still controlled by Catholic Spain, Peeter Heyns moved first to Frankfurt after the fall of Antwerp and then to Stade, on the River Elbe near Hamburg, before finally coming to rest in Protestant Haarlem near Amsterdam in 1594. This was where one of his sons-in-law had started a new school for girls, once again called De Lauwerboom (The Laurel Tree). Another son-in-law, Zacharias, who was a former apprentice of Plantin, had also moved north and had set up a bookshop in Amsterdam, and it was he who arranged for a number of his father-in-law's works to be published, including the three plays for girls mentioned in Chapter 5, which had first been performed in Antwerp between 1578 and 1583 (see p. 107).[359] While Lipsius was writing in favour of imposing religious conformity by whatever means were necessary, Heyns was publishing plays that suggested comparisons of Philip II to the Pharaoh, who ordered the murder of all male Israelite babies, and of Philip's general, Alba, to the invading Assyrian general Holofernes, who met a gruesome death at the hands of the patriotic Judith. The civilised group of authors who had gathered around Plantin had been well and truly scattered.

The three artists
Maerten de Vos

The print of de Vos engraved by Aegidius Sadeler from a painting by the Swiss painter Joseph Heintz shows us a man in his sixties looking out at the world in a jaundiced and slightly world-weary way, with a furrowed brow and bags under his eyes (ill. 25). Nevertheless, after the decline and death in 1570 of Frans Floris, who had been the foremost painter in Antwerp, de Vos became well established as his successor. As a Lutheran, he presumably followed his church's instructions to conform to the religion of the ruling authority while Alba was in power and, unlike the Calvinists, would not have objected as a matter of principle to painting religious scenes such as would have been required to replace the altarpieces destroyed in the *Beeldenstorm*. He had, after all, played a major part in decorating the Lutheran chapel at Celle (see pp. 53–6). Lutherans were tolerant of images so long as they were not the subject of idolatrous worship, unlike the Calvinists, who, when they took control in 1581, followed the earlier uncontrolled destruction of paintings with the *stille Beeldenstorm*, during which religious paintings continued to be removed from churches albeit in a manner controlled by the authorities (that is to say, the paintings were sometimes sold rather than being indiscriminately destroyed by mob action, as had happened in the *Beeldenstorm*). De Vos's treatment of the left exterior wing of the altarpiece triptych that he painted for the Furriers' Guild soon after the *Beeldenstorm* provides an implicit comment on the earlier destruction of statues (ill. 31). When the outer panels are closed, as they normally would be except for festivals, the figures of St Thomas and St Stephen are visible. These are grisailles, the neutral tones and shadows of which painted against a plain red background make them look remarkably like statues, the *trompe l'oeil* effect making them stand out as if in relief. They would not have been painted by anyone who thought statues should be destroyed. A much later painting, *St Luke Painting the Virgin* (1602), shows empty niches in the background and might well be taken as a rebuke of those who had emptied them since the apostle himself was a painter (according to legend).[360]

De Vos could also find other work in a time of religious uncertainty, since not all of his subjects were religious. In 1577, for example, he paints a charming family group portrait of Antonius Anselmo, his wife, Joanna Hooftman (a daughter of Gillis Hooftman from an earlier marriage) and their two children (ill. 32). Antonius was to be the guardian of Anna Hooftman (the girl kneeling in the left foreground of the *Paneel*, who was later to marry Palavicino). As well as portraits, he also painted scenes from classical mythology and a number of what are described as 'allegorical' paintings. In about 1590, he was to paint his striking picture of the *Allegory of the Seven Liberal Arts*, a smaller painting than the *Paneel*, but by no means diminutive (200 cm wide), and extremely impressive in its confident grouping of figures, painted in strong reds and greens. A number of his paintings of scenes from classical mythology were subsequently engraved and circulated widely as prints; there had also been a series of animal prints, probably made in 1572 (that is the date given on two of them, of a leopard and a deer). Other paintings also formed sets, such as the 'Four Elements' and the 'Four Temperaments', the former engraved by Adriaen Collaert and the latter by Raphaël Sadeler.[361] It is tempting to think that the marvellously realistic painting of so many kinds of birds in 'Air' influenced Joris Hoefnagel in his own paintings of groups of creatures (ills. 33 & 34).

De Vos appears to have made his peace with the Catholic authorities after the fall of Antwerp, not out of religious conviction but rather as a matter of expediency. He had first intended to go to Germany, but having a large family, including several grown-up (but presumably unmarried) daughters and much business to sort out, he had run out of time, and so he stayed on.[362] Nevertheless, his true feelings about Spain's violent assertion of authority may perhaps be deduced from the prints of some of his earlier work that were used to illustrate *Tyrannorum praemia. Den loon der tyrannen* ('The Rewards of Tyranny'), which was published in 1578. The stories are taken from a variety of biblical and classical sources, but each one tells of a victory over a tyrant; as such, while the criticism of Spain is only implicit, it is still not hard to find.[363]

After the return of Plantin to Antwerp, de Vos cooperated with him on a number of projects, one of which was a picture Bible published in 1585, Gerard de Jode's *Thesaurus veteris et novi Testamenti* ('A Treasury of the Old and the New Testament').[364] Later, he also worked with a Roman print designer called Bernardino Passeri to produce the images for *Evangelicae historiae imagines* ('Pictures of the Gospel Stories'),[365] a book intended as a companion aid for Ignatius Loyola's *Spiritual Exercises*, which had been written by another Jesuit, Jerome Nadal. The Ignatian approach involved using the senses to place oneself mentally and emotionally in a biblical situation (e.g. at the foot of the Cross) as a prelude to earnest prayer, and the prints were intended as prompts to the imagination. Since the author of the exercises was St Ignatius Loyola, founder of the Jesuits (the 'crack troops' of the Counter-Reformation as they have been described), it might seem that de Vos's involvement in the project was a clear demonstration of his recently acquired Catholic convictions, but this is not conclusive evidence since Loyola's *Spiritual Exercises* were widely admired and quite often used by Protestants as well in an adapted form; moreover, to illustrate scenes from the Gospels was certainly not a betrayal of Lutheran principles. The actual engraving of the prints for this book was done by the Wierix brothers, whose skill was so admired that the Jesuits in Rome asked if they could be sent to Rome for further work. Plantin advised against it, however, writing that as soon as he had paid them a couple days' wages at the going rate for skilled craftsmen, they would disappear to spend it on drink and debauchery. He suggested that if one needed them to do more work, one had to find them and then redeem their pawned belongings, even their clothes, which he describes with evident distaste as 'leurs hardes' ('their rags').[366]

However debauched he may have been, it was nevertheless Hieronymus Wierix who produced a much-copied print in 1584 of a painting by de Vos of the Archangel Michael treading down the defeated Lucifer. This print was dedicated to Montano and was widely influential, being copied in a great variety of ways all over the Spanish Empire.[367]

It is clear that de Vos carried on living a very productive life after the fall of Antwerp. He continued to take apprentices into his studio and produce a steady stream of work. His painting of the *Worship of the Three Kings* in 1599 has already been mentioned (**ill. 18**), and perhaps is intended to remind us of the submission that even kings must make to God, although it is hard to read too much into a subject that was popular with so many artists. Perhaps more can be made of the altarpiece that he painted for the Guild of the Minters in 1602, the subject of which is the time when Jesus was asked the trick question about whether it was right to pay tribute to Caesar. Jesus' response was to ask for a coin and ask whose image was on it – it was Caesar's. He then replies, 'Give to Caesar the things that are Caesar's and to God the things that are God's.' In this way, he avoids getting into trouble with the Roman authorities or with the crowd around him, who were devout Jews and loathed the Roman occupiers. Although the subject was an obvious one for the guild of those who made coins themselves, Christ's words here could be seen as indicative of de Vos's own feelings that there was divine sanction for a pragmatic acceptance of the Habsburg rulers as long as one reserved a space in one's heart for true religion. This was certainly the view of the Family of Love, but, as so often, there is no evidence at all to suggest that de Vos himself was a Familist.

Joris Hoefnagel

If de Vos managed to make a good living from his art by staying in Antwerp, Joris Hoefnagel was to discover that his own quite different art had a monetary value further afield. It is hardly surprising that after his family's wealth was lost in the Spanish Fury, he chose to travel to Italy with Ortelius the following year in the hope of finding some employment in Venice. Passing through Augsburg on their way to Venice, they met Hans Fugger, a member of the extremely wealthy merchant and banking family and also a patron of the arts. Fugger provided them with a letter of introduction to the region's elector, Albrecht V of Bavaria. In his *Schilderboek*, van Mander describes how Hoefnagel, when asked to show some evidence of his talent, showed Albrecht a picture of himself with his first wife and also a miniature of some animals and trees painted on vellum. The miniature so impressed Albrecht that he sent a messenger after them in order to buy it. According to van Mander, Hoefnagel had not really thought of himself as an artist and was unsure what to do, but Ortelius told him to ask for 100 gold crowns, which he was promptly paid. Albrecht then offered him a post at his court, additionally offering the princely sum of 200 gold crowns to defray the costs of his wife moving from the Low Countries to join him in Munich. Hoefnagel agreed to accept this offer after he had visited Italy. In Rome the following year, he received a further offer of employment from Cardinal Alessandro Farnese, another great patron of the arts (and, coincidentally, an uncle of the Farnese who was to secure the surrender of Antwerp in 1585). Farnese was clearly eager to gain Hoefnagel's services since, according to van Mander, he offered him up to 1,000 gold crowns per year. Even so, Hoefnagel declined, saying that he had given his word to Albrecht.

On his return to Albrecht's court in Munich, he was paid a handsome pension and was not prevented from doing work for other people. He was, for example, commissioned by Archduke Ferdinand of Innsbruck to decorate a very fine manuscript missal (Mass book) with miniature illuminations; these are emblematic, referring sometimes to the religious text and sometimes to his patron. Since the missal consisted of 658 vellum folios, it is not surprising that he was working on it for eight years. According to van Mander, it was such an 'extraordinarily perfect' work that one might well ask if a whole lifetime of work would be sufficient for a single man to make it. Ferdinand evidently shared this high opinion since he paid 2,000 gold crowns and a golden chain worth a further one hundred crowns for it.

Hoefnagel stayed on at the court in Munich under Albrecht's successor, Wilhelm V, but chose to leave in 1591 when all members of the court were required to proclaim their loyalty to the Catholic Church. He then entered the service of the Emperor Rudolf II, first living in Frankfurt, where there was a Flemish exile community that included the botanist Charles de l'Ecluse, a friend of Dodoens. De l'Ecluse had entered the service of Rudolf's father, Maximilian II, to supervise the imperial botanical garden in Vienna, but later moved to Frankfurt soon after Rudolf succeeded his father. Their friendship may have contributed to Hoefnagel's own impressively accurate depictions of plants.

Hoefnagel continued his remarkable work as a miniaturist at Vienna, adding illuminations to the *Mira Calligraphiae Monumenta*, a *Schriftmusterbuch* (handbook of writing styles) by Georg Bocskay, master calligrapher and secretary to Emperor Ferdinand I, the grandfather of Rudolf II. If Bocskay's work can be seen as asserting his own pre-eminence as a scribe and extolling the power of the written word, Hoefnagel's delicate illustrations of plants and flowers, animals, and even cityscapes, using ink, tempera, watercolour and gold and silver ink could be interpreted as a counterclaim, vaunting the power of the visual image over the written word, rather as d'Heere did in *Den hof en boomgaerd der poësien* (although, ironically, d'Heere had used words to make his point, while Hoefnagel's use of illustrations is perhaps more persuasive).

There remains one more major artistic achievement, perhaps Hoefnagel's greatest, which we know he was working on from at least 1575 until 1589, based on the dates on some of its images. It is a work that he seems to have done for his own satisfaction and not for a patron, although some pages were removed from the work in progress and given to others. It is the *Four Elements*, a collection of four manuscript volumes, each given the name of one of the four traditional elements, and which between them offer small but detailed and astonishingly beautiful images of every form of life: thus *Ignis* (fire) has insects, *Aqua* (water) has fish and shellfish, *Terra* (earth) has mammals and reptiles, and *Aier* (air) has birds. Each volume is only about 14 x 18 cm, and each vellum page has delicate illustrations of a variety of creatures in watercolour and gouache within an oval of gold.[368] These exquisite volumes might seem the ultimate demonstration of the superiority of the image as opposed to the written word were it not for the fact that on the verso of each image is a space prepared for writing, which Hoefnagel sometimes uses to explore an idea. Exploration is, in fact, an appropriate description, for in some cases the verso of image has no writing, and sometimes there is writing but no image on the opposite page; in other words, this remains a work in progress, the ongoing working out of Hoefnagel's thoughts. Just as this work crosses the boundaries between art and literature, so too does it transcend those between art and science. This can be seen above all in his detailed images of insects, which are works of art but which also stand comparison for scientific accuracy with those in *Micrographia* by the Englishman Robert Hooke, a book that was not published until much later in 1665 and which was prepared with the aid of a microscope, a late sixteenth-century Dutch invention of which Hoefnagel may or may not have been aware (**ill. 35**).

Lucas d'Heere

When Lucas d'Heere first left the Low Countries in 1568 to avoid Alba's persecution of Protestants, he went to France, where he had drawn cartoons for tapestries for Catherine de Medici. He then joined the Dutch Protestant community in London, where, like Radermacher, he was an elder in the stranger church at Austin Friars. He also became a member of the strongly Calvinist political group that gathered around his patron, Edward Seymour, Earl of Hertford, to whom a number of the poems in *Tableau Poetique* are addressed (see Chapter 8). By 1577, he felt able to return to Ghent, his native city, after the Pacification of Ghent the year before (see p. 142). Given his religious and political views, and the fact that he was an accomplished artist and poet, it is no surprise that he was chosen to design the pageants for the entry of William the Silent into Ghent, and that afterwards he published the verses written in his honour together with a description of the celebrations.

William's visit to Ghent was an unsuccessful attempt to moderate the Calvinists' persecution of Catholics; William was trying to hold the predominantly Catholic states of the south together with the more Calvinist northern states after the intervention of Don Juan, who was working on the principle of 'divide and rule' and doing his best to separate them. D'Heere also played a part in arranging the 'joyous entry' of the Duke of Anjou, who had been invited by William in 1582 to become titular ruler of the Low Countries in a further attempt to hold the vying states together. William hoped that both Catholics and Protestants would see him as an acceptable overlord and that Anjou, as brother of the French king, might be able to call upon French support against Spain. His hopes were thwarted not only by Calvinist suspicions of a Catholic Frenchman, but by Anjou's perfidious behaviour in trying unsuccessfully to seize control of Antwerp for himself, after which he fled back to France, dying shortly afterwards.

Frances Yates proposed the hypothesis that d'Heere was the designer of the tapestries known as the Valois Tapestries, and that they were intended by William the Silent as a gift for Catherine de Medici in anticipation of her son, the Duke of Anjou, being invited to become ruler of the Low Countries in the place of Philip II. Yates draws attention to the careful portrayal of different costumes as being typical of d'Heere. However, her suggestion that they were made in Antwerp was queried by Roy Strong on the grounds that the maker's marks on the tapestries are those of Brussels and not of Antwerp. In addition, Lisa Jardine and Jerry Brotton take issue with Yates's hypothesis on the grounds that the tapestries can be interpreted much more naturally as being typical of a number of similar ones used to celebrate military power and possibly the defeat of the Protestants, rather than fitting with William's agenda of reconciliation.[369]

Van Mander tells us in his life of d'Heere that he got on well with princes, who often appointed him to important positions. A Ghent taxation list from 1585 describes him as 'greffier de la chambre des comptes et pensionnaire du prince d'Orange et de Sainte-Aldegonde'.[370] The precise nature of the responsibilities of the *greffier* (clerk) of this financial office is not clear, but it sounds more like a genuine job than simply a sinecure awarded as a thank-you for his work in preparing for the joyous entries and writing encomiastic verse. In fact, it seems probable that, like Panhuys and Radermacher, his conscience led him to devote time to public service. The fact that he was working for William and his right-hand man, Marnix van St Aldegonde, rather than for the intolerant Calvinist council, suggests that, while he was certainly Protestant, he is likely to have wanted William to succeed in his attempt to achieve unity through moderation.

In 1584, d'Heere left Ghent once more when the city was forced to surrender to Farnese. He died shortly afterwards, probably in Paris. The artists were scattered as well.

CHAPTER 13

Epilogue:

An 'invisible college' – three albums, last letters, stoic virtue, a poem and a painting

There is merit in keeping alive the
memory of those days.

– J.K Galbraith[371]

The expression 'invisible college' is a term sometimes used to describe the network of friends and correspondents who exchanged their research and questions through Samuel Hartlib in London between about 1630 and 1660. The idea was not a new one, though. Van Meteren had provided just such a link as the 'postmaster' of the Netherlandish community in London, and the assiduous correspondence of Ortelius and Plantin with so many of their friends, including Montano, also supported a wider 'invisible college'. Apart from their letters, the reality of their shared friendship, which survived their dispersal by the ideologically rigid persecution of Philip II, is to be found in their *alba amicorum*, those books of friendship that unite them not merely across space but also though time, as Ortelius's epitaph on Bruegel shows.

I started this book with the likenesses that are brought together in de Vos's magnificent group portrait, but I propose to finish it with letters; not just letters in the common modern sense of correspondence, but first of all the written contributions that they made to each other's *alba amicorum*, in particular those of Ortelius, van Meteren and Radermacher, as they laboured to maintain the 'college' that had been scattered from Antwerp.[372]

* * *

The entries in Ortelius's *album amicorum* date from 1574, around the time that the *Paneel* was being painted, and they continue into the 1590s. At the beginning of his *album* is the Christian monogram of the chi/rho (the first two letters of Christ in Greek) with an alpha and an omega on either side, and below it is the Latin 'Vitae Scopus' ('the Aim of Life'). This means that Christ, who is the beginning and end (alpha and omega), is also the aim of life, and this is something that all his friends, regardless of their differing denominational allegiances, would have agreed upon. Underneath, Ortelius has written that it is his wish that his nephew Ortelianus should take the book and keep it. That he specifies in this way that his favourite nephew should take and preserve the book makes clear how important it was to him. Further light is thrown on the book's significance in a long entry made by his first cousin once removed, Daniel Rogers, in the form of an ode in Latin praising the concept of friendship books, addressed to the *philophylacium* of Abraham Ortelius. I take this unusual Latin word to be derived from *philia* (the Greek for love or friendship) and *phulakē* (Greek) or *phylaca* (Latin), both of which mean prison. Hence, Rogers is saying that the *album* is like a jewel case holding the jewels of friendship (literally, a friendship prison) since it encloses the names of those linked by friendship to its owner (or perhaps, by extension, *philophylacium* refers to that circle of friends tightly bound by affection). Whether or not it is a neologism of his own invention, Rogers evidently liked the word since it also appears in the title of the similar ode that he inscribed in the *album amicorum* of Lucas d'Heere. Such an *album*, he writes in the ode for Ortelius, will preserve mutual affection even after death. In future years, descendants will read his name amongst the others, a token of everlasting love. The *album* is not just a record of mutual affection but of shared ideals, and so Rogers declares that a triple pact between 'Natura, Amor, Pallas' ('Nature, Love and Pallas Athene [the goddess of wisdom]') binds them together by ties of family (*generis*), creative talent (*genii*) and intelligence (*ingenii*). The conscious art with which he writes can be seen in the careful echoing of the triple pact in the wordplay on the root 'gen-' that appears in the final line below:

Nam nos, Abrame, triplice foedere
Natura, Amor, Pallasque, ligant duos
Vincloque stamus copulati
Et generis, genii, ingeniique.[373]

Early modern education was centred on teaching Latin and Greek by means of translation both in and out of these languages, and frequently involved turning passages into verse. Thus, all educated people were familiar with the conventions of writing poetry and frequently used it to encapsulate their thoughts. Such verse was valued not for its sentimental qualities, but for the freedom it gave to express one's ideas memorably and forcefully, as in the wordplay employed by Rogers above.

Not all is wordplay and ingenious poetry, however. One of the most moving entries is that of the humanist Andreas Dycchius, who in straightforward prose recalls with gratitude the encouragement that he was given on the first occasion that Ortelius spoke to him when he was young and inexperienced. Even now, he is flattered to have been invited to join Ortelius's distinguished friends in contributing to the *album*.[374]

The emotional value of these albums is also made clear by van Meteren's reaction to the loss of his in 1575, when he was arrested in Antwerp. His indignation at losing this prized personal possession is made clear by his use of the word 'eripuissent', which means 'snatched by force', as if he had been mugged in the street: 'Cum Hispani hoc anno Antverpiae inter caetera Album amicorum illi eripuissent' ('Since this year the Spaniards in Antwerp snatched the *album amicorum* from me amongst other things').[375]

Once back in England, he immediately set about making a new *album*, dated that same year. Just as the exiled d'Heere insisted that he was still a painter of Ghent, so van Meteren resists any attempt by the Spanish (or others) to exile him or change his identity, defiantly describing the *album* as the property of a 'Mercatoris Antverpiani' ('Antwerp merchant').

In the *album*'s opening sonnet, written in Dutch and addressed to lovers of virtue, art and godly living, he writes, 'I invite and request you to make with your hand some fine device [i.e. a motto or pictorial emblem].' The strongly personal nature of the request is apparent in the phrase 'with your hand'. For van Meteren, this is not an abstract business: the book is a physical object that has been handled by all those who contribute to it, and this makes it more precious as a lasting symbol of friendship. Marisa Anne Bass points out that the word he uses for the *album*, 'bandt', signifies not only the 'bound' leaves of the book, but also the friends who have contributed to what is bound in it and who are, in a sense, bound together by it.[376] Six of the first seven entries are then made by members of his immediate circle: Daniel Rogers, Ortelius, Johan Vivien, Hoefnagel, d'Heere and Radermacher. Others who contributed include Lipsius, Peeter Heyns and Marnix, as well as some of van Meteren's English friends, including William Camden, the author of *Britannia* (see p. 159).

Another Englishman invited to contribute to van Meteren's book was Richard Mulcaster, the first headmaster of Merchant Taylors' School and then of St Paul's School. Like Radermacher, who started to write a Dutch book on grammar, Mulcaster values the vernacular and wishes it to be used for weightier purposes. With this in mind, he writes the *Elementarie* (published in 1598), which puts forward the case for teaching children 'the right writing of our English tung'[377] so that it can be used instead of Latin. This is because, as he argues passionately in the peroration that concludes the book, 'I do not think that anie language be it whatsoever, is better able to utter all arguments, either with more pith, or greater planeness, then our English tung is, if the English utterer be as skillfull [knowledgeable] in the matter which he is to utter as the forren utterer is.'[378] This is not an argument for not learning other languages, but a wish to make English their equal; elsewhere in the book, he points out the importance of having a good grasp of the grammar of one's own language before trying to learn the grammar of other languages. There is a real sense in which Mulcaster and his Dutch friends are part of a shared civilisation in their passion for language and recognition of the need to be 'better able to utter all arguments'.

Amongst the many other contributors are family and friends, such as van Meteren's own cousin once removed, Godevaert Montens, who was the father-in-law of Johan Panhuys (see p. 164), Ortelianus, the nephew of Ortelius, and Raphelengius, the son-in-law of Plantin.

If van Meteren's *album* is a roll call of the learned as well as a collection of their affectionate good wishes, Radermacher's is more of an anthology of their poetic endeavours. Much early modern poetry remained unprinted but was circulated in manuscript collections, of which his *album* is typical. It not only contains entries written by his contributors but also verse that has caught his eye when looking at other people's albums and which he has copied down. The nature of the book is revealed by the first entry, a lengthy translation by Johan Vivien of almost the whole of the Book of Proverbs. The work, which covers the first eighty-one pages, is a substantial example of the predominantly Protestant custom of translating parts of the Bible into Latin verse. Tantalisingly, it finishes at the bottom of folio 41r in the middle of Chapter 30 with only one and a half chapters to go. Whether the poem was unfinished at the time, or whether the copyist's patience or pen-nib gave up the ghost, is unknown to me, but the poem itself is a substantial reminder of the shared friendship, scholarship and Protestant faith of Vivien and Radermacher.[379] There are another dozen or so poems by Vivien, as well as several from another manuscript collection, Lucas d'Heere's *Tableau Poetique* (see pp. 130–2), and many more, some anonymous and some copied from other people's albums. In other words, Radermacher's album is not exactly an *album amicorum* but more of a notebook for recording things that he wished to preserve. Its value to Radermacher must, however, have been very similar since many of the items are poems written by his friends, as well as copies of letters, carefully composed epitaphs by Radermacher himself for members of his family, and even a Latin verse letter written by Vivien to Lipsius to console him for the death of a son; it is indeed a record of friendship.

Undoubtedly, however, the most emotionally powerful of the three albums is that of Ortelius. It is also the longest, consisting of 136 texts in Latin, twenty in Greek, eleven in Dutch, four partly or entirely in Hebrew, three in French, two in German, and one in Italian. What emerges through all the mottoes, anagrams, emblems and linguistic erudition is both the respect in which Ortelius is held for his learning and the very real affection with which he is regarded. To illustrate this, I shall turn to the entry by Janus Dousa (Jan van der Does). This poet, scholar and diplomat was a friend of Daniel Rogers when they were both in Paris as young men, a friendship that was to be renewed when they met again in England. It was Dousa who led the citizens of Leiden during the Spanish siege of 1574, stiffening their resistance at a desperate time, and later that year, he was chosen as president of Leiden's newly founded university. His poem begins by describing how Ortelius's *Theatrum* has enabled him to traverse the world in his imagination; in what far corners of seas, mountains or forests is his friend Abraham to be found, he asks with pardonable poetic hyperbole.[380] He would even follow him without fear to the 'tables of cannibals'.[381] At the end of considerable flights of fancy, he enquires: 'Non credis nobis? Abraämi at crede Theatro' ('You don't believe me? Then believe in Abraham's *Theatrum*'). His florid style of compliment is not to today's taste, but its evident enthusiasm and good humour give it a certain charm, and we have no difficulty believing him when he finishes by saying that 'Nec capiet plausus Axis interque tuos' ('the whole world from pole to pole cannot contain your praises').[382]

However, a final question remains, for although the albums help to bring alive the portrait of the civilisation that we have been looking at, can they really preserve it? For the participants and for assiduous writers of letters such as Plantin and Montano, it seems that something *can* be preserved at a distance, and yet Montano writes nostalgically of his eight sweet years in the Netherlands and tells Lipsius how much he misses Plantin for whose company he feels 'heu perpetuum desiderium' ('alas, perpetual desire').[383] Lipsius, for his part, writes to Ortelius and declares that although 'Raro scribo, semper amo, te veterem, te fidus et probum amicum, quod Europam totam velim scire' ('I do not often write, but I will always love my old, faithful and virtuous friend and would wish the whole of Europe to know of my affection').[384] In his final letter, Plantin writes to Lipsius in a faltering hand, which is hard to read: 'Amicus amico s[alutat]' ('a friend greets his friend').[385] From this, we see friendship in absence is sustained by the letters and tangible albums that 'bind' together the handwriting and thoughts of friends, despite their sense of sadness and loss. The memory of the civilisation that depended on these close personal friendships and the trust that enabled the willing sharing of knowledge could just survive when its members were scattered, but the chance of its renewal through the development of new face-to-face friendships across confessional boundaries was clearly lost.

This balance of lost opportunities and acquired alternatives is demonstrated on the one hand by the posthumous painting of Lipsius by Peter Paul Rubens in the room at the Plantin press where the great humanist liked to study and discuss philosophy (*The Four Philosophers*, **ill. 36**), and on the other by the collections of letters that Lipsius started to publish. The Rubens picture shows Lipsius sitting at a table with three books, one of which is open in front of him; he has his finger on the passage to which he is referring. Above him on a shelf is a bust of Seneca, whose works he edited, and on either side of him are Joannes Woverius (who would oversee the posthumous publication of various works by Lipsius) with another book in his hands, and Philip Rubens, the painter's brother who died that year. Standing to the left of the picture is a self-portrait of the painter himself. It is in these intimate surroundings that ideas can be discussed face to face, and disciples not only taught but personally enthused.

It is hard to imagine that anything could replace the impact of such personal teaching, but Lipsius also did a lot to develop the art of letter writing, not only as a means of expressing friendship and feelings but also as a more formal way of setting out philosophical principles. To this end, he collected and published a number of his letters in sets of one hundred (*Centuriae*), and it is from these that we know he wrote to people whom he could have never met in Antwerp, such as the French neostoic and essayist Michel de Montaigne, whose essays are not entirely dissimilar in combining personal thoughts with more serious philosophical ones. We have evidence of Montaigne's response to Lipsius not in specific letters but in comments on Lipsius's wider writings; for example, he describes Lipsius's *Politica* with its copious use of classical quotations as being 'ce docte et laborieux tissue de ses Politiques' ('this learned and carefully woven fabric').[386]

Apart from losing the willingness to tolerate unorthodox opinions which had allowed ideas to be freely debated, Antwerp had lost something else: the merchant wealth that had allowed Plantin to spread knowledge by setting up a prosperous publishing business there had now moved to Amsterdam.[387] Yes, there was a new university at Leiden, where Plantin's son-in-law, Raphelengius, continued publishing, but the enlightened tolerance that marked Leiden's early days under Dousa was not to last. Bruised by controversy, Lipsius moved from Leiden to Leuven. Ortelianus in Protestant London could not be reunited with his uncle in Catholic Antwerp. It had become inconceivable that Hoefnagel, now in Vienna, would ever again meet Montano, who was living at the El Escorial. And while de Vos stays in Antwerp, d'Heere dies an exile in Paris.

Nothing, of course, can last forever, and not all is lost. Lipsius still publishes in Antwerp through the Plantin press, now run by his son-in-law, Moretus, although the main output of the Antwerp press would in future be safely orthodox: a steady stream of missals and psalters, beautifully printed but hardly ground-breaking. Nor, of course, is the presence of Rubens, Van Dyck and Jordaens in Antwerp to be scorned. Nevertheless, one is left with the inescapable feeling that learning and civilisation have moved away. It has to be recognised that dogma-driven persecution destroyed something of great value when, after the violence of the *Beeldenstorm* and Spanish Fury, the trade wars and the fourteen-month siege, half the population of Antwerp emigrated. Old networks and friendships could be preserved by diligent correspondents, but Plantin and Ortelius were to die in 1589 and 1598, respectively, and by 1603, de Vos was dead as well. New networks and friendships could no longer be so easily made. Cosmopolitan Antwerp, buzzing with commercial and intellectual energy, had become a relative backwater, albeit a cultured one.

* * *

It is necessary to draw lessons from history if we are not to repeat similar idiocies time after time, but to do so risks distorting history as well as offending those with committed beliefs. For example, C.V. Wedgwood's *William the Silent* is a splendid example of an enormously readable narrative history.[388] Nevertheless, writing during the Second World War as she was, Wedgwood almost inevitably presents William as a principled and heroic leader of a small European country invaded by a brutal hostile power, whose self-sacrificing leadership paves the way for the independence of the future Netherlands. Although she never makes a specific comparison of Philip's armies with the Nazi invaders, her sympathies with William as the plucky underdog lead her, I suspect, to present an unduly idealised picture of his motives in struggling to establish a free, tolerant and united country. Although her sympathies are clear, she wisely avoids specific comparisons, and I shall follow her example.

Nevertheless, the destruction of Antwerp's position as a prosperous financial centre at the heart of a civilised, international culture by an unyielding ideology suggests lines of thought that some readers will wish to pursue but others to resist. There are always those who wish to set aside anything from the past that might point to the folly of their insisting on ideological purity in the face of reality. As J.K. Galbraith, that wry observer of human nature and chronicler of the Great Crash of 1929, observed ironically in *A Short History of Financial Euphoria*: 'Past experience, to the extent that it is part of memory at all, is dismissed as the primitive refuge of those who do not have the insight to appreciate the incredible wonders of the present.'[389] In fact, as R.H. Tawney argues in *Religion and the Rise of Capitalism*, to examine the issues of the past, 'even in the narrow field of a single country and a limited period is not mere antiquarianism. It is to summon the living, not to invoke a corpse, and to see from a new angle the problems of our own age, by widening the experience brought to their consideration.'[390]

The subjects of this book embodied what used to be referred to as 'love of the brethren and all sound learning' (quaintly old-fashioned though that gendered language sounds today),[391] and few, I imagine, would disagree with the assertion that strong friendships across confessional boundaries and national borders were an integral part of Antwerp's civilisation, paving the way for the fruitful exchange of knowledge.

Where different opinions were held, a certain degree of detachment must have been a pre-condition for these learned friendships to flourish; a willingness to allow the warmth of personal affection to override religious and political disagreements. Lipsius, for his part, certainly tested the tolerance of some of his friends when he argued that any dissent that threatens national unity must be 'cut out and burnt'. Despite the unfortunate and tactless image of burning that he borrows from Cicero, his tone is normally more moderate, writing as he does that 'Virtus autem media via ingreditur. & cautè cavet nequid in actionibus suis defiat aut excedat' ('virtue must strike the middle path between over-reaction and mere inertia') (*Constantia* I, 4).

Plantin sums up what this calm pursuit of the middle way means in personal terms when he describes what he sees as happiness in this world in a poem of stoic detachment:

'*Le Bonheur de ce monde*'

Avoir une maison commode, propre & belle,
Un jardin tapissé d'espaliers odorans,

Des fruits, d'excellent vin, peu de train, peu d'enfans,
Posséder seul, sans bruit, une femme fidèle.

    N'avoir dettes, amour, ni procés, ni querelle,
Ni de partage à faire avecque ses parens,
Se contenter de peu, n'espérer rien des Grands,
Régler tous ses desseins sur un juste modèle.

    Vivre avecque franchise et sans ambition,
S'adonner sans scrupule à la dévotion,
Domter ses passions, les rendre obéissantes.

    Conserver l'esprit libre, et le jugement fort,
Dire son Chapelet en cultivant ses entes,
C'est attendre chez soi bien doucement la mort.

'This world's Happiness'

    To have a comfortable, clean and attractive house,
a garden adorned with sweet-smelling espaliers,
their fruit, good wine, few hindrances or children,
to have to yourself without fuss a faithful wife;
    To have no debts, no passionate desires, neither law-suits nor quarrels,
no property disputes to settle with relatives,
to be satisfied with little, and expect nothing from the great,
to act justly in all one's schemes;
    To live without deceit or ambition,
to commit yourself to a devout life,
to control your desires, making them obey your will;
    To keep the mind free and the judgement firm,
to tell one's beads while cultivating new growth,
that is what it is to wait peacefully at home for death.[392]

As you look round what was once Plantin' s sheltered, courtyard garden at the Plantin-Moretus Museum, it is not difficult to imagine the peace that Plantin may just occasionally have found time to enjoy, surrounded by his blossoming fruit trees. There is every reason to suppose that Jeanne de la Rivière was indeed 'une femme fidèle' and that she would have contributed largely to this peaceful and idyllic environment (when it was not being rudely interrupted by outside forces). Nevertheless, there is something indubitably sad in the thought that he considers 'peu d'enfans' to be a requirement for happiness, while his desire to avoid family quarrels about money and to put aside memories of his shabby financial treatment by Philip II ('n'espérer rien des Grands') hints at past unhappiness. Whether the *persona* of the poet here truly represents Plantin is open to argument. Although what he describes here sounds like the calm of an old man, all passion spent, it may have been written in about 1579, some time before the end of his life.

A more positive understanding of mutual affection and a love of learning is to be found in Hoefnagel's picture entitled *Amicitiae monumentum* ('Monument of Friendship'), which is dedicated to Abraham Ortelius (ill. 37). In it, we see the elements of civilisation – both its scholarship and the friendship that enables it to thrive. Although perhaps more positive than Plantin's poem, there is a hint of doubt in what is written at the top in gold leaf: 'Ars neminem habet osore[m] nisi ignora[n]tia' ('Art has no enemy but ignorance'). *Ars* is difficult to translate; it means more than fine painting or the skill of the map illustrator, and refers to all the skills and understanding that should, for example, make a graduate a *magister artium* (a master of the arts). These are the arts that the groups around Ortelius, Plantin and Radermacher valued and fostered in mutual affection and the exchange of ideas. Here at the centre of Hoefnagel's painting is the owl of Minerva or Pallas Athene, the goddess of wisdom, which carries the *caduceus*, the staff entwined by two serpents that is the rod of Hermes, messenger of the gods. The owl, as it says below, is *Hermathena*, combining the two gods' functions as the messenger of wisdom and sharer of knowledge. The *caduceus* itself is made from a paintbrush, implying that painting is perhaps the means by which the message of wisdom is shared. The owl is perched upon a globe, no doubt the orb of the whole world that is shown in Ortelius's *Theatrum Orbis Terrarum*. On either side of it are the dividers used in cartography and further brushes for art, both surrounded by the shells used to hold the pigments but which were also studied by the new biologists. Further up at the sides are a pair of butterflies facing each other, accurately observed but also symbols of new life (butterflies emerge from chrysalides) and matching each other in perfect friendship. Is the phrase 'Ars neminem habet osore[m] nisi ignora[n]tia' written above as reassurance or in defiance? Ignorance is not in short supply, which may explain why the owl, balanced on the globe, which is in turn balanced on a book, looks so precarious. In an uncertain world, where civilisation is so insecure, wealth is destroyed, and learning hindered by unyielding ideology, perhaps we must settle for the modest, stoically understated wishes of the aged Plantin when he describes all that can be hoped for in this world – but we should also enjoy the remarkable beauty of Hoefnagel's art and vision.[393]

Postscript

In a letter of 8 July 1589, François Raphelengien, Plantin's grandson (the son of his daughter Marguerite and Raphelengius), writes to Ortelianus to express his disappointment that his planned visit to Italy has been cancelled because, after his grandfather's death, he is 'utilem domui et familiae' ('needed at home in the family business'). He describes his grandfather's illness, stricken with a painful abscess, and how about eight days later he developed a high fever, which only left him just before death: 'Metuebamus mortem duram et laborosiam; sed, laus Deo, placide in vocibus O Jesu, O Jesu, expiravit' ('We feared that he would have a drawn out and painful death, but, God be thanked, he died quietly saying with his last breath, O Jesus, O Jesus').[394]

Some nine years later, in 1598, Ortelius wrote to his nephew Ortelianus to express his disappointment that the latter had gone straight back home from Amsterdam without coming south to visit him; he urges him to return from London to live with him, but the committed Protestant could not safely return to Catholic Antwerp and his uncle never saw him again. In June that year, Ortelius writes to him again, but this time about normal business matters. Then, at the end of that month, he died at the age of seventy-one. The engraver Philip Galle writes to van Meteren to tell him of the death and expresses the wish that Ortelianus could be there to comfort Ortelius's unmarried sister Anne, who had always lived with him.[395] Despite his disappointment that Ortelianus could not return to him, Ortelius's death seems to have been a peaceful one, summed up by the motto on his tombstone, which read 'Quietis cultor sine lite, uxore, prole' ('He was a cultivator of peace without accusers, wife or children').

Eight years later, in March 1606, Lipsius was to die at Leuven, accompanied, like Plantin, by the prayers of Jesuit priests. According to the account of those at his deathbed, he displayed the 'Christiani roboris constantia' ('constancy of Christian strength'). They also reported that when encouraged to respond to death with the stoicism that he had advocated, he replied that 'illa sunt vana ... haec est vera patientia' ('those things are vain ... here is true patience [in Christ's suffering on the Cross, which was portrayed in the crucifix held before him]'). There may well have been a touch of propaganda in this edifying account of his death, but it would be unreasonably cynical to suggest that he did not die peacefully, as a faithful Catholic.[396]

Among Lipsius's papers at his death was found that last letter from Plantin ('A friend greets a friend'[397]). Affectionate friendship had survived death as well as the fall of Antwerp, but the group who had appeared in the *Panhuys Paneel* had long been scattered. Radermacher himself was to live on until 1617 as an elder of the church in Middelburg, but his erstwhile master, Hooftman, was long since dead, as were Panhuys himself and his wife, exhausted after their flight from Antwerp in 1585. Van Meteren was to live a little longer in London, but the civilised community epitomised by those whom Radermacher had gathered together for de Vos to paint in the *Paneel* had come to an end.

Montaigne, one of Lipsius's many correspondents and admirers, seems to suggest the cause for this sad end in his essay 'De l'Art de Conferer' in Book 3 of the *Essais*, when he pleads for tolerance of differing opinions regardless of who is actually right. The fault lies in what he calls 'aigreur tyrannique': 'car c'est tousjours un'aigreur tyrannique de ne pouvoir souffrir une forme diverse à la sienne' ('for it is always a tyrannical sourness to be unable to endure a way of thinking different from one's own').

Appendix

The political background: A timeline of the events leading up to the Dutch Revolt and first part of the Eighty Years' War (until 1609)

This attempt to summarise the religious, political and military upheavals associated with the power struggles of the late sixteenth century inevitably distorts at times by simplifying what is complex, but I hope it will be helpful. It is necessary to go back about a century before the events described in this book to see their origins.

The rebels believed that the revolt (or series of revolts) had its roots in the decision of Philip II of Spain to use force to eradicate Calvinism and to ride roughshod over the privileges and freedoms that had been granted to the cities by earlier Dukes of Burgundy. Philip, however, was hereditary ruler of the Netherlands by virtue of being the heir of the Dukes of Burgundy and felt entitled to enforce his authority and restore order after the *Beeldenstorm* (the iconoclastic destruction of images in churches across the Low Countries) in order to protect what he considered to be true religion, namely Catholicism. Apart from the struggle for political control and between differing religious beliefs, commercial interests and taxation were also triggers of the dispute.

Year	Low Countries	England, France, Germany and elsewhere
1477	Charles the Bold, Duke of Burgundy, whose territories include the Low Countries, is killed at the Battle of Nancy. Charles's sole child, Mary of Burgundy, is recognised at Ghent as his successor, but has to grant the Great Privilege, which restores to the provinces and cities of the Netherlands rights that had been gradually abolished by previous dukes in their efforts to create a centralised state. Faced with aggression from Louis XI of France, who takes control of Burgundy itself, she chooses to find support by marrying Maximilian of Austria, a member of the Habsburg dynasty.	
1478	Birth of Philip the Fair (son of Mary and Maximilian).	
1482	Philip the Fair becomes the first Habsburg Duke of Burgundy upon the death of his mother.	
1489		*By the treaty of Medina el Campo between England and Spain, Arthur (elder son of Henry VII of England) and Katherine of Aragon are betrothed.*
1496	Philip the Fair marries Joanna, second daughter of Queen Isabella of Castile and King Ferdinand of Aragon. On the subsequent death of her siblings, Joanna becomes heir presumptive to both Spanish kingdoms.	
1500	The son of Philip and Joanna, the future Charles V, is born in Ghent. He is brought up a fluent Dutch speaker.	
1501		*The 15-year-old Prince Arthur marries the 16-year-old Katherine of Aragon.*
1502		*Arthur dies less than five months after the marriage.*
1503		*Papal dispensation is given for the betrothal of Arthur's younger brother (the future Henry VIII) to Katherine of Aragon.*
1506	Charles inherits the lordship of the Burgundian territories, which includes the Low Countries.	

1509		Death of Henry VII and accession of Henry VIII, who later marries Katherine of Aragon.
1514		Mary Tudor (sister of Henry VIII) marries Louis XII of France.
1515	Charles takes an oath on his Joyous Entry as Duke of Brabant to guarantee the freedom and privileges of his Netherlandish subjects.	
1516	Charles becomes King of Spain.	Katherine of Aragon gives birth to Princess Mary. Following the death of Louis XII, Henry VIII's sister, Mary Tudor, marries Charles Brandon without Henry's permission. (Their daughter, Frances, will be the mother of Lady Jane Grey.)
1517		Luther nails his ninety-five theses to the church door at Wittenberg, an act usually taken as the start of the Reformation.
1519	Charles, now also Archduke of Austria, is elected Holy Roman Emperor. Discontent grows in the Low Countries at heavy taxes to fund Charles's endless wars against France, Protestant German princes, and the Ottoman Empire.	
1521		Luther excommunicated.
1525		François I of France is defeated and captured at the Battle of Pavia by the imperial forces of Charles V.
1526		The Treaty of Madrid forces the captured François I to renounce all claims in Italy. Once freed, however, he forms an alliance with Henry VIII of England and the Pope, and resumes hostilities.
1527		Charles V sacks Rome and forces the Pope to withdraw from this alliance. Henry VIII asks the Pope unsuccessfully for an annulment of his marriage to Katherine (aunt of Charles V).
1530		Schmalkaldic League formed by German Protestant princes to resist Charles V's attempts to impose Catholic conformity throughout the Holy Roman Empire.
1531		Parliament recognises Henry VIII as Supreme Head of the Church of England.

1533		*Henry VIII divorces Katherine of Aragon and marries Anne Boleyn.*
		Thomas Cranmer is appointed Archbishop of Canterbury. Both Henry and Cranmer are excommunicated.
		Anne Boleyn gives birth to Princess Elizabeth.
1536		*Death of Katherine of Aragon.*
		Anne Boleyn beheaded.
		Henry marries Jane Seymour.
1537		*Birth of Prince Edward and death of Jane Seymour in childbirth.*
1540–3		*Henry marries his last three wives, none of whom bear him a child.*
1547		*Henry dies and his young son Edward VI accedes to throne. The Duke of Somerset is Lord Protector and the new government is strongly Calvinist.*
		The first stranger church for foreign Protestants is set up by the Italian Bernardino Ochino with Cranmer's approval.
1549	The Pragmatic Sanction of Charles V formally unites all the territories of which he was personally ruler into one 'state'.	
	The Joyous Entry into Antwerp of the future Philip II as Charles V's heir apparent.	
1550	A second Reformed stranger church, which would become the mother church of the Dutch Reformed Church, is established at Austin Friars in London.	*Edward's council authorises Calvinist exiles from the Low Countries to use the former Augustinian priory at Austin Friars in London as a stranger church under their own supervision.*
1553		*Edward VI dies, naming the Protestant Lady Jane Grey as his successor.*
		Mary I accedes to throne after an unsuccessful attempt to put Jane Grey on throne. Leading Protestants flee to the continent.
1554		*Lady Jane Grey executed.*
		Mary marries Philip of Spain, son of Charles V.

1555	After the Peace of Augsburg ends the second Schmalkaldic War, Charles V abdicates and is succeeded by his brother Ferdinand as Emperor, while he passes the throne of Spain and Duchy of Brabant (which had feudal overlordship of a large part of the Low Countries, including Antwerp) to his son, Philip II (educated in Spain and unable to speak Dutch).	*The Schmalkaldic Wars end with the Peace of Augsburg. Charles V agrees that the ruler of each territory within the Holy Roman Empire may determine its own religious allegiance.*
1558	The Netherlands States General resists Philip's tax proposals. Following this, the Counts of Egmont and Hoorn and William of Orange withdraw from States General.	*Mary I of England dies childless and Elizabeth I accedes to the English throne.*
1559	Philip moves from the Low Countries to Spain and appoints his illegitimate half-sister, Margaret of Parma, Regent of the Low Countries.	*Elizabeth I permits Protestants from the Low Countries to use the church at Austin Friars again, but under the supervision of the Bishop of London.*
1560s	Protestantism spreads widely in the Netherlands, followed by harsh repression.	
1562		*Massacre of Huguenots (French Protestants) at Vassy (modern spelling Wassy) by troops under command of François, Duke of Guise, ignites the French Wars of Religion. French Calvinist refugees flee to the southern Netherlands, spreading Calvinism.*
1565	Bad harvest adds to discontent.	*Ongoing war between Denmark and Sweden damages Dutch trade by closing the Baltic to merchant vessels.*
1566	The 'Wonder Year': in an outburst of Protestant confidence, 400 nobles petition Margaret of Parma to suspend the persecution of Protestants until peace is restored. The petitioners are scornfully called beggars or *Geuzen*, which they ironically take as a proud title. Hedge priests (open-air preachers) preach Calvinism and iconoclasm. The *Beeldenstorm* (iconoclasm) follows and much damage is done to church art.	

1567	Calvinist *Gueux* rebels are overwhelmed at Oosterweel (just outside Antwerp) by an army of Spanish mercenaries and troops provided by Count Egmont. Many Protestants and William of Orange leave Antwerp. Margaret restores order, but the Duke of Alba is sent to the Low Countries with 10,000 Spanish soldiers by Philip II. Alba sets up the Council of Troubles (also known as the Council of Blood); the Counts of Egmont and Hoorn are executed. NB: Both were Catholic rather than Protestant, but were reluctant to yield too much power to Philip. William withdraws to his father-in-law's territory of Saxony. Margaret resigns as Regent after swearing in Alba as her successor. Antwerp taxed 400,0000 guilders to pay for a new citadel for Spanish troops.	
1568	William of Orange returns, but is defeated. Spanish control is established.	
1570	Alba overrides the States General by introducing a new tax (the Tenth Penny) to pay his troops, which provokes fierce discontent.	*The Pope excommunicates Elizabeth I and calls upon English Catholics to remove her from the throne.*
1572	Revolt breaks out again in the Low Countries: at the insistence of the Spanish, Elizabeth I drives out the *Watergeuzen* (Sea Beggars) from English ports and they seize the undefended port of Brielle (Brill). This gives heart to the rebels. William returns and establishes his court at Delft. *Gueux* based at Vlissingen (Flushing) on the Scheldt estuary stifle trade with Antwerp.	*Henri, King of Navarre and a Protestant, marries Margaret of Valois, daughter of Henri II of France and Catherine de Medici in Paris on 18 August. On 24 August, the St Bartholomew's Day Massacre begins: Coligny, the Huguenot leader, and thousands of other Huguenots in Paris and across France are murdered. Henri of Navarre saves his life by converting to Catholicism. He is held in Paris. French Protestants are unable to support the Dutch rebels any longer.*
1573	Philip II replaces Alba with Luis de Requesens as his commander in the Low Countries.	
1574	In April, mutinous Spanish troops demanding their back pay take possession of Antwerp Town Hall; they are eventually paid off with difficulty. No English merchant ships sail up the Scheldt thereafter.	*Charles IX of France dies without an heir and is succeeded by his brother Henri III.*

1576	March: Requesens dies. Philip II declares Spain bankrupt. In November, unpaid troops riot in Antwerp, causing great damage and many deaths in the Spanish Fury. This and similar atrocities elsewhere so enrage the seventeen provinces of the Low Countries that they agree the Pacification of Ghent by which all provinces (regardless of whether they were predominantly Catholic or Protestant) combine to demand the withdrawal of Spanish troops.	*Henri of Navarre escapes Paris, renounces Catholicism and resumes leadership of the Huguenots. The Catholic League is formed with Spanish support to oppose Henri III after he made concessions to the Huguenots in the Edict of Beaulieu.*
1579	Union of Arras: Provoked by Reformed intolerance, the ten predominantly Catholic southern provinces return to Spain. Union of Utrecht: The seven northern provinces remain united against the Spanish.	
1581	The Duke of Anjou, younger brother of Henri III of France, is invited by the States General of the United Provinces to rule in place of Philip. He first insists on the Act of Abjuration, in which Philip is formally deposed as sovereign.	
1583	Anjou is not accepted by all the provinces and tries to seize power by capturing Antwerp by a ruse, but suffers a humiliating defeat. Elizabeth I is then invited to rule, but refuses. A new Spanish army is sent under the Duke of Parma to reconquer the Netherlands.	
1584	William of Orange assassinated (he had been declared an outlaw by Philip).	*The death of the Duke of Anjou, the last of Henri III's brothers, means that Henri, the Protestant King of Navarre, becomes heir presumptive to the throne of France.*
1585	Fall of Antwerp to Parma. Protestants given four years in which to leave.	

1587	Treaty of Nonsuch: England agrees to aid Dutch rebels. The Earl of Leicester is dispatched with over 5,000 soldiers. (This was in response to an alliance between Spain and the French Catholic League aimed at destroying the Huguenots. Leicester, however, has little understanding of the importance of trade and manages to antagonise Catholic moderates; he returns to England a year later.) In the absence of foreign royalty to become ruler, William of Orange's son, Maurice, is appointed Captain General of the Dutch army; the Netherlands now functions as a republic.	*England intervenes on behalf of the United Provinces.*
1588	Parma pauses war against the Dutch rebels to prepare for the planned invasion of England.	*The Armada fails to enable Parma's Spanish army from Flanders to invade England. Henri, Duke of Guise, leader of the Catholic League, enters Paris and Henri III is forced to flee. He joins with Henri of Navarre in resisting the Catholic League.*
1589		*Assassination of Henri III by a Catholic fanatic. Upon his death, the House of Valois dies out. Henri of Navarre becomes Henri IV of France (the first Bourbon), but civil war continues.*
1593–4		*Henri IV converts to Catholicism in order to bring the French Wars of Religion to an end and is crowned at Chartres. Paris submits.*
1596	Triple Alliance of England, France and the Dutch northern provinces against Spain. Philip grants the Low Countries to Archdukes Albert and Isabella (Philip's nephew and elder daughter), who rule well and consolidate Habsburg control of the southern provinces. In the meantime, Maurice's military successes secure control of the northern provinces, which had become *de facto* a separate state.	
1598		*Edict of Nantes grants certain privileges to Huguenots.*
1609	Start of the Twelve Years' Truce between the United Provinces and Spain.	
1610		*Assassination of Henri IV by a Catholic fanatic.*

Bibliography

Primary sources (including transcriptions and translations)

Boderie, Guy Lefèvre de la, 'Encyclie', in Dudley Wilson (ed.), *French Renaissance Scientific Poetry* (London: The Athlone Press, 1974)

Cisneros, Francisco Jiménez de, *Complutensian Polyglot Bible* (Alcalá de Henares, 1517), available online at https://archive.org/details/polyglotcomplutensis/Vol%201/page/n7/mode/2up (accessed 24.04.2023)

Erasmus, *Ten Colloquies*, trans. Craig R. Thompson (Indianapolis: The Library of Liberal Arts, 1957)

Foxe, John, *Actes and Monuments* (London: John Day, 1563)

Guicciardini, Lodovico, *Descrittione di M. Lodovico Guicciardini, Gentilhuomo Fiorentino, di Tutti I Paesi Bassi, Altrimenti Detti Germania Inferiore* (London: FB&c. Ltd, 2018)

Haecht, Godevaerd van, *De Kroniek van Godevaerd van Haecht over de troebelen van 1565 tot 1574 te Antwerpen en elders*, ed. Rob van Roosbroek (1929/30), available online at https://www.dbnl.org/tekst/haec002kron01_01/#Literatuur_&_Taal (accessed 17.07.2023)

Heere, Lucas d', *Den hof en boomgaerd der poësien* (Ghent: Ghileyn Manilius, 1565)

——, 'Tableau Poetique', in Frederica van Dam and Werner Waterschoot (eds), *Lucas d'Heere, Tableau Poetique: Verzen van een Vlaamse migrant-kunstenaar voor de entourage van de Seymours op Wolf Hall* (Ghent: Koninklijke Academie voor Nederlandse Taal-en-Letterkunde, 2016)

Hessels, Jan Hendrick, *Epistulae Ortelianae Ecclesiae Londino-Batavae Archivum, Volume I, Parts 1 and 2* (Cambridge: Cambridge University Press, 2009)

Hexham, Henry, *The Great Word Book: Set in 't Nederduytsch, ende in 't Engelsch* (Rotterdam: Arnout Leers, 1648), transcription available online at https://www.dbnl.org/tekst/hexh001gro001_01/colofon.php

Heyns, Peeter, *Spieghel der Werelt, Ghestelt in Ryme door M. Peeter Heyns* (Antwerp: Plantin for Philips Galle, 1577)

Mander, Karel van, 'Het Schilder-boek', in *Karel van Mander and his Foundation of the Noble, Free Art of Painting*, trans. Walter S. Melion (Leiden & Boston: Brill, 2023)

——, *Het Schilder-boek*, trans. Henri Hymans (Paris: Librairie de l'Art, 1884; facsimile reprint)

Manningham, John, *Diary of John Manningham*, ed. W. Tite (London: Camden Society, 1868)

Marot, Clément, *Oeuvres poétiques, Tome II*, ed. Gérard Defaux (Paris: Clasiques Garnier, 1993)

Meteren, Emanuel van, *Album Amicorum* (MS Douce 68, Bodleian Library, Oxford)

——, 'Album Amicorum', in H.C. Rogge (ed.), *Het Album van Emanuel van Meteren* (The Hague: Netherlands Institute for Art History, 1898)

——, *Comentarius dat is ghedaechtenis boek ofte register vande gheschiedenissen, handel ende wesen etc. van mij Emanuel Demetrius* (MS 237, Auckland Public Library, Sir George Grey Special Collections)

Montaigne, Michel de, *Essais*, transcribed from the Bordeaux copy (Ēdition Viley-Saulnier) by the Montaigne Project, Chicago University, available online at https://www.lib.uchicago.edu/efts/ARTFL/projects/montaigne

Mulcaster, Richard, *The First Part of the Elementarie* (Menston: Scolar Press, 1970),

Ortelius, Abraham, *Album Amicorum* (MS LC.2.113, Pembroke College Library, Cambridge), available online at https://cudl.lib.cam.ac.uk/view/MS-LC-00002-00113/11

——, *Album Amicorum: Abraham Ortelius*, ed. Jean Puraye (Amsterdam: A. L. van Gendt, 1969)

——, *Theatrum Orbis Terrarum Abrahami Orteli Antverp: The Theatre of the Whole World* (London: Iohn Norton, 1606), available online at https://iiif. lib.harvard.edu/manifests/view/drs:50211907$1i

Plantin, Christophe, *Biblia Sacra Hebraice, Chaldaice, Graece, & Latine* (Antwerp: Ex officina Christophori Plantini, 1569–72)

——, *Correspondance de Christophe Plantin*, eds M. Rooses and J. Denucé (Antwerp: J.E. Buschmann, 1883–1914)

——, *Supplément à la Correspondance de Christophe Plantin*, ed. M. van Durme (Antwerp: De Nederlandsche Boekhandel, 1955)

——, *Thesaurus Theutonicae Linguae: Schat der Neder-duyt-scher spraken* (The Hague: Mouton, 1972).

Rogers, Daniel, *De laudibus Antverpiae oda sapphica* (Antwerp: Plantin, 1565)

Stow, John, *A Survey of London. Reprinted from the Text of 1603*, ed. C.L. Kingsford (Oxford, 1908)

Vasari, Giorgio, *Lives of Seventy of the Most Eminent Painters, Sculptors and Architects*, vol. 2, eds E.H. Blashfield, E.W. Blashfield, and A.A. Hopkins (New York: Charles Scribner's Sons, 1911)

Other works cited

Arber, Agnes, *Herbals, their Origin and Evolution* (Cambridge: Cambridge University Press, 1912)

Archer, Ian W., 'Palavicino, Sir Horatio', in *Oxford Dictionary of National Biography* (2008), available online at https://www.oxforddnb. com/display/10.1093/ref:odnb/9780198614128.001.0001/odnb-9780198614128-e-21153 (accessed 24.06.18)

Bass, Marisa Anne, *Insect Artifice: Nature and Art in the Dutch Revolt* (Princeton & Oxford: Princeton University Press, 2019)

——, 'Justus Lipsius and his silver pen', *Journal of the Warburg and Courtauld Institute* 70 (2007), pp. 157–94

——, 'Mimetic obscurity in Joris Hoefnagel's *Four Elements*', in Karl A.E. Enenkel and Paul J. Smith (eds), *Emblems and the Natural World* (Leiden & Boston: Brill, 2017), pp. 521–46

——, 'Patience grows: The first roots of Joris Hoefnagel's emblematic art', in Walter S. Melion, Bret Rothstein, and Michel Weemans (eds), *The Anthropomorphic Lens, Anthropomorphism, Microcosmism and Analogy in Early Modern Thought and Visual Arts* (Leiden: Brill, 2015), pp. 145–78

Batavia Illustrata ofte Oud Batavien (The Hague: Johan Veely, Johan Tongerloo en Jasper Doll, 1685), available online at https://www.google.co.uk/books/edition/Batavia_illustrata_ofte_Verhandelinge_va/MGNUAAAAcAAJ?hl=en&gbpv=1&dq=Batavien&pg=PA44&printsec=frontcover (accessed 19.04.2023)

Battilana, Natale, *Genealogie delle Famiglie Nobili di Genova* (Genova, 1825)

Berens, Willi, 'Ein großer Eupener: Gillis Hooftman', in *Geschichtliches Eupen* I (1968)

Besse, Jean-Marc, *Les Grandeurs de la Terre: Aspects du savoir géographique à la Renaissance* (Lyon: ENS Éditions, 2003)

Binding, Paul, *Imagined Corners: Exploring the World's First Atlas* (London: Headline Review, 2003)

Biographie Nationale de Belgique, Tome 9 (Brussels: Emile Bruylant, 1886/7), available online at https://academieroyale.be/Academie/documents/FichierPDFBiographieNationaleTome2050.pdf (accessed 05.05.23)

Boersma, Owe, 'Florio, Michael Angelo' in *Oxford Dictionary of National Biography* (2004), available online at https://www.oxforddnb.com/view/10.1093/ref:odnb/9780198614128.001.0001/odnb-9780198614128-e-9759?rskey=1tSgM4&result=3, (accessed 02.12.2022)

Bostoen, Karel, *Bonis in Bonum: Johan Radermacher de Oude (1538–1617), humanist en koopman* (Hilversum: Verloren, 1998)

Bracken, Susan, 'Lucas de Heere' in *Oxford Dictionary of National Biography* (2004), available online at https://www.oxforddnb.com/display/10.1093/ref:odnb/9780198614128.001.0001/odnb-9780198614128-e-7424?rskey=zgRIRi&result=1 (accessed 03.03.23)

Brotton, Jerry, *A History of the World in Twelve Maps* (London: Penguin, 2013)

Brummel, L., *Twee Ballingen's Lands Tijdens Onze Opstand Tegen Spanje: Hugo Blotius (1534–1608); Emanuel van Meteren (1535–1612)* (The Hague: Martinus Nijhof, 1972)

Buchanan, Iain, 'A portrait of Emanuel van Meteren and his wife, Hester van Corput, by Joris Hoefnagel', *The Burlington Magazine* 161 (March 2019), pp. 201–05

Büttner, M, 'The significance of the Reformation for the reorientation of geography in Lutheran Germany', *History of Science* 17 (1979), pp. 151–69

Castro, Jean de, *Chansons, stanses, sonets, et épigrammes à deux parties... livre second* (Anvers: Pierre Phalèse et Jean Bellère, 1592)

——, *Harmonie joyeuse et délectable, contenant aucunes stanzes et chansons à quatre parties* (Anvers: Pierre Phalèse et Jean Bellère, 1595)

——, *Sonets, avec une chanson, contenant neuf parties l'une suivant l'autre le tout à deux parties... livre premier* (Anvers: Pierre Phalèse et Jean Bellère, 1592)

Church, Alfred J. and Brodribb W.J. (eds), *The Agricola and Germania of Tacitus* (London: Macmillan & Co., 1889).

Clair, Colin, *Christopher Plantin* (London: Cassell, 1960)

Clark, Kenneth, *Moments of Vision* (London: John Murray, 1981)

Cordier, Jean-Yves, 'Nicolas de Malapert, Ami de Joris Hoefnagel à Séville. Eléments Biographiques. A propos de la Vue de Séville par Hoefnagel du *Civitates Orbis Terrarum*, vol. V, planche 7 (1598)', *le blog de jean-yves cordier* (2015), available online at https://www.lavieb-aile.com/2015/03/nicolas-de-malepert-ami-de-joris-hoefnagel-a-seville-elements-biographiques-les-vues-de-seville-par-hoefnagel-volume-v-du-civitates (accessed 18.03.23)

Curry, Helen Anne, Jardine, Nicholas, Secord, James Andrew, and Spary, Emma C. (eds), *Worlds of Natural History* (Cambridge: Cambridge University Press, 2018)

Dam, Frederica van and Waterschoot, Werner (eds), *Lucas d'Heere, Tableau Poetique: Verzen van een Vlaamse migrant-kunstenaar voor de entourage van de Seymours op Wolf Hall* (Ghent: Koninklijke Academie voor Nederlandse Taal-en-Letterkunde, 2016)

Davies, Horton, *Worship and Theology in England, Volume 1: From Cranmer to Hooker* (Grand Rapids, MI & Cambridge, UK: William B. Eerdmans Publishing Company, 1970)

Denucé, J., *L'Afrique au XVIe Siècle et le commerce anversois* (Antwerp: De Sikkel, 1937)

D'Ewes, Sir S. (ed.), *The Journals of All the Parliaments during the Reign of Queen Elizabeth* (London: Irish University Press, 1973)

Dickens, A.G., *The Age of Humanism and Reformation: Europe in the Fourteenth, Fifteenth and Sixteenth Centuries* (London: Prentice-Hall International, 1977)

Dorsten, J.A. van, *Poets, Patrons and Professors: Sir Philip Sidney, Daniel Rogers and the Leiden Humanists* (Leiden: Leiden University Press, published for the Sir Thomas Browne Institute, 1962)

——, *The Radical Arts: First Decade of an Elizabethan Renaissance* (Leiden: Leiden University Press, published for the Sir Thomas Browne Institute, 1970)

——, *The Anglo-Dutch Renaissance* (Leiden: R. J. Brill & Leiden University Press, 1988)

Duke, A.C. and Tamse C.A., *Clio's Mirror: Historiography in Britain and The Netherlands* (Zutphen: De Walburg Pers, 1985)

Dunthorne, Hugh, *Britain and the Dutch Revolt 1560–1700* (Cambridge: Cambridge University Press, 2013)

Dutch Church, 'Adriaan van Haemstede', available online at https://www.dutchchurch.org.uk/adriaan-van-haemstede/ (accessed 02.01.2023).

Egmond, Florike, 'European exchanges and communities', in Helen Anne Curry, Nicholas Jardine, James Andrew Secord, and Emma C. Spary (eds), *Worlds of Natural History* (Cambridge: Cambridge University Press, 2018), pp. 78–93

Elliott, J. H., *Europe Divided* (London: Collins, 1968)

Enenkel, Karl A.E. and Smith, Paul J. (eds), *Emblems and the Natural World* (Leiden & Boston: Brill, 2017)

Farrer, Austin, *A Science of God* (London: Geoffrey Bles, 1966)

Filedt Kok, J.P., 'Jan Jansz Mostaert, *Portrait of an African Man*, Mechelen, *c.*1525–*c.*1530', in J.P. Filedt Kok (ed.), *Early Netherlandish Paintings* (2010), available online at hdl.handle.net/10934/RM0001.COLLECT.431086 (accessed 06.05.2021)

Freedberg, David, 'Art and iconoclasm, 1525–1580: The case of the Northern Netherlands', in J.P. Filedt Kok, W. Halsema-Kubes, and W.T. Kloek (eds), *Kunst voor de Beeldenstorm* (Amsterdam: Rijksmuseum, 1986), pp. 69–84

Galbraith, John Kenneth, *A Short History of Financial Euphoria* (London: Penguin, 1990)

——, *The Great Crash 1929*, 2nd edn (London: Penguin, 1975)

Gelderblom, Oscar, *Cities of Commerce: The Institutional Foundations of International Trade in the Low Countries, 1250–1650* (Princeton: Princeton University Press, 2013)

Gibson, Walter S., 'Artists and *rederijkers* in the age of Bruegel', *The Art Bulletin* 63(3) (2014), pp. 426–46

Göttler, Christine, 'Imagination in the chamber of sleep: Karel van Mander on Somnus and Morpheus', in Christoph Lütty, Claudia Swan, Paul Bakker, and Claus Zittel (eds), *Image, Imagination and Cognition: Medieval and Early Modern Theory and Practice* (Leiden & Boston: Brill: 2018), ch. 6

Grell, Ole Peter, *Calvinist Exiles in Tudor and Stuart England* (Aldershot: Scolar Press, 1996)

Haar, Alisa van de, 'Beyond nostalgia: The exile publications of the Antwerp schoolmaster Peeter Heyns (1537–1598)', *De Zeventiende Eeuw* 31(2) (2015), p. 327

Hale, John, *The Civilization of Europe in the Renaissance* (New York: Atheneum, 1994)

Ham, Gijs van der, et al., *80 jaar oorlog* (Amsterdam: Rijksmuseum/Atlas Contact, 2018)

Hamilton, Alastair, *The Family of Love* (Cambridge: James Clarke & Co Ltd, 1981)

——, 'Hiël and the Hiëlists: The doctrine and followers of Hendrik Jansen van Barrefelt', *Quaerendo* 7 (1977), pp. 243–86

Hanou, Jos, 'Moses, muiten en munten. De Wet in Maerten de Vos' Panhuyspaneel volgens de "methode Radermacher"', *Oud Holland – Quarterly for Dutch Art History* 127(2–3) (October 2014), pp. 61–78

Harkness, Deborah E., *The Jewel House: Elizabethan London and the Scientific Revolution* (New Haven & London: Yale University Press, 2007)

Harris, Jason, 'The religious position of Abraham Ortelius', in Arie-Jan Gelderblom, Jan L. de Jong, and Marc van Vaeck (eds), *The Low Countries as a Crossroads of Religious Belief* (Leiden: Brill, 2004), pp. 89–139

Hart, Marjolein 't, *The Dutch Wars of Independence: Warfare and Commerce in The Netherlands, 1570–1680* (London & New York: Routledge, 2014)

Helmers, Helmer, *De Comentarius van Emanuel van Meteren* (Hilversum: Verloren, 2023)

——, 'History as diplomacy in early modern Europe: Emanuel van Meteren's *Historia Belgica* and international relations, 1596–1640', *Renaissance Studies* 36 (2021), pp. 27–45

——, 'Urbanization', in Helmer J. Helmers and Geert H. Janssen (eds), *The Cambridge Companion to the Dutch Golden Age* (Cambridge: Cambridge University Press, 2018)

Herendeen, Wyman H., 'Camden, William', in *Oxford Dictionary of National Biography* (2008), available online at https://www.oxforddnb.com/display/10.1093/ref:odnb/9780198614128.001.0001/odnb-9780198614128-e-4431 (accessed 09.02.2023)

Hondius, Dienke, 'Black Africans in seventeenth-century Amsterdam', *Renaissance and Reformation* 31(2) (2008), pp. 87–105

Horace, *Horace: Satires, Epistles, Art of Poetry*, rev. edn, trans. H. Rushton Fairclough (Cambridge, MA: Harvard University Press, 1929)

Imhof, Dirk, *Christophe Plantin's Correspondence* (Ghent: Academia Press, 2020)

Janssen, A.E.M., 'A "trias historica" on the revolt of the Netherlands: Emanuel van Meteren, Pieter Bor and Everhard van Reyd as exponents of contemporary historiography', in A.C. Duke and C.A. Tamse (eds), *Clio's Mirror: Historiography in Britain and The Netherlands* (Zutphen: De Walburg Pers, 1985)

Jardine, Lisa and Brotton, Jerry, *Global Interests: Renaissance Art between East and West* (Ithaca, NY: Cornell University Press, 2000)

Jeannin, Pierre, 'Usages et instruments du négoce', in Jacques Jacques Bottin and Marie-Louise Pelus-Kaplan (eds), *Marchands d'Europe, Pratiques et Savoirs à l'époque moderne* (Paris: Editions Rue d'Ulm, 2002)

Jones, David Martin, 'Aphorism and the counsel of prudence in early modern statecraft: The curious case of Justus Lipsius', *Parergon* 28(2) (2011), pp. 57–85

Jones, Emrys, '"A world of ground": Terrestrial space in Marlowe's *Tamburlaine* plays', *The Yearbook of English Studies* 38(1/2) (2008), pp. 168–82

Jonkheere, Koenraad, *Antwerp Art after Iconoclasm: Experiments in Decorum, 1566–1585* (New Haven & London: Mercatorfonds, 2012)

Kamen, Henry, *Philip of Spain* (New Haven & London: Yale University Press, 1997)

Kaminska, Barbara A., '"That there be no schisms among you": St Paul as a figure of confessional reconciliation', *Journal of Early Modern Christianity* 3(1) (2016), pp. 99–129

Kaufmann, Miranda, 'African freedom in Tudor England: Dr Nunes' petition', *Early Modern Migrations 1500–1750*, available online at https://www.ourmigrationstory.org.uk/oms/african-freedom-in-tudor-england-dr-hector-nuness-request (accessed 06.05.2021)

Keats, John, *The Poems of John Keats*, ed. H.W. Garrod (London: Oxford University Press, 1956)

Koch, Ebba, 'Being like Jesus and Mary: The Jesuits, the Polyglot Bible and other Antwerp print works', in Margit Kern and Klaus Krüger (eds), *Transcultural Imaginations of the Sacred* (Leiden: Brill, 2019), pp. 197–230

Knecht, R.J., *Catherine de'Medici* (Harlow: Pearson Education Ltd, 1998)

Koenigsberger H.G., Mosse, George L., and Bowler G.Q., *Europe in the Sixteenth Century*, 2nd edn (London: Longman, 1989)

Kossman, E.H. and Mellink, A.F. (eds), *Texts Concerning the Revolt of the Netherlands* (Cambridge: Cambridge University Press, 1974)

Leeflang, Micha, *From Antwerp to Amsterdam: Painting from the Sixteenth and Seventeenth Centuries*, catalogue of the *Ode aan Antwerpen* exhibition at the Catherijneconvent Museum in Utrecht (Veurne: Hannibal, 2023)

Leeuwen, Rudie van, '*Moses and the Israelites* by Maerten de Vos: the *Portrait Historié* of the Panhuys Family from 1574', in Volker Manuth, Rudi Van Leeuwen, and Jos Koldeweij (eds), *Example or Alter Ego? Aspects of the*

Portrait Historié in *Western Art from Antiquity to the Present* (Turnhout: Brepols, 2016)

——, 'The *portrait historié* in religious context and its condemnation', in Katlijne van der Stighelen, Hannelore Magnus, and Bert Watteeuw (eds), *Pokerfaced: Flemish and Dutch Baroque Faces Unveiled* (Turnhout: Brepols Publishers, 2011), pp. 109–24

Linden, David van der, 'Coping with crisis: Career strategies of Antwerp painters after 1585', *De Zeventiende Eeuw* 31(1) (2015), pp. 18–54

Lockyer, Roger, *Habsburg & Bourbon Europe 1470–1720* (London: Longman, 1974)

Loudon, Mark, 'Rogers, Daniel', in *Oxford Dictionary of National Biography* (2006), available online at https://www.oxforddnb.com/display/10.1093/ref:odnb/9780198614128.001.0001/odnb-9780198614128-e-23970 (accessed 03.08.2023)

Louis, Armand, 'La Vie et l'Oeuvre Botanique de Rembert Dodoens (1517–1585)', *Bulletin de la Société Royale de Botanique de Belgique / Bulletin van de Koninklijke Belgische Botanische Verenigin* 82(2) (March 1950), pp. 271–93

MacCulloch, Diarmaid, *Thomas Cromwell: A Life* (London: Allen Lane, 2018)

Maclean, Ian, *Scholarship, Commerce, Religion: The Learned Book in the Age of Confessions* (Cambridge, MA & London: Harvard University Press, 2012)

Magalhães, Joaquim Romero, 'Africans, Indians, and slavery in Portugal', *Portuguese Studies* 13 (1997), pp. 143–51

Marnef, Guido, *Antwerp in the Age of Reformation: Underground Protestantism in a Commercial Metropolis, 1550–1577*, trans, J. C. Grayson (Baltimore: John Hopkins Press, 1996)

——, 'Gresham and Antwerp', a lecture given at Gresham College, 19 June 2008; video and transcript available at https://www.gresham.ac.uk/watch-now/gresham-and-antwerp (accessed 03.12.2010)

McGowan, Margaret M., 'Review of "*Psaumes mis en vers français (1551 1562)*, ed. Pierre Pidoux (Travaux d'Humanisme et Renaissance, 199) Geneva, Librairie Droz, 1984"', *Renaissance Quarterly* 40(1) (Spring 1987), pp. 141–2

Meganck, Tine Luk, *Erudite Eyes: Friendship, Art and Erudition in the Network of Abraham Ortelius (1527–1598)* (Leiden & Boston: Koninklijke Brill NV, 2017)

Melion, Walter S., *Karel van Mander and his Foundation of the Noble, Free Art of Painting* (Leiden & Boston: Brill, 2023)

Melion, Walter S., Rothstein, Bret and Weemans, Michel (eds), *The Anthropomorphic Lens, Anthropomorphism, Microcosmism and Analogy in Early Modern Thought and Visual Arts* (Leiden: Brill, 2015)

Mercator, Gerhard and Ortelius, Abraham, *The Mercator Atlas of Europe* (1570), available online at https://www.bl.uk/collection-items/mercator-atlas-of-europe (accessed 24.05.2021)

Meskens, Ad, 'Liaisons dangéreuses: Peter Heyns en Abraham Ortelius', *De Gulden Passer* 76–77 (1998–99), pp. 103–04, available online at https://www.dbnl.org/tekst/_gul005199801_01/_gul005199801_01_0003.php (accessed 15.11.2023)

——, *Practical Mathematics in a Commercial Metropolis: Mathematical Life in late 16th Century Antwerp* (Dordrecht: Springer, 2013)

Municipality of Genoa, 'Genoa and its treasures' (2011), available online at http://www.visitgenoa.it/sites/default/files/Genoa%20and%20its%20treasures_0.pdf

Murray, John J., *Antwerp in the Age of Plantin and Bruegel* (Newton Abbot: David & Charles, 1972)

Netpoint, *Jean de Castro: Muziek en Mecenaat in de 16de eeuw*, available online at https://www.netpoint.be/abc/castro/en/n_30.htm (accessed 02.11.2022).

–––, *The Genoese* Nation, available online at https://www.netpoint.be/abc/castro/en/n_06.htm (accessed 04.09.2024).

Olusoga, David, *Black and British: A Forgotten History* (London: Macmillan, 2016)

Orrock, Amy, 'Homo ludens: Pieter Bruegel's Children's Games and the Humanist Educators', *Journal of Historians of Netherlandish Art* 4(2) (2012)

Opsopäus, Johannes, *Stirpium historiae pemptades sex. Sive libri XXX / [Rembert Dodoens]* (1583), available online at https://archive.org/details/hin-wel-all-00000420-001/page/n179/mode/2up (accessed 01.11.2023)

Papy, Jan, 'Justus Lipsius', in *The Stanford Encyclopedia of Philosophy*, ed. Edward N. Zalta (Spring 2019), available online at https://plato.stanford.edu/archives/spr2019/entries/justus-lipsius/ (accessed 08.05.2023)

——, 'Justus Lipsius', in *The Stanford Encyclopedia of Philosophy*, eds Edward N. Zalta and Uri Nodelman (Fall 2023), available online at https://plato.stanford.edu/archives/fall2023/entries/justus-lipsius/ (accessed 09.12.2023)

Parker, Geoffrey, *The Dutch Revolt* (London: Allen Lane, 1977)

Parsons, Ben, 'Dutch influence on English literary culture in the early Renaissance, 1470–1650', *Literature Compass* 4(6) (2007), pp. 1577–96

Porras, Stephanie, 'Going viral: Maerten de Vos's "St. Michael the Archangel"', in *Nederlands Kunsthistorisch Jaarboek* (NKJ) / *Netherlands Yearbook for History of Art*, vol. 66, Netherlandish Art in its Global Context / De mondiale context van Nederlandse kunst (Leiden: Brill, 2016), pp. 54–79

Puttevils, Jeroens, *Merchants and Trading in the Sixteenth Century* (London: Routledge, 2015)

Pye, Michael, *Antwerp: The Glory Years* (London: Allen Lane, 2021)

Ramakers, Bart, 'Art and artistry in Lucas de Heere', in *Nederlands Kunsthistorisch Jaarboek* / *Netherlands Yearbook for History of Art*, vol. 59 (Leiden: Brill, 2009), pp. 164–92

Ramsay, G.D., *The City of London in International Politics at the Accession of Elizabeth Tudor* (Manchester: Manchester University Press, 1975)

——, *The Queen's Merchants and the Revolt of the Netherlands: The End of the Antwerp Mart, Vol 2* (Manchester: Manchester University Press, 1986)

Rekers, B., *Benito Arias Montano* (London & Leiden: The Warburg Institute & E.J. Brill, 1972)

Riggs, David, *Ben Jonson: A Life* (Cambridge, MA: Harvard University Press, 1989)

Sabbe, Maurice, 'Les rapports entre B. Arias Montanus et H. Jansen Barrefelt (Hiël)', *De Gulden Passe* 4 (1926), pp. 19–43

Seaton, Ethel, 'Marlowe's map', *Essays and Studies* 10 (1924), pp. 13–35

Serebrennikov, Nina Eugenia, 'Imitating nature / Imitating Bruegel', in *Nederlands Kunsthistorisch Jaarboek* / *Netherlands Yearbook for History of Art*, vol. 47 (Leiden: Brill, 1996), pp. 222–46

Simoni, Anna (ed.), 'The Radermacher Catalogue 1634: Introduction', available online at https://www.johanradermacher.net/introduction/ (accessed 03.12.2022)

Slenk, Howard, 'Christophe Plantin and the Geneva Psalter', Tijdschrift van de Vereniging voor Nederlandse Muziekgeschiedenis 20(4) (1967)

Smolderen, L, 'Deux Médailles de l'Armateur Anversois, Gilles Hooftman', Revue Belge de Numismatique et de Sigillographie CXIV (1968), pp. 95–112

Soen, Violet, 'Challenges to clemency: Seneca, Lipsius and the Dutch Revolt', in Astrid Steiner- Weber (ed.), Acta Conventus Neo-Latini (Leiden: Brill, 2012), pp. 1039–48

Steiger, Johann Anselm, Die Schlosskapelle in Celle: Ein Bild- und Schriftraum der Reformation (Regensburg: Schnell & Steiner, 2018).

Stockmans, J. B., Notice historique sur le château de Cleydael (Anvers, 1892),

Stone, Lawrence, An Elizabethan: Sir Horatio Palavicino (London: Oxford University Press, 1956)

Stow, John, A Survey of London. Reprinted from the Text of 1603, ed. C.L. Kingsford (Oxford, 1908)

Strong, Roy, Art and Power: Renaissance Festivals 1450–1650 (Woodbridge: Boydell Press, 1984)

——, Gloriana: The Portraits of Queen Elizabeth I (London: Pimlico, 1987)

Stubbs, John, John Donne: The Reformed Soul (New York & London: W.W. Norton & Company, 2006/7)

Swart K.W., 'William the Silent's Statecraft' in Theo Hermans and Reinier Salverda (eds), From Revolt to Riches: Culture and History of the Low Countries (London: UCL Centre for Low Countries, 1993), pp. 65–73

Szykuła, Krystyna, 'Anthony Jenkinson's unique wall map of Russia and its influence on European cartography', Belgeo, Revue belge de géographie 3–4 (2008), pp. 325–40

Tawney, R.H., Religion and the Rise of Capitalism (London & New York: Verso, 2015)

Verduyn, W.D., Emanuel van Meteren (The Hague: Martinus Nijhoff, 1926)

Verwey, H. de la, 'Le siege de Valenciennes et l'imprimerie clandestine de Plantin à Vianen', *Revue française d'histoire du livre* 1 (1971), pp. 9–25

Wedgwood, C.V., *William the Silent: William of Nassau, Prince of Orange, 1533–1584* (London: Jonathan Cape, 1945)

Wijnroks, Eric H., *Handel Tussen Rusland en de Nederlanden 1560–1640* (Hilversum: Uitgeverij Verloren, 2003)

Willmott, Richard, *William Blake: Songs of Innocence and of Experience*, rev. edn (Oxford: Oxford University Press, 2011).

Wilson, Dudley (ed.), *French Renaissance Scientific Poetry* (London: The Athlone Press, 1974)

Wouk, Edward H., 'From *nabeeld* to *kopie*: The after-image and the copy in early modern Netherlandish art', *Word & Image*, 35(3) (2019), pp. 223–42

Yates, Frances, *The Valois Tapestries* (London: The Warburg Institute University of London, 1959)

Zondervan, J.W., 'Het Panhuys-paneel van het Mauritshuis: beeld van een snel vervlogen droom', *Jaarboek Centraal Bureau voor Genealogie* 36 (1982), pp. 74–116

——, 'Montens, Panhuysen en Vosbergen: Verwante vertrouwelingen van Prins Maurits', *Jaarboek van het Centraal Bureau voor Genealogie en het Iconographisch Bureau: Deel 36* (1982)

Zweite, Armin, *Marten de Vos als Maler* (Berlin: Gebr. Mann Verlag, 1980)

Endnotes

Chapter 1

1   The Eighty Years' War (1568–1648) was the secession war in which the Dutch Republic gained independence from Habsburg Spain.

2   Vasari 1911, pp. 213–14. Not all critics agree with Vasari's identification, but they do agree that the painting includes Medici portraits.

3   Hessels 2009. Volume 1 has been reprinted in two parts, but the page numbering runs consecutively through both parts.

4   See Parker 1977, pp. 30–7.

5   If you want to know more about the sequence of events that led to Philip's father, Charles V, becoming not only the Holy Roman Emperor and King of Castile and Aragon, but also the Duke of Brabant and therefore overlord of the Low Countries, there is a timeline in Appendix A. When Charles abdicated, his brother Ferdinand became the new Emperor, and his son, Philip, became King of Spain (Castile and Aragon) and Duke of Brabant.

6   For many of these ascriptions, I am indebted to Hanou 2014; van Leeuwen 2016; and Zondervan 1982. There is also a discussion of the *Paneel* in Zweite 1980.

7   Consulted online from *Batavia Illustrata ofte Oud Batavien*.

8   For the detective work establishing details of the Hooftman family, see Berens 1968, especially pp. 58–64.

9   See Göttler 2018, p. 153.

Chapter 2

10   Daniel Rogers, from 'De magnificentia urbis Handoverpianae' ('On the magnificence of the city of Hanover') and 'De frequentia omnium gentium in Ianimedo, vulgo die Burse' ('On the gathering of nations within the Bourse at Antwerp'), both in Rogers 1565, B3r and B4r. The 'new Rome' is Antwerp, and 'The great globe flourishes within the smaller one' means that the merchants who gathered from all over the world to do business in the Bourse formed a microcosm of the whole world, the 'great globe'. For further information about the poet and diplomat Daniel Rogers, see Chapter 10 and Dorsten 1962.

11   A retrospective letter from Radermacher to Ortelianus, 14 August 1603, in Hessels 2009, Letter 331, p. 782.

12   Ironically, despite all this wealth, Philip II of Spain defaulted on his debts much more often than Elizabeth I of England, perennially hard-up though the latter was. Both suffered from the problem of all early modern rulers in Europe in that no effective and accepted means of taxation had been developed. For an account of the financial pressures on Philip II when he came to the throne, see Elliott 1968, pp. 25–7.

13   Plantin 1955, p. 333.

14   See Marnef 1996, p. 24.

15 'Finishing' involved shearing the nap to produce a finer and smoother-feeling cloth, which was often then dyed. The shearing was a skilled and labour-intensive task. See Puttevils 2015, p. 56.

16 See Gelderblom 2013, p. 29.

17 The archaic term, East Indies, refers in particular to the islands of Southeast Asia, visited first by merchants and subsequently colonised, but was used very loosely.

18 Puttevils 2015, p. 69.

19 Stow 1908, p. 132, quoted in MacCulloch 2018, p. 30.

20 Saaftinghe was a town at the mouth of the Scheldt estuary, but which now no longer exists, being known as Verdronken Land ('Drowned Land') van Saeftinghe. It was built on reclaimed land, but never recovered after the final dyke was deliberately breached as a defensive measure against the Spanish in 1584. This second shipwreck is recorded by the contemporary chronicler, Godevaerd van Haecht, in his entry for 1 December; see Haecht 1929/30.

21 They were owed thirty-seven months' wages; see Parker 1977, pp. 164 and 172.

22 The medallions can be seen at the Museum aan de Stroom, Antwerp.

23 Berens 1968, p. 75.

24 See Biographie Nationale de Belgique 1886/7), cols. 49–50.

25 Thijs quoted in Zondervan 1982, p. 108.

26 Unfortunately, no trace of it remains today, since the street that it was on projected out into the river like two sides of a flattened triangle and was dug away when the banks were straightened for new wharfs to facilitate trade at the end of the nineteenth century. Similarly, only the gatehouse of Het Steen now remains – and the site of the busy scene painted by Sebastiaan Vrancx (ill. 3) no longer exists.

27 For an account of the political threats to trade in the Baltic, see Elliott 1968, pp. 43–50.

28 Hessels 2009, Letter 330, pp. 776–7.

29 Ibid., Letters 330 and 334, pp. 773 and 787. Biographie Nationale de Belgique 1886/7, vol. 18, p. 542.

30 Hessels 2009, Letter 330, pp. 775–6.

31 I have used the transcription of Algemeene Rijksarchief, 1ste afd: Familiearchief Van Panhuys, nr. 2 in the second appendix of Zondervan 1982, pp. 136–45.

32 Alba had set up the Council of Troubles to deal with any religious or political opposition. It soon became known as the Council of Blood. This was not just Protestant propaganda, since it was responsible for the execution of more than 1,000 Protestants and political opponents.

33 Rijksarchief Zeeland, Familie Archief Schorer, 157, quoted in Bostoen 1998 (my translation).

34 A similar situation existed in France, but in reverse, where all Reformers tended at first to be called Luthériens, although many of them were not Lutherans, but Calvinists; later, they were called Huguenots. Dickens 1977, p. 165.

35 For a survey of the manifold skills needed by early modern merchants and the many manuals written to help them, see the third part of Jeannin 2002. There is also a useful summary in an afterword by Marie-Louise Pelus-Kaplan (p. 420).

36 This interest is described by Radermacher in one of his letters to Ortelianus: Hessels 2009, Letter 330, p. 776.

37 See Meskens 2013, p. 16.

38 This is the attribution in the display at the Museum aan de Stroom in Antwerp (visited 2019), but had been questioned earlier by Smolderen in an article in Revue Belge de Numismatique at de Sigillographie CXIV (1968), p. 106.

39 Attribution in display at Museum aan de Stroom.

40 Smolderen 1968, p. 109.

41 For a description of the reverse of the medallion see Smolderen 1968, pp. 108–9.

42 See van Mander 1884, p. 101.

43 Sonets, avec une chanson, contenant neuf parties l'une suivant l'autre le tout à deux parties... livre premier (Anvers: Pierre

Phalèse et Jean Bellère, 1592) was dedicated to Cornelis, and *Chansons, stanses, sonets, et épigrammes à deux parties... livre second* (Anvers: Pierre Phalèse et Jean Bellère, 1592) was dedicated to Marguerite and Beatrice. A third volume dedicated to all three children – *Harmonie joyeuse et délectable, contenant aucunes stanzes et chansons à quatre parties* (Anvers: Pierre Phalèse et Jean Bellère, 1595) – was published three years later.

44 See Netpoint, *Jean de Castro.*

45 Denucé 1937, pp. 14ff; Wijnroks 2003, pp. 112–13.

46 The ruling oligarchy (subject to the overall lordship of the Duke of Brabant, who was in fact the King of Spain) were known to the English as the 'lords of Antwerp'. They were landed gentry owning property both within and without the city and did not usually take part in trade themselves (unlike the nobility of Genoa, such as Orazio Palavicino; see Chapter 11). See Ramsay 1975, pp. 11–12; Ramsay 1986, pp. 22–4.

47 Puttevils 2015, pp. 154–5.

48 Ramsay 1986, pp. 22–4.

49 *Geuzen* (literally, beggars) was originally a term of contempt (in French *des gueux*) used by one of Margaret of Parma's councillors, Berlaymont, for those members of the nobility who had petitioned her to suspend further persecution of Protestants, but a name proudly taken on by them as an act of defiance.

50 Quotations from Marnef 2008.

51 Puttevils 2015, p. 75.

52 Ramsay 1986, pp. 9–51.

53 After the Calvinists seized power in March 1567, their ministers wanted Hooftman to support them, which he was evidently reluctant to do. Van Haecht called him 'the foremost of the Mertinists' ('*de overste der mertinisten*'). 'Mertinist' was a term used to describe the followers of Martin Luther. See Haecht 1929/30.

54 See Bostoen 1958, p. 20.

55 Quoted in Tawney 2015, pp. 103–4. The whole of this paragraph draws on what Tawney has to say about the different teachings and influence of Luther and Calvin; see pp. 89–139.

56 *Ibid.*, p. 113.

57 *Ibid.*, pp. 115–17 and 128.

58 See Zondervan 1982, pp. 140, 128 and 131.

59 Emanuel van Meteren, quoted in Smolderen 1968, p. 102.

60 Pounds Artois was the currency of a northern French province adjacent to Flanders; coins varied slightly in weight and therefore in value from region to region.

61 See Jos Hanou 2014, pp. 66–78. Although I reach a slightly different conclusion, I am deeply indebted to this article, which served as the stimulus and starting point for my consideration of de Vos's painting.

62 For a summary of Familism, see Hamilton 1981, pp. 34–39.

Chapter 3

63 Zondervan 1982. Although I disagree with Zondervan's identification of Lipsius, I found his article helpful and instructive. Se also van Leeuwen 2016, p. 289.

64 See Leeflang 2013, p. 18.

65 van Mander 1884, p. 192 (my translation from the French).

66 Guicciardini 2018, p. 117.

67 van Mander 1884, p. 289.

68 Carlo Ridolfi's *La Vita di Giacopo Robusti* (Tintoretto's real name) was published considerably later, in 1642.

69 Guicciardini notes that de Vos was 'a good master of colour and invention'; see Guicciardini 2018, pp. 129–30.

70 Meganck 2017, p. 5.

71 See Hessels 2009, vol. 1, part 2, Letters 330 and 331, pp. 772–83. For a fuller account see p. 63–4.

72 The surviving pictures are *St Paul in Malta* (Louvre Museum) and *St Paul in Ephesus* (Musées Royaux des Beaux-Arts, Brussels) and, less certainly, *Sts Paul and Barnabas in Lystra* (in private ownership).

73 For a discussion of the motives behind iconoclasm, including the suggestion that the underlying motive was not simply theological, but partly the desire to rebel against established authority by attacking what the old order valued (not untouched by vandalism), see Clark 1981, pp. 30–49 ('Iconophobia').

74 Quoted in Erasmus 1957, p. xxiii.

75 *Ibid.*, p. 150.

76 Ruytinck's plans are transcribed and commented on in Grell 1996, pp. 191–200.

77 Quoted from the State Papers in MacCulloch 2018, p. 152.

78 Zweite accepts that this picture (in private ownership) is by de Vos and that thematically it could well be one of the five paintings, but suggests that with its much lower horizon, it would not fit in well with the others and might even be part of a different, but similar, series (Zewite 1980, p. 78). Without knowing how Hooftman's pictures were arranged (alongside or above each other, or with one over a door, for example), I think it hard to be sure that this is a serious difficulty. Barbara A. Kaminska includes this picture as a part of the same series in her article, '"That There Be No Schisms among You", St Paul as a Figure of Confessional Reconciliation' (2016). The dimensions of the three paintings are almost identical.

79 See his letter to Ortelianus of 14 August 1603, in Hessels 2009, Letter 331, pp. 780 and 782.

80 See Zweite 1980, p. 80.

81 Steiger 2018, p. 9.

82 Most Lutherans had a much more positive attitude to both art and music than the Calvinists. Luther himself was not unaware of the potential abuse of images, but recognised their educational value as the Bible of the illiterate. See Freedberg 1986, pp. 69–84.

83 There are excellent photographs of the paintings in Steiger 2018.

84 Interestingly, de Vos follows the division of the Commandments into the same ten sections used by the Lutherans as opposed to the different organisation followed by Calvinists and the Church of England. This involves running together the first two commands as they appear in the *Book of Common Prayer* and splitting the Commandment about not coveting into two. This appears to be further confirmation that both de Vos and Panhuys were likely Lutheran at the time of painting the *Paneel*. For a discussion of this point and a very informative study of changing interpretations of the painting, see van Leeuwen 2016. I am very grateful to the author for sending me this in an English translation.

85 See Zweite 1980, pp. 97–8.

86 Dickens 1977, pp. 147–8.

87 Magalhães 1997, pp. 144–5.

88 See Koenigsberger, Mosse and Bowler 1989, pp. 260–1.

89 See Kamen 1997, pp. 30 and 60–61.

90 Quoted in Koenigsberger, Mosse and Bowler 1989, p. 262.

91 This is the first known image of a black Englishman; see Olusoga 2016, pp. 59–60.

92 See report in *The Times* newspaper of 5 May 2021, pp. 16–17.

93 See Olusoga 2016, p. 118 and Kaufmann, 'African freedom in Tudor England'.

94 For an account of this episode, see Dienke Hondius 2008.

95 For a brief summary of current thinking, see Filedt Kok 2010.

96 Held at the Museum Boijmans Van Beuningen in Rotterdam.

97 I am indebted to the research of Bendor Grosvenor for information about the Joos van Cleve painting, which formed part of 2021 BBC 4 programme as part of the series, *Britain's Lost Masterpieces*. There is also a thoughtful looking Balthazar by Pieter Coecke van Aelst in his *Triptych with the Adoration of the Magi, c.* 1530 (The Phoebus Foundation, Antwerp) and doubtless others.

98 Hale 1994, p. 12.

Chapter 4

99 D'Ewes 1973, quoted in Dunthorne 2013, p. 110.

100 The full title of van Meteren's *memorieboek* is *Comentarius dat is ghedaechtenis boek ofte register vande gheschiedenissen, handel ende wesen etc. van mij Emanuel Demetrius* (Auckland Public Library, Sir George Grey Special Collections, MS 237). The article drawing attention to it is by Iain Buchanan (2019). See also Zondervan 1982, and van Leeuwen 2016 and 2011. For a modern transcription of the *Comentarius*, see Helmers 2023.

101 For an account of Radermacher's religious commitments throughout his life, see Grell 1996, pp. 69.

102 See Behrens, 1968, p. 59.

103 Hessels 2009, p. 774.

104 For an account of van Meteren's life, see Verduyn 1926.

105 Hessels 2009, Letter 330, p. 774.

106 *Ibid.*, pp. 772–4.

107 *Ibid.*, p. 775.

108 Bostoen 1998, pp. 33–5. Contrary to this claim, Parker says that the first West Dutch grammar was published in 1553, but gives no further details; see Parker 1977, p. 36.

109 Latin, Greek, Hebrew, Dutch, English, French, German, Spanish and Italian. See Simoni (ed.), 'The Radermacher Catalogue'.

110 Hessels 2009, p. 775.

111 Ortelius 1606.

112 As part of their encouragement of overseas trade, the Antwerp authorities provided bases in the city where merchants from different nations could stay and could store their goods. (An equivalent in London was the Steelyard, where the Hanseatic merchants had a base.)

113 This was at the time that Philip II was in London as husband of Mary, but he appears to have been less willing to execute heretics at this time than his wife. The Sunday after Rogers was burnt, Philip's confessor, Fray Alfonso de Castro, preached a sermon at court strongly opposed to the burning of heretics, saying that such actions lacked biblical authority, and that they should live in order that they might be converted. For all his faults, Philip seems generally to have been willing to listen to advice even when he chose not to follow it. On this occasion, he appears not to have taken exception and in due course promoted de Castro to Bishop of Santiago, the second-most important see in Spain. See Kamen 1997, pp. 61–2.

114 Hessels 2009, pp. 17–19.

115 *Ibid.*, pp. 37–9.

116 *Ibid.*, pp. 52–5.

117 *Ibid.*, p. 513.

118 Binding 2003, p. 19. St. Luke is the patron saint of painters and Maerten de Vos's *St Luke Painting the Virgin*, which was painted for the guild's altar, can still be seen in the Cathedral of Our Lady in Antwerp.

119 Hessels 2009, pp. 773–7.

120 *Ibid.*, pp. 773 and 777.

121 See Mercator and Ortelius 1570; Binding 2003, pp. 84–7.

122 Binding 2003, p. 87.

123 Ortelius, *Album Amicorum* (MS LC.2.113), p. 71v.

124 For a much fuller discussion of this dispute, see Brotton 2013, pp. 186–227.

125 Quoted in Koenigsberger, Mosse and Bowler 1989, p. 256.

126 Quotations are taken from the first English edition of the *Theatrum Orbis Terrarum* (Ortelius 1606). I have modernised spelling and occasionally inserted clarifications in square brackets.

127 See Seaton 1924, pp. 13–35; Jones 2008, pp. 168–82.

128 Quoted in Büttner 1979, p. 160.

129 Further changes to the coastline mean that Ortelius's drawing of the foundations is the only record that there is of this Roman fort. For a survey of Ortelius's intellectual interests, see Besse 2003, pp. 261–72.

Chapter 5

130 For a picture of the Dutch community in London, see Harkness 2007, pp. 15–56.

131 See van Meteren, *Comentarius*, pp. 13–14 (44). For ease of reference, I follow the numbering of Helmers 2023); the number in brackets is the page number of the modern book.

132 Their son Jan was to be apprenticed to Lucas d'Heere and became Serjeant Painter at the court of James I and VI in London. Their daughter Magdalena was to marry Marcus Gheeraerts the Elder, who was to become another fashionable court painter and who may also have been an apprentice of d'Heere. This last couple in turn had a daughter, named Sara, who married Isaac Oliver, a pupil of Nicholas Hilliard and painter at the court of Anne of Denmark, queen of James I and VI. See van Dorsten 1970, pp. 51–2.

133 See van Dorsten 1988, p. 46

134 *Comentarius*, p. 21 (50).

135 For a summary, see Dutch Church, 'Adriaan van Haemstede' on the website of the Dutch Church in London: https://www.dutchchurch.org.uk/adriaan-van-haemstede/ (accessed 02.01.2023).

136 See Grell 1996, pp. 6–8.

137 See Harris 2004, p. 17.

138 See Loudon 2006; Davies 1970, p. 16.

139 See Ramsay 1986, pp. 17–33.

140 Murray 1972, p. 39.

141 The account that follows is based on the account in Ramsay 1986, pp. 85–115.

142 See Kamen 1997, p. 74.

143 Elizabeth was probably born in 1551 at Wittenberg when her father was studying there. Sources disagree about the number and order of birth of John Rogers' children, but this contemporary record at least proves that she existed.

144 Kamen 1997, pp. 104 and 141.

145 I have been unable to find out any more about this. It may be that van Meteren misremembered the date of the Battle of Flushing, which took place in 1573.

146 Kamen 1997, p. 145.

147 Antwerp's council responded by offering the new Spanish governor, Requesens, a loan of 400,000 pounds Artois. Gillis Hooftman not only contributed to the loan but was subsequently part of a committee to review the city's finances in order to raise income and reduce expenses. Among those depicted on the *Paneel*, Hooftman and Plantin contributed 1,500 and 140 guilders respectively; neither will have expected their money to be repaid, and Philip II in effect announced himself bankrupt the following year.

148 Those who wish to know more about this period of French history will find an account in Knecht 1998, pp. 166–90.

149 He was not a fully naturalised English subject, but had received a letter patent of denization, which meant that he had certain legal rights in England.

150 For Zwevegem's earlier involvement in trying to restore the *Intercursus*, see Ramsay 1975, pp. 278–9. Details of the visit of Zwevegem and Boischot can be found at https://folgerpedia.folger.edu/mediawiki/media/images_pedia_folgerpedia_mw/5/54/ECDbD_1574.pdf; for Boischot's visit in 1575, see https://folgerpedia.folger.edu/mediawiki/media/images_pedia_folgerpedia_mw/2/20/ECDbD_1575.pdf (both accessed 14.02.22)

Chapter 6

151 Clair 1960, p. 68.

152 *Ibid.*, pp. 8–9.

153 Quoted in Parker 1977, p. 26 and p. 281, n. 3.

154 Guicciardini 2018, p. 161.

155 See Clair 1960, pp. 14 and 241–2, n. 7. Another possible source of money for setting up his printing business is discussed on p. 96.

156 There was a lengthy correspondence between Margaret of Parma and the Margrave about this; see Plantin 1955, Letters 2–8, pp. 12–18. However, it seems the city became tired of paying the costs of imprisoning the guilty trio while the

investigation continued and, reading between the lines, it sounds as though they probably slipped quietly away to another jurisdiction.

157 Clair 1960, pp. 27–36, n. 9, and p. 246.

158 For a much fuller account of this split in the Family of Love and of Barrefelt's links with Plantin's own family, see Hamilton 1977, pp. 243–86.

159 Hessels 2009, p. 48; Plantin 1883–1914, Letter 30, p. 80.

160 Plantin 1883–1914, vol. 1, Letters 31 and 33, pp. 82–4 and 86–9.

161 Ibid., Letter 74, pp. 157–60.

162 For a translation of the letter and commentary, see Imhof 2020, pp. 40–4.

163 See Verwey 1971, pp. 9–25; referenced in Parker 1977, pp. 96 and 291, n. 23.

164 In fact, Donne might well have been a good deal less troubled by his 'descent' when publishing the First and Second Anniversaries if he had not been mocked for idolising a dead teenager in a shameless pursuit of patronage from her mourning parents. See Stubbs 2006/7. p. 281.

165 See Marot 1993, pp. 566, 574 and 600; see also McGowan 1987, pp. 141–2.

166 See Plantin 1955, Letter 9, p. 19.

167 See Slenk 1967, p. 226.

168 Paulus Manutius was the third son of the famous Venetian printer, Aldus Manutius.

169 Plantin 1883–1914, vol. 2, Letters 153 and 155, pp. 5–7 and 12.

170 The breadth of Granvelle's interests is revealed in a letter of 29 December 1568, when he asks what has happened to his request for a copy of Carmina novem illustrium feminarum, a selection of poems by Sappho and other classical poetesses that Plantin had published earlier that year, which he requested be 'well bound'. Plantin 1955, letter 79, pp. 100–01.

171 Evidence of the close links between Plantin and Granvelle can be seen in the steady exchange of letters between them in 1568/9; see Plantin 1955, Letters 75–81, pp. 95–111.

172 Plantin 1883–1914, vol. 2, Letter 280, p. 221.

173 Ibid., Letter 280, pp. 221–4; see also Maclean 2012.

174 Wilson 1974, p. 25, Epistre dédicatoire, ll. 175–82. William Paley was still using the same argument in England in Natural Theology (1802), where he famously argued that the construction of a watch inescapably implies the creative mind of the watchmaker who designed it.

175 Wilson 1974, Cercle premier, p. 51, ll. 293–310.

176 Ibid., Cercle second, p. 67, ll. 151–62.

177 'Aut prodesse volunt aut delectare / aut simul et iucunda et idonea dicere vitae' (Horace, Ars Poetica, ll. 333–4).

178 See Louis 1950, pp. 271–93.

179 Ibid., p. 275

180 Plantin 1883–1914, vol. 1, Letter 125, p. 273.

181 For an account of the networks of exchange of botanical specimens, see Egmond 2018.

182 For a description of the Netherlandish community in London and its cooperative approach to the advancement of learning, see Harkness 2007), pp. 15–56.

183 Cited in Marnef 1996, p. 33; Guicciardini 2018, p. 143.

184 Marnef 1996, p. 34.

185 Guicciardini 2018, p. 141.

186 Plantin 1883–1914, vol. 3, Letter 386 (misnumbered 186), p. 106.

187 See Clair 1960, p. 178.

188 See Parker 1977, p. 21.

189 See Marnef 1996, p. 34.

190 See Meskens 2013, p. 31.

191 The rhyme-scheme is abab/bcbc/cdcd/dede.

192 Heyns 1577, p. 6.

193 Chambers of rhetoric were guilds responsible for staging 'improving' plays.

194 Erasmus, De utilitate Colloquiorum (The Usefulness of Colloquies, first printed 1526); quoted in Orrock 2012. Radermacher owned a copy of Erasmus's

Colloquia (see Simoni (ed.), '*The Radermacher Catalogue*').

195 Mirror here means 'an ideal example'.

196 Consider, for example, this damningly dismissive comment on Galba, the first of the four emperors in the year named after them: 'There would have been general agreement that he would have made an excellent emperor, if he hadn't actually reigned as emperor.' The last two words of the much terser Latin give it a stinging epigrammatic bite: *Omnium consensu capax imperii, nisi imperasset* (*Histories* I, 49).

197 *Agricola XXX*, in Church and Brodribb (eds) 1889, p. 21.

Chapter 7

198 The Jewish Tanakh, or Bible, is regarded from the Christian point of view as a precursor of the Christian New Testament and is therefore called the Old Testament by Christians. Since this is how it would have been thought of by the compilers of the polyglots, the Christian term is used here, but no disrespect is intended.

199 Syriac developed from a dialect of Aramaic and became the principal liturgical and literary language of the Christian communities in the Near East. Plantin refers to this language as Chaldean.

200 The Council of Trent was held between 1545 and 1563, and laid down the direction and principles of the Catholic Church's own internal reformation (the Counter-Reformation).

201 *Rex Catholicissimus* ('Most Catholic King') was a title first bestowed on the kings of Spain by Pope Alexander VI in 1493.

202 In the end, there were to be eight volumes, and publication was not completed until six years later, in 1572.

203 Plantin 1883–1914, vol. 1, Letter 20, pp. 48–52.

204 *Ibid.*, Letter 22, pp. 57–60.

205 *Ibid.*, Letter 64, pp. 142–3.

206 *Ibid.*, Letter 83, p. 180.

207 *Ibid.*, Letters 30, 31 and 33, pp. 80–84 and 86–9 for his correspondence with Postel, and Letter 74, pp. 157–60 for his letter addressed to Niclaes.

208 *Ibid.*, Letter 84, pp. 183–8.

209 *Ibid.*, Letter 85, pp. 188–92.

210 *Ibid.*, Letter 108, p. 241.

211 *Ibid.*, Letter 123, pp. 269–71.

212 *Ibid.*, Letter 107, pp. 237–8.

213 A letter quoted and translated by Rekers 1972, pp. 48 and 147.

214 Plantin 1883–1914, vol. 1, Letters 131 and 133, pp. 285 and 287.

215 Rekers 1972, Letter 1, 'Montano to Philip II, 6 July 1568', pp. 15 and 131. (The bowels were thought to be the seat of pity.)

216 *Ibid.*, pp. 16 and 131.

217 *Ibid.*, Letter 5, pp. 132 and 17.

218 *Ibid.*, Letter 12, pp. 18–23 and p. 133.

219 I have referred to vol. 1 of the Complutensian Polyglot; see Cisneros 1517.

220 Koch 2019.

221 See Soen 2012, pp. 104.

222 Hart 2014, p. 15.

223 Undated letter, quoted and translated in Rekers 1972, pp. 24 and 134.

Chapter 8

224 There were no fewer than 1,305 in the final edition published in Latin in 1583; see Clair 1960, p. 116.

225 Clark 1981, p. 18.

226 Van Dam and Waterschoot (eds) 2016, p. 139.

227 This pithy summation of what poetry can do is from Farrer 1966, p. 11.

228 *Ars Poetica*, l. 360, in Horace 1929, p. 480. Horace follows Plutarch in saying this, who in turn attributes the idea to the Greek poet, Simonides (fifth century BCE): see Plutarch's *De Gloria Atheniensium*.

229 Guicciardini 2018, p. 131, and van Mander 1884, 'Lucas De Heere'.

230 See Bracken 2004, 'Lucas de Heere'.

231 D'Heere 1565. A scan of the original book can be found at https://books.google.

co.uk/books?id=SN4dI6Kveq4C&print-sec=frontcover&source=gbs_ge_summa-ry_r&cad=0#v=onepage&q&f=false and an annotated transcription at https://www.dbnl.org/tekst/heero01denh01_01/heero01denh01_01_0012.php.

232 van Dorsten 1970, pp. 76–9, and Parsons 2007, p. 1585.

233 D'Heere 1565, p. 4 (translation taken from Ramakers 2009, p. 173). This article has influenced my thoughts on *Den hof en boomgaerd der poësien*.

234 See Wouk 2019.

235 van Mander 1884, ch. 6, stanza 5; translated version in Melion 2023, p. 261 (my glosses in brackets).

236 Ortelius, *Album Amicorum* (MS LC.2.113), 13v.

237 There are various versions of this painting. The one held in the British Royal Collection is thought to be the only one by Bruegel himself (albeit with the slaughtered babies painted over) and shows the standard most clearly.

238 D'Heere 1565, p. 3.

239 *Ibid.*, p. 60. D'Heere's own poem in French appears, quite possibly in a revised version, in the later manuscript collection that he put together in England after migrating there to escape persecution; see d'Heere 2016, p. 155.)

240 Jesus met den Balsenblomme ('Jesus with the Balsam Flower').

241 See Gibson 2014, p. 431.

242 D'Heere 1565, pp. 117–9.

243 Van Dam and Waterschoot (eds) 2016, p. 203, 'Le filz de l'auteur parle', ll. 7–8,

244 *Ibid.*, p. 161, ll. 5–8.

245 See Meganck 2017, p. 109.

246 See Bracken 2004, 'Lucas de Heere'. D'Heere appears in the *Oxford Dictionary of National Biography* because of the work he did at the court of Elizabeth I.

247 Van Dam and Waterschoot (eds) 2016, p. 274; and Strong 1987, pp. 71–7.

248 Nevertheless, he was later to be dismissed from the court of the Catholic Duke Wilhelm V of Bavaria when he

refused to make an open profession of faith. See Bass 2019, p. 12.

249 Meganck 2017, p. 95.

250 This and the next two translations are taken from Bass 2015, p. 154. The commentary that follows is indebted to this chapter.

251 As in Blake's *Songs of Innocence and of Experience*, each page is an artistic whole, the artist writing out his own poetry and drawing the images to create a completely integrated work of art in which verse and image throw mutual light on each other. Blake's *Songs* can be studied at *The William Blake Archive* (blakearchive.org). For an introduction to the text of the poems see Willmott 2011.

252 Ortelius, *Album Amicorum* (MS LC.2.113), 7v. For a fuller discussion of this see Serebrennikov 1996, pp. 222–46.

253 Bass points out that *fantasijen* can mean mental agonies as well as creative imaginings (Bass 2015, p. 45).

254 Keats, 'Ode to a Nightingale', p. 209; 'The Fall of Hyperion', p. 408.

255 See Bass 2015, pp. 174–7.

256 Ortelius, *Album Amicorum* (MS LC.2.113), 7r; the French poem is on 7v.

Chapter 9

257 See Lockyer 1974, p. 281. Much of what follows in this brief summary is drawn from pp. 232–53.

258 For a description of the causes of the frequent mutinies, see Parker 1977 *passim* and especially pp. 171–4.

259 Lockyer 1974, pp. 246–7.

260 Parker 1977, p. 215.

261 For an introduction to the convoluted constitutional debates that the northern Netherlanders engaged in to justify their invitation to Anjou, as earlier to Henri III and after Anjou's death to Elizabeth I, see the introduction to Kossman and Mellink (eds) 1974.

262 Pye 2021, p. 214.

263 The Ruckers started making harpsichords in Antwerp in 1579 and continued until 1667; they were generally

painted considerably later; see Murray 1972, p. 151).

264 A concise summary of the complexities of the Wars of Religion in France is given in Lockyer 1974, pp. 254–76, but is beyond the scope of this book. In view of Farnese's earlier military successes in the Netherlands, Oscar Gelderblom considers Philip's decision to send him to France to be the decisive element that secured the independence of the Dutch Republic; see Gelderblom 2013, p. 162.

Chapter 10

265 For example, see *Biographie Nationale de Belgique, Tome 9* 1886/7, 'Hoofman [sic] (Gilles)', p. 450.

266 This is according to Manningham 1868, and is referred to in Stone 1956, p. 30.

267 Szykuła 2008; Dunthorne 2013, p. 110.

268 We know, for example, that Hooftman was the first person to import smoked salmon into Antwerp; this is according to the display on the history of Antwerp port in the Museum aan de Stroom in Antwerp. See also Smolderen 1968, p. 97.

269 The details of these purchases are given in the introductory section of Smolderen 1968, p. 99. Smolderen refers to Stockmans 1892, pp. 66–9.

270 Parker 1977, p. 47.

271 See *Biographie Nationale de Belgique, Tome 9* 1886/7, p. 450.

272 After 1578, he would merely record that his children were baptised without mentioning either a church where it took place or the name of a priest, although he does usually name the godparents. See the transcription in Zondervan 1982, p. 141.

273 I am much indebted in what follows to Bostoen 1998.

274 See Boersma 2004, 'Florio, Michael Angelo'.

275 Quoted in Bostoen 1998, pp. 56–7 (my translation).

276 The immediate cause of her execution was actually political and not religious, in that it only took place after Wyatt's

unsuccessful rebellion, when the danger of leaving alive the claimant to the throne whom Mary's brother, Edward VI, had nominated as his successor was made very obvious.

277 Bostoen 1998, pp. 22–24.
278 *Ibid.*, p. 21.
279 *Ibid.*, p. 24.
280 Quoted in Bostoen 1998, pp. 59–60 (my translation).
281 See Stone 1956, pp. 191–2.
282 Henri III of France was assassinated in 1589 by a Catholic who objected to any hint of compromise with the Huguenots. Henri IV was assassinated in 1610 by another fanatical Catholic for similar reasons.
283 Hessels 2009, Letter 66, pp. 155–7.
284 See Helmers 2021.
285 Quotations from the preface to the Reader of the 1608 edition, in Brummel 1972, p. 118.
286 See Janssen 1985, pp. 15–16.
287 Hessels 2009, Letter 136, p. 315.
288 Janssen 1985, p. 18.
289 This and the subsequent quotations from the 1599 preface are taken from the translation in *ibid.*, pp. 16–17.
290 Hessels 2009, Letter 262, p. 617.
291 Hessels 2009, Letter 148, pp. 341–2.
292 For a much fuller account of this journey, see Meganck 2017, pp. 49–63.
293 Richard Hakluyt, the geographer who wrote about various voyages of exploration, grumpily complains that Ortelius had gone to London for 'no other end than to pry and look into the secrets of Frobisher's voyage'. Meganck 2017, p. 252, n. 56.
294 Quoted in Herendeen 2008, 'Camden, William'.
295 Besse 2003.
296 *Ibid.*, p. 270.
297 See Meskens 1998-9, pp. 103–04.
298 Hessels 2009, Letter 212, pp. 508–9, and Letter 214, pp. 512–14). Ortelius's use of initials may well have worked, as Hessels took 'S.F.' to refer to St Francis.

299 For a more thorough and very scholarly review of the debate about Ortelius's beliefs, see Harris 2004.

300 See van Dorsten 1962, *passim* and Loudon 2006, 'Rogers, Daniel'.

Chapter 11

301 The transcription of the complete *memorieboek*, including the later section, can be found in Zondervan 1982, pp. 136–46.

302 *Ibid.*, p. 138.

303 Other members of the Malapert family set up a trading branch in Seville, where a cousin, another Nicolaas, had met Hoefnagel, who dedicated a view of Seville to him; see Cordier 2015.

304 Details of the Pallavicini family tree (the number of 'l's varies) can be found in Battilana 1825. Details are not always easy to reconcile with accounts of the family's business in other books.

305 See Municipality of Genoa 2011, p. 12.

306 Much of the information that follows is drawn from Stone 1956 and Archer 2008.

307 It was most unusual for Elizabeth I to default on interest payments, although fairly normal for Philip II of Spain to do so.

308 Anjou had been invited by the seven predominantly Calvinist northern states to be their ruler. His intervention was not a success. Given his history of changing of sides during the French Wars of Religion, the invitation is more surprising than its failure. He was described by the historian Motley as 'the most despicable person who had ever entered the Netherlands' (quoted in Clair 1960, p. 145).

309 See Stone 1956, pp. 212–24.

310 *Ibid.*, pp. 8–9.

311 See in Battilana 1825, 'Famiglia Pallavicini', table 20.

312 See Stone 1956, p. 61.

313 See Parker 1977, p. 136.

314 Stone 1956, p. 27 (my translation).

315 *Ibid.*, p. 28.

316 *Ibid.*, p. 34.

317 *Ibid.*, p. 28.

318 The tapestries were destroyed when Parliament burnt down in 1834.

319 Quoted in Stone 1956, pp. 107–08.

320 Henri finally solved his problem with the Guise family by having them assassinated at Blois three years later in 1588. However, he was himself assassinated the following year.

321 The Spanish support of the Catholic League was a way of keeping France preoccupied with internal matters and unable to challenge Spanish interests, not least in the Low Countries.

322 This was a short-lived agreement of German Lutherans and Calvinists to form a defensive alliance.

323 Some idea of sixteenth-century spying can be deduced from the story of how, in 1579, Palavicino arranged for the theft of a letter from Mendoza, the Spanish ambassador to England, who had himself arranged for the theft of Palavicino's letters and was less than impressed to find his own letter amongst them. Stone 1956, p. 234.

324 State Papers France, 22, f.18, in Stone 1956, pp. 240–1.

325 Stone 1956, p. 129.

326 *Ibid.*, pp. 159–63,

327 Parma had suggested that the endless warfare could only be ended by offering a degree of religious tolerance, something that Philip had uncompromisingly rejected. Parker 1977, pp. 222–23.

328 The Genoese *natie* in Antwerp was one of the wealthiest and was assessed for the largest contribution towards the cost of maintaining Spanish soldiers in Antwerp (30,000 pounds Artois). For the Register of Loans, see Netpoint, *The Genoese Nation*.

329 The dramatist Ben Jonson joked about James's 'thirty-pound knights' in his play *Eastward Hoe*, a gag that eventually landed him in prison. See Riggs 1989, pp. 122–4.

Chapter 12

330 Clair 1960, p. 133. For Moretus's letter, see Plantin 1883–1914, vol. 5, Letter 745, pp. 210–13. On Perez, see Sabbe 1926, p. 28.

331 Clair 1960, p. 135.

332 See Plantin 1883–1914, vol. 5, Letter 787, pp. 294–7.

333 Plantin 1883–1914, vol. 1, Letter 20, p. 52.

334 See Chapter 3 of this book, Clair 1960, p. 139.

335 Clair 1960, p. 146; see also Chapter 5 of this book.

336 Arber 1912, quoted in Clair 1960, p. 116.

337 Clair 1960, p. 149.

338 Plantin 1883–1914, vol. 7, Letter 1045, pp. 213–15.

339 Clair 1960, p. 166.

340 Hessels 2009, p. 139. *Arctis* is a variant form of *artis* ('tight').

341 Plantin 1883–1914, vol. 7, Letter 663, pp. 33–5.

342 *Ibid.*, Letter 801, p. 317.

343 Rekers 1972, pp. 38–9.

344 Plantin 1883–1914, vol. 7, Letter 1011, p. 103–11.

345 See Sabbe 1926, p. 35.

346 Plantin 1883–1914, vol. 7, Letter 1071, p. 271.

347 Plantin 1883–1914, vols 8/9, Letter 1263, p. 235. For a further discussion of the links between Montano and Hiël, see Rekers 1972, pp. 88–94.

348 Rekers 1972, pp. 10 and 119–21.

349 *Ibid.*, pp. 100 and 156.

350 Quoted in Jones 2011, p. 75. The source of the advice is Seneca.

351 Quoted in Papy 2019.

352 Jones 2011, p. 58.

353 See Soen 2012, pp. 1045–8.

354 The above two paragraphs are drawn from an article by Bass 2007, pp. 157–94.

355 *Pemptades* is a Latinised form of the Greek word for sets of five. The 'books' are probably better thought of as chapters.

356 The 1583 edition with its illustrations can be seen at Opsopäus 1583.

357 See Harkness 2007, pp, 15–56.

358 Plantin 1883–1914, vol. 7, Letter 1045, p. 214.

359 *Miroir des mesnageres* (1595), *Miroir des meres* (1596) and *Miroir des vefves* (1596); see van de Haar 2015.

360 On the use of grisaille, see Jonkheere 2012, pp. 221–3.

361 These are to be found in an *album* probably compiled by Jean de Poligny in the Rijksmuseum.

362 See Zweite 1980, p. 27, n. 42. For a detailed analysis of painters' career decisions after the fall of Antwerp, see van der Linden 2015, pp. 18–54.

363 Jonkheere 2012, p. 64.

364 *Ibid.*, p. 50

365 Printed in 1593 and reprinted the following year as *Adnotationes et meditationes in Evangelia*.

366 Plantin 1883–1914, vol. 8/9, Letter 1188, p. 114.

367 For an account of this phenomenon, see Porras 2016, pp. 54–79.

368 See Bass 2019, p. vii. This beautifully produced book is generously illustrated with images from the *Four Elements*, showing in each case the accompanying inscriptions on the verso. The images can also be seen on the website of the National Gallery of Art, Washington, DC: https://www.nga.gov/collection/art-object-page.69762.html.

369 See Yates 1959; Strong 1984, pp. 98–125; Jardine and Brotton 2000, pp. 122–31.

370 See Yates 1959, p. 31. Yates quotes the French translation of the entry.

Chapter 13

371 Galbraith 1975, p. ix.

372 Although Ortelius does not appear on the *Panhuys Paneel* himself, his ability to make friends and his intellectual interests are at the heart of the varied gathering of friends portrayed by it. He does, however, appear in another *portrait historié* by de Vos (see p. 52).

373 Ortelius, *Album Amicorum* (MS LC.2.113), f4r. There is also a helpful facsimile in Ortelius 1969 (the Pembroke College

website draws attention to an error in the pagination of this facsimile).

374 Ortelius, *Album Amicorum* (MS LC.2.113), f44r.

375 Van Meteren's *Album Amicorum* is held at the Bodleian Library, but I have referred to the transcriptions in van Meteren 1898.

376 See Bass 2019, p. 84.

377 Mulcaster 1970, Dedicatory Epistle.

378 *Ibid.*, p. 258.

379 The pair had got to know each other well when they both lived in Aachen, having both been driven from Antwerp. They went on to become close friends, and in a letter to Ortelius, Radermacher calls Vivien 'my *alter ego*' (Hessels 2009, p. 496).

380 Ortelius, *Album Amicorum* (MS LC.2.113), f84r

381 *Ibid.*, f84v.

382 *Ibid.*, f85r.

383 Rekers 1972, Letter 87, p. 155.

384 Hessels 2009, Letter 277, p. 663.

385 Plantin 1883–1914, vol. 8/9, Letter 1475, p. 540.

386 Book 1, Essay 25. 'De l'institution des enfants', quoted in Papy 2019.

387 See Parker 1977, pp. 249–51.

388 Wedgwood 1945. Despite my reservations, this is a book that I recommend. Her account of the siege of Leiden is gripping and her description of William's final days very moving. For a much briefer but more dispassionate assessment of William as 'a highly pragmatic politician', see Swart 1993, pp. 65–73.

389 Galbraith 1990, p. 13

390 Tawney 2015, p. 19.

391 The college prayer of St John's College, Cambridge.

392 This poem may have been printed as a specimen to show William the Silent when he visited Plantin's press in 1579; see Plantin 1955, pp. 327–8. The translation is mine.

393 I realise that this section is indebted to a similar passage in Binding 2003, pp. 291–2.

Postscript

394 Hessels 2009. pp. 396–7.

395 *Ibid.*, pp. 759–60.

396 See Papy 2023.

397 See p. 197.

Index

Image credits